RACE MIXTURE IN

NINETEENTH-CENTURY U.S.

AND SPANISH AMERICAN

FICTIONS

RACE MIXTURE IN NINETEENTH-CENTURY U.S. AND SPANISH AMERICAN FICTIONS

Gender, Culture, and Nation Building

DEBRA J. ROSENTHAL

The University of North Carolina Press

Chapel Hill and London

© 2004 The University of North Carolina Press
All rights reserved
Manufactured in the United States of America
Set in Cycles by Keystone Typesetting, Inc.

The paper in this book meets the guidelines for permanence
and durability of the Committee on Production Guidelines for Book Longevity
of the Council on Library Resources.

Parts of this book have been reprinted with permission in revised form from the
following works: "Race Mixture and the Representation of Indians in the U.S. and
the Andes," in Monika Kaup and Debra J. Rosenthal, eds., *Mixing Race, Mixing Culture:
Inter-American Literary Dialogues* (Austin: University of Texas Press, 2002), 122–39;
"Floral Counterdiscourse: Miscegenation, Ecofeminism, and Hybridity in Lydia
Maria Child's *A Romance of the Republic*," *Women's Studies* 31, no. 2 (Mar.–Apr. 2002):
221–45; and "The White Blackbird: Miscegenation, Genre, and the Tragic Mulatta in
Howells, Harper, and the Babes of Romance," *Nineteenth-Century Literature* 56, no. 4
(Mar. 2002): 495–517, © 2002 by the Regents of the University of California.

Library of Congress Cataloging-in-Publication Data
Rosenthal, Debra J., 1964–
Race mixture in nineteenth-century U.S. and Spanish American fictions:
gender, culture, and nation building / Debra J. Rosenthal.
p. cm.
Includes bibliographical references and index.
ISBN 0-8078-2899-8 (cloth : alk. paper) — ISBN 0-8078-5564-2 (pbk. : alk. paper)
1. American fiction—19th century—History and criticism. 2. Miscegenation in
literature. 3. Spanish-American fiction—19th century—History and criticism.
4. Literature, Comparative—American and Spanish American. 5. Literature,
Comparative—Spanish American and American. 6. Racially mixed people
in literature. 7. Race relations in literature. 8. Slavery in literature.
9. Racism in literature. 10. Race in literature. I. Title.
PS374.M53R67 2004
813'.3093556—dc22
2004005104

cloth 08 07 06 05 04 5 4 3 2 1
paper 08 07 06 05 04 5 4 3 2 1

THIS BOOK WAS DIGITALLY PRINTED.

To Ariana, Nathaniel, and Glenn

CONTENTS

Acknowledgments *ix*

Introduction. Inter-American Interracial Intercourse *1*

CHAPTER 1
Race Mixture and the Representation of Indians in the
United States and the Andes *18*

CHAPTER 2
Temperance and Miscegenation in Whitman's *Franklin Evans* *52*

CHAPTER 3
Cuban Slave Fiction: Race Mixture in *Sab* *69*

CHAPTER 4
Floral Counterdiscourse: Miscegenation, Ecofeminism, and
Hybridity in Lydia Maria Child's *Romance of the Republic* *95*

CHAPTER 5
The White Blackbird: Miscegenation, Genre, and the Tragic
Mulatta in Howells, Harper, and the Babes of Romance *115*

Conclusion *143*

Notes *149*

Works Cited *157*

Index *179*

ACKNOWLEDGMENTS

It is difficult to express sufficient gratitude for the exceptional intellectual talents and caring guidance of Lee Clark Mitchell, Maria DiBattista, and A. Walton Litz, under whose direction this book started as a doctoral dissertation at Princeton University. I can only hope that the merits of this book pay homage to their erudition, tutelage, and friendship. Any shortcomings of the book point back only to me.

Chapters 1 and 5 could not have been written without the perceptive critiques, literary insights, and culinary skills of Martha Cutter and Carolyn Sorisio, whose demands for excellence and clarity strengthened my arguments.

I owe many, many thanks to my friend and colleague Monika Kaup, who exemplifies rigorous comparative thinking. Our conversations, both scholarly and otherwise, continuously broaden my perspectives and offer ample opportunity for mirth.

I am indebted to a geographically diverse community of scholars for their comments, criticism, and suggestions: Mary Beadle, Lauren Bowen, Jeanne Colleran, Michael J. Davey, Susan Gillman, Steve Hayward, Carolyn L. Karcher, Dan Kilbride, Robert J. Kolesar, Peter Kvidera, Maryclaire Moroney, David S. Reynolds, David Robson, Karen Sánchez-Eppler, Doris Sommer, and Brenda Wirkus.

Anna Hocevar deserves much of my gratitude: her wealth of knowledge, organizational skills, interpersonal savvy, and ability to take pleasure in life carved for me daily a happy and composed place to work.

The friendship and perspective offered by Ellen Kloppman, Grant Kloppman, Anne Kugler, and Carin Ruff remain central to my ability to think, teach, and write. Much of the intellectual equanimity needed to hold me aloft through the difficult phase of revision came from Doris Donnelly, Chris Roark, and Tami Schneider.

Gracious thanks to Lois Percaciante, Norma Piccirillo, and Lana Riebe for their professionalism in handling the various stages of my manuscript and for their unending good cheer and friendship. At

John Carroll University's Grasselli Library, Elaine Minichiello and Kathy Skerkoski were always extremely helpful. Amore Haydu generously provided much-needed bibliographic assistance.

Munificent financial support came from John Carroll University, which awarded me three summer research fellowships to work on this book.

I am extremely indebted to Sian Hunter, Paula Wald, Becky Standard, and the anonymous readers for the University of North Carolina Press for being such intelligent, caring, and critical readers. Their intimate knowledge of my manuscript rivaled mine and pushed me to improve every page.

With its concern for genealogy and inheritance, this project inevitably leads me back to my own relatives. I am so grateful to my family, especially to my parents, Marvin Rosenthal and Joan Rosenthal, for their optimism, interest, pride, and belief in my work.

The most unwavering, enduring, and loving support has come from my children, Nathaniel and Ariana, who urge me to do my best work and who provide the most compelling reasons for putting it down. The blissful world they shape for me elicits a benevolence of spirit and unburdens troubles.

Ultimately, I owe everything to Glenn Starkman, my husband, best friend, and ideal reader. Although his work on time and the early universe is theoretical, he is able to conjure for me actual work time from a void in which none had existed. The sustaining pressure of his confidence and trust generates abundant light both to share life's joys and to illuminate the darker moments.

INTRODUCTION
Inter-American Interracial Intercourse

Why study race mixture in nineteenth-century novels of the Americas? Whether New and Old World inhabitants recounted stories of first contact with anger or with triumph, the meeting of cultures and peoples opened new chapters in history. European explorers entangled their lives with those native to the Americas for a variety of purposes: religious proselytization, expanded trade, increased wealth, imperial glory. But another consequence transpired from the conjunction of the two civilizations: sexual desire for people understood to be racial and cultural Others. Although race mixture has starred in world conflicts and in world literature, it was formative in the history of the Americas primarily in terms of cultural constitution, political organization, nation building, civil identity, and, most important to the concerns of this book, literary expression.[1] Central to these hemispheric notions of cultural structure and the incorporation of persons into a constituency, race mixture and its denial or repression figure prominently in nineteenth-century literary expression. In fact, in the United States this literary tradition, with its repudiation of race mixture, is virtually founded upon the denial it appropriates for its very existence. And since many early pan-American poems and novels, and even earlier explorers' travel narratives, are concerned with race mixture, racial hybridity can be situated at the heart of the literature of the Americas.

The burgeoning field of comparative literature of the Americas rezones the hemisphere to identify the intersections and overlapping concerns among the diverse literatures of the New World.[2] *Race Mixture in Nineteenth-Century U.S. and Spanish American Fictions: Gender, Culture, and Nation Building* examines selected nineteenth-century authors in the United States and Spanish America who, in textually simultaneous moves, struggle to give voice to contemporary dilemmas about interracial sexual and cultural mixing. In the novels engaged here, narrative unease surrounding miscegenation coincides with heated debates over national identities and race reform, so that miscegenation fiction participates discursively in issues of social reform and national identity in the Americas. The selected authors from North and South America employ discourses of miscegenation that yield analogies with concurrent political and social developments in nation building.

Written primarily for specialists of U.S. literature, this book is distinctive in that in it I discuss novels from Ecuador, Peru, and Cuba to anchor interpretations of the U.S. works. While aimed at readers of U.S. literature, this book will also be of interest to readers of Spanish American literature and studies, Latino/Latina literature and studies, and comparative literature of the Americas who want to see a comparative pan-American context. In Deborah N. Cohn's words, the Americas constitute "neighboring spaces" (2), sharing a history of slavery, racism, colonialism, and racial and cultural hybridity. Celeste Olalquiaga argues that our bicontinental hemisphere results in the influence of the United States on other countries as well as the "latinization of the United States," a phenomenon she describes as "a process whereby U.S. culture and daily practices become increasingly permeated by elements of Latin American culture imported by Spanish-speaking immigrants from Central and South America as well as the Caribbean" (76). Thus a comparative reading of the hemisphere results in fruitful thematic dialogue among literatures.

In this work, I aim to fill in narrative and theoretical gaps in current thinking about race mixture and to initiate scholarly methods for conceptualizing U.S. literature in a more interdisciplinary, hemispheric context. I find useful the shared history Cohn identifies between the U.S. South and Latin America: one of "dispossession, of socioeconomic hardship, of political and cultural conflict, and of the export of resources to support a development of a 'North'" (5). Present here as well are some of the most pressing issues in literary and cultural studies of the Americas: relations between the United States and Spanish America, the nature of "race" as a social and an identity category, racial mixture as both fortifying and threatening such categories, the nexus of race and sexual desire, and the role of race and gender in configuring nationalism.

Nation-building societies in the Americas had to account for or circumscribe the inevitable contact between constituents understood to be of different races, and writers took up the challenge of voicing their concerns in fictional form. Whereas autobiography demands a "coherent, centered image of the self," these authors enfold and test their beliefs in the novel, which permits them "to distribute the elements of subjectivity among a number of fictional characters" (Kirkpatrick, *Las Románticas* 147). In North and South American countries the contexts in which the anxiety of race mixture occurs are culturally distinct, but often narratively analogous. For example, some authors map a myth of national origin by locating their novels and concerns about racial heterogeneity in the distant past. The fictions in this study express and participate in debates on race issues and nation building and demonstrate the symmetry between the body politic and the body human by providing a corporeal metaphor for national and literary identity. By reading against each other works that offer compellingly dissonant views of race mixture, I demonstrate how the anxiety of miscegenation is perceived politically and framed novelistically.

In Spanish America of the 1800s, issues of national identity culminated in the many wars of independence. As newly created nations, the various countries had to define themselves, which encompassed, among other things, understanding their populations' racial mixtures. This process took on different forms in each nation since even neighboring countries had different histories. Poetry enjoyed a rich tradition in Spanish America; fiction, not widely written during the colonial period, flourished late in the nineteenth century. Scholars estimate that more than 80 percent of nineteenth-century Spanish American novels appeared after 1850 (Brushwood 3). These novels posed some particularly challenging questions since many authors sought to represent the ongoing changes in society that were shaping national identity. For example, as the century progressed the Latin American novel increasingly demonstrated "an openness toward the market and new readers, a marked didacticism, and political, social, or extra-literary content. . . . Most of the novels of that century, from Lizardi to Matto de Turner, sought to educate the people, to improve their *costumbres* (customs/mores), and to better their societies" (Unzueta 26). In the United States, the years of debate leading up to the Indian Removal Act of 1830, and its subsequent passage, greatly influenced the imaginations of such writers as Lydia Maria Child, James Fenimore Cooper, and Catharine Maria Sedgwick, who were interested in the "noble savage" and the "Indian question." Later in the century, the Civil War and the settling of the West generated bloody disputes about nationhood and race. The bitter prejudice of the postwar Reconstruction period and the taboo against interracial mixing left deep marks on the fiction of the 1890s.

The *Oxford English Dictionary* traces the word "miscegenation" back to the Latin roots *miscere*, meaning to mix, and *genus*, meaning race, and defines the term as a "mixture of races; esp. the sexual union of whites with Negroes." The earliest citation of the word occurred in 1864 in the title of a pamphlet intended to incite racial hatred, "Miscegenation: The Theory of the Blending of the Races, Applied to the American White Man and Negro" (Croly).[3] The *New York Daily Graphic* editor David Croly, trying to discredit antislavery Republicans, published the pamphlet anonymously but labeled it the work of an abolitionist who advocated interracial sexual practices. In the pamphlet Croly argued that interracial sex would ensure the prosperity of the country by granting physical freedom to blacks and sexual freedom to both races, particularly to white women, who would be able to indulge their secret passion for black men.

"Miscegenation" did not appear until relatively late in the history of interracial sex, which suggests the power of words to ossify reality or to organize hatred into a neatly quasi-scientific phrase. Noting that the word was coined not long after the Emancipation Proclamation, Eric Sundquist argues that "amalgamation means simply a mixing, but miscegenation quite clearly meant interracial *sexual* mixing, and the term therefore quickly acquired a contagious and derisive force, one that expressed the nation's most visceral fears, paradoxical or not, about emancipation" (107; see also Sidney Kaplan). Similarly, Catharine MacKinnon defines "miscegenation" as "a sexual model for racial integration." To some critics the term connotes sexual exploitation by a dominant group (Solaún and Kronus 50).

Although "miscegenation" was not coined until 1864, many scholars use it in reference to works that appeared earlier because no other term accurately describes the phenomenon. Other terms in critical usage include *métissage*, creolization, transculturation,[4] racial syncretism, amalgamation, mixed-blood, and, perhaps most commonly, hybridity, which will be discussed below. These assorted words are not necessarily analogous; rather, these various imbricated discourses of race mixture reflect attendant cultural fluidity and cross-fertilization. As Monika Kaup and I argue in our introduction to *Mixing Race, Mixing Culture: Inter-American Literary Dialogues*, "hybridization suggests a nonexclusive, plural, dialogic, or multicultural model of culture" and "some terms, like mixedblood, miscegenation, or amalgamation, evoke the biological union of different races; others, like creolization, *métissage* and *mestizaje*, hybridity, and transculturation, are used to refer to the mixing of cultures in cross-cultural formations" (xvi, xvii).

Although Child, Cooper, and Sedgwick wrote forty years before "miscegenation" first appeared in print, for clarity and convenience I use the term with reference to their works. I deliberately risk anachronism to pose larger questions about issues of race mixture but nonetheless recognize that even when "miscegenation" is historically appropriate, the word still recalls its racist origins and thus may arouse discomfort.

The Spanish language does not have a word to describe a mixed-race procreative act. Instead, Spanish contains many words to depict the offspring of such a union. The familiar terms *mestizaje* and *mezcla*, for example, simply denote a mix. The *Enciclopedia del idioma* defines *mestizaje* as a "mezcla de razas" (mix of races), while there are no racial overtones in the definition of *mezclar*: "hablando de familias de linajes, enlazarse unos con otros [in the case of family lineage, to tie one to another]."[5] The word *mestizo/mestiza*, which first appeared in print in 1680, is defined as "la persona nacida de padre y madre de raza diferente, y con especialidad al hijo de hombre blanco e india, o de indio y mujer blanca [a person born of a father and mother of different races, especially a child of a white man and Indian woman, or of an Indian man and a white woman]." The word *mulato* etymologically derives from an Arabic word meaning "mule" and refers specifically to black-white mixture.

Thus, while *mestizaje* and *mestizo* originated without a negative value attached, "miscegenation" was coined to exploit racial fears, leading Doris Sommer to describe it as "an unfortunate translation for *mestizaje*, which is practically a slogan for many projects of national consolidation" (*Foundational* 22). Reflecting North and South America's different obsessions with race, "miscegenation" describes black and white mixing, while *mestizaje* refers primarily to Indian and white mixture. The different linguistic incarnations of such terms parallel the distinct purposes race mixture served in these areas. The Catholic monarchy did not send women with the conquistadors, leaving the men free to marry, cohabit with, or rape native women. According to Magner Morner, "In a way, the Spanish conquest of the Americas was a conquest of women. The Spaniards obtained the Indian girls both by force and by peaceful means. The seizure of women was simply one element in the general enslavement of Indians that took place in the New World during the first decades of the 16th century" (22). In fact, because of the Spaniards' legacy of coupling with native women, *mestizo* "became associated with illegitimacy as out-of-wedlock mestizo kids were left with their mothers" (55). Similarly, *mestizaje* was central to the Andean social and literary movement of *indigenismo* (Rama 138–58).

In contrast, English women accompanied their men to the New World, perhaps arguing for what Richard M. Morse terms "Protestant and Catholic versions of Americanization" (2).[6] Such practice also minimized interracial mixing and kept Anglo Protestant bloodlines "pure." Although seventeenth-century Spainiards were more concerned than other Europeans with "limpieza de sangre" (blood purity) because of the presence of Arabs and Jews, Mauricio Solaún and Sidney Kronus theorize that Spaniards did not adhere to these ideologies of purity to the extent that the British did because of Spain's historical conquest by the Moors: "There is a powerful logic behind the assumption that precolonial Iberian mingling with dark human groups, which had themselves miscegenation with Negroid populations, could have affected Iberian racial attitudes. The shifting and ill-defined boundaries that characterize Latin American race relations require perceptions of race as part of a continuum" (56). The importance of racial hybridism "lies in its intimate relationship with two social processes: *acculturation*, the mixture of cultural elements, and *assimilation*, or the absorption of an individual or a people into another culture. In Latin America, miscegenation became an important vehicle in acculturation, and very often racial mixture and cultural mixture coincided" (Morner 5).

Like "mulato," "hybrid" also derives from bestiality: its origins refer to the offspring of a tame sow and a wild boar. The word appeared early in the seventeenth century but its use remained uncommon until it began to circulate widely in the nineteenth century. Hybridity as an intellectual construct reminds us that nineteenth-century science emphasized essentialist studies of human racial biology. Essentialized race-based identity necessitated an ideology of racial and cultural purity, especially of "pure" whiteness. Ironically, one of the most influential racial scientists, Arthur de Gobineau, complicates his arguments when he admits that even Anglo-Saxons themselves, as indicated by the hyphen, are a hybrid race: "It would be fruitless to try to identify [features] today in the hybrid agglomeration that constitutes what we call the 'white race' " (147).[7]

In the view of Néstor García Canclini, "Hybridity can imply a space betwixt and between two zones of purity in a manner that follows biological usage that distinguishes two discrete species and the hybrid pseudo-species that results from their combination. . . . On the other hand, hybridity can be understood as the ongoing condition of all human cultures, which contain no zones of purity because they undergo continuous processes of transculturation (two-way borrowing and lending between cultures). Instead of hybridity versus purity, this view suggests that it is hybridity all the way down" and that it is the construction of "ideological zones of cultural purity" that is harder to understand (xv). Because hybridity "shows the connections between the racial categories of the past and contemporary cultural discourse" (Robert J. C. Young, *Colonial Desire* 27), we can examine how writers imaginatively converted scientific discourse into racial rhetoric.

Because the existence of white and nonwhite bodies in close proximity so vexed people in both the North and the South, representing such closeness fictively inevitably took on political dimensions. Novels with miscegenation themes tend to fall into two overlapping categories: those that, often in ideologically unsuspect ways, defend the status quo and those that advocate social transformation, usually via assimilation. Assimilationist endings coinciding with nation-building policies comprise what Sommer calls "foundational fictions." In such conciliatory conceptions of miscegenation, the Native American or black surrenders him- or herself in the arms of the white lover, thereby deflecting anxiety about the dark other taking up arms. In both categories, commitment to miscegenation themes drives political agendas. Themes of race-based identity lead Diana Paulin to think about hybridism in terms of "a process of substitution and reformulation" she calls "surrogacy" and defines as the way in which "racial substitutions enabled writers to rehearse the possibility of interracial desire and all the conflicts surrounding it without articulating any explicit resolution" (418). The novels I examine engage this process of surrogacy in the way that their authors present and tease readers with the potential coupling of opposite-race protagonists.

In many of the fictions I examine, discussions of race quickly devolve into meditations on the semiotics of blood. Writers imagine race not as socially constructed but as essentially contained in the blood, so that one can talk about blood in terms of skin color ("black blood"), eliding the fact that blood is neither black nor white. Blood thus becomes construed as epidermally visible. Skin and blood color may diverge after repeated miscegenation: one who is socially white can have a drop of what is legally considered black blood. Since the human body is a vehicle for the transmission of material inheritance as well as of genetic heredity, property is linked to blood. Blood relatives inherit estates, making miscegenous desire a threat to white familial and national property distribution (Saks 49). Finally, miscegenation is not the only taboo transgressed by improper mixing of blood; incest represents another type of taboo blood mixture. Miscegenation and incest redouble in the same confounded family romance.

Many novels in the Americas featuring race mixture also thematize incest. I will examine the conflation of these two blood taboos in Juan León Mera's *Cumandá; o, Un drama entre salvajes*, Clorinda Matto de Turner's *Aves sin nido*, Gertrudis Gómez de Avellaneda's *Sab*, and Lydia Maria Child's *Romance of the Republic*. Werner Sollors discusses incest between black and white relatives and deduces "at least three different ideological explanations" for the reliance of one theme upon the other: "a 'pragmatic' state-interventionist [trajectory], a 'realistic' abolitionist-liberal [trajectory], and a 'paranoid' proslavery-racialist-fascist trajectory" (*Neither* 314). The first explanation refers to governmental laws that legislated family relations: in having an interest in preventing incestuous relations, the government as well had an interest in prohibiting cross-racial marriages. Thus, the law equated incest with miscegenation by decrying both as deviations and hence subjected them to the same restrictions. Sollors's second explanation gestures toward abolitionist agendas that sought to reinforce the link between consanguinity and interracial rape to raise awareness of the reality of slavery that justified slave masters' abuse of their slaves and even of their own mixed-blood descendants. Finally, white supremacists benefited from equating the two blood ties "to make miscegenation seem 'unnatural' and 'repulsive'" and "to make hybridism seem as 'heinous' as incest" (320). Generally speaking, the novels under consideration in *Race Mixture in Nineteenth-Century U.S. and Spanish American Fictions* fall into Sollors's second category: the authors fictively portray consanguineous hybridity to proffer a vision—of thwarted love (*Cumandá*), of white society's abuse of native peoples (*Aves sin nido*), of white society's enslavement of and inability to grant subjectivity to a noble soul (*Sab*), or of a progressive mixed-race generation in which cousins can marry and skin color does not preclude acceptance into elite society (*A Romance of the Republic*).

Yet incest may figure differently when it is portrayed as Indian-white incest, not black-white incest. According to Renata Wasserman, in fiction incest plots are important to acculturation plots (142). In her discussion of European romances of the Americas—Bernadin de Saint-Pierre's *Paul et Virginie* (1787) and Chateaubriand's *Atala* (1801) and *René* (1805)—Wasserman argues that "if the prohibition of incest is, as Claude Lévi-Strauss maintains, the threshold between nature and culture, one should expect it to hover, as it does, over these tales of contact" (12). If, as Wasserman suggests, "marriage is a metaphor for contact with the exotic other," then marriage in these novels mediates between the Old World and the New (12), and incest functions simultaneously to enhance exoticism and facilitate acculturation, especially to Catholicism. For example, in *Paul et Virginie*, even though the potential lovers are not consanguineous, they were raised in the New World as siblings. Since the two come from different social classes, the novel still toys with endogamy and exogamy. *Atala* presents the Indian Chactas, who is orphaned and captured by an enemy tribe but subsequently rescued and adopted by a Spaniard named Lopez. When Chactas's enemies recapture him, they give him the Indian maiden Atala to enjoy on his last night and they fall in love. Atala wears a cross—she has converted to Christianity—and thus, "proud like a Spaniard and an Indian" (49), represents hybridity. Atala reveals that her mother was raped by a Spaniard named Lopez, the same man who raised Chactas. The incest theme intensifies their love: "Daughter of my benefactor! . . . This fraternal friendship which had come to visit us and to join its love with ours was too much for our hearts" (48). A thunderstorm prevents their lovemaking, but Atala cannot marry Chactas: her mother made Atala swear to maintain her Christian virtue by never marrying. Atala ingests poison and a missionary intones, both to her and by extension to readers, that "this extreme passion to which you have abandoned yourself is seldom correct. . . . Religion does not demand superhuman sacrifices" (66). A final example of the predominance of the incest theme in European romantic imaginings of the Americas is Chateaubriand's novel *René*, in which the eponymous hero is attracted both miscegenously to an Indian maiden, Céluta, and incestuously to his sister, Amélie, a love some critics suggest biographically parallels Chateaubriand's relationship with his sister Lucille.

The persistence of the incest theme serves as an exemplary study in transoceanic dialogue: the Americas inspire and exoticize the idea of "natural man" in the writings of European writers (although Chateaubriand's five-month journey throughout France's North American empire cannot be precisely reconstructed, he gathered much material for his writings from his trip to the "primitive" civilization there), who in turn influence writers of the Americas who reflect and refract Europeans' images of the Americas. Although Jean-Jacques Rousseau's works did not specifically address the Americas or contribute to an exoticization of the Americas, Rousseau does refer to the New World to undergird his assertions about human nature (Wasserman 74). Peter Hulme argues that underlying the European colonial discourse of the Americas was "the presumption that during the colonial period large parts of the non-European world were *produced* for Europe through a discourse that imbricated sets of questions and assumptions, methods of procedure and analysis, and kinds of writing and imagery" (2). Thus, writers of the Americas inherited from the Europeans a discourse of the romanticization of race and its conflation with incest, a discourse that was itself spawned by the Americas.

The merging of blood, which threatens to dissolve difference, represents a loss or destabilization of identity. A body that claims both whiteness and otherness threatens the foundations of white supremacy; the eponymous hero of *Sab*, for instance, finds himself simultaneously a family member and a piece of property. In this sense, miscegenation can be seen as a corporeal metaphor for equalizing hierarchy. Although racial heterogeneity has been construed as a fixed synthesis of the thesis and antithesis of white and nonwhite merging, it can also be a source of instability since it is the concentration of opposites. Antonio Benítez Rojo casts *mestizaje* as insoluble differential equations that repeat their unknowns so that it is impossible to assume a constant identity (26). Helen Hunt Jackson's heroine in *Ramona*, for instance, belongs to the highborn Mexicans, the Scottish upper class, and the exploited Native Americans.[8]

To a large extent, then, this study gains its traction from bodies and the fear of mixed-race bodies.[9] In texts with miscegenation themes, the body becomes an instrument for narrative signification. Color-coded, the fleshly identity of the body defines and circumscribes personhood and social convention. As a dangerous repository of desire, the body must be contained and prevented from expressing inappropriate desire. Simultaneously, the proximity of opposite-sex, opposite-race bodies, or the yearning for such proximity, causes social consternation yet propels narratives forward. Mikhail Bakhtin emphasizes the body's centrality in establishing and overthrowing authority (Bakhtin; Bauer and McKinstry). Although Bakhtin refers to language in the novel, his terms can also apply to the difficulty of determining racial identity in society because the expression of identity always takes place within language. His theory of dialogism can be read as a dialogism of race in which competing discourses of race become somatized. That is, the threat of miscegenation parallels the threat of collapsing dialogisms. Racially distinct bodies correspond to ideologically distinct discourses, just as racial heterogeneity can be an analogue to heteroglossia. The tension between contesting discourses and races takes place within the language used to constitute the tension. What Bakhtin refers to as the hybrid construction of an utterance can also be used to describe racial hybridity: a single entity that contains two elements. The body of the product of miscegenation comprises two different races, so that in this study, mixed-race characters embody double-voiced discourse, simultaneously descending from the conqueror and the conquered.

Nowhere is the anxiety of miscegenation concentrated greater than in the female body. Women's bodies bear the evidence of miscegenation, with race literalized as a woman's "issue." In all the novels discussed here, concerns about race mixture and racial heredity are articulated in terms of female sexual identity. In fact, such issues of ethnicity and race permitted freer discussion of sexuality. Since miscegenation plots narratively link themes of (female) sexuality with nationality, these novels present the territory of the white female body, which is being fought over when race mixture is an issue, and the geographical territory of the Americas as analogous. This analogy between the land and women's bodies, and the need to govern both, has received considerable scholarly attention (for example, Annette Kolodny posits that the U.S. psyche is "bound" "by the vocabulary of a feminine landscape and the psychological patterns of regression and violation that it implies" [*Lay* 146]). Because nation building depends on legitimizing state-sanctioned sexuality to assure the transference of inheritance and to create the proper citizenry, nationhood depends on the regulation of womanhood.

Perhaps for these reasons, women intellectuals in the nineteenth century were committed to miscegenation themes. Middle-class women supported many social reforms, including racial justice, suffrage, abolition, and temperance. Women intellectuals' devotion to such reforms undoubtedly stemmed from the realization that nationalism was based on sexism because "the inequality of sexual roles in conjugal love and child-rearing constitutes the anchoring point for the juridical, economic, educational, and medical mediation of the state" (Balibar 102). Unable to vote and confined to domesticity, many women intellectuals picked up their pens to inscribe themselves in the polity.

Benedict Anderson argues that an emerging print culture helped "invent" nations by consolidating onto a reproducible page all that the state imagined as relevant to its existence and that the establishment of a print community ushered the development of nationalism and reified feelings of patriotic cohesion. Claudio Lomnitz outlines some inaccuracies when Anderson's theory is applied to Latin America; particularly relevant here is Lomnitz's claim that "the concept of 'empty time' was present in the Spanish world long before print capitalism, beginning with the decline of empire and Spain's failure to attain a universal monarchy" (352). Yet Mary Louise Pratt corrects Anderson where Lomnitz does not: the idea of a print community, whether a contributor to or a predecessor of nationalism, opens the possibility of studying women's roles in nineteenth-century national identity formation, which Anderson ignores, for women in the Americas were often prominent writers and journalists ("Women, Literature, and National Brotherhood" 50). Denied access to the political sphere, many women found political and cultural representation in the public sphere of literacy. Nationhood and womanhood, while often at odds, coalesce in the written word. To contribute to the ongoing nineteenth-century process of national self-definition, the middle-class women authors discussed in this book addressed issues of racial oppression. Although their own rights as women were suppressed, they nevertheless championed the causes of Indians and slaves, with whom they frequently felt a common bond of subjugation. In both North and South America, nationhood and womanhood merged and emerged in women intellectuals' public literary engagement with national policy on race-based persecution and social attitudes toward race mixture.

At a time when the United States, Peru, and Cuba were either recovering from or about to embark on wars of national formation, these countries were searching for ways to define themselves and their racial policies. For example, many nineteenth-century Latin American novels "radically democratize[d] literature by portraying lower social classes, previously excluded from serious representation (they were included only in the comic mode, as the objects of ridicule or of exemplary lessons), and by broadening its reading public" (Unzueta 26). Women authors, in addition, challenged the figure of the "statesman," a concept that neatly articulates the oneness of nation and masculinity, by using their pens to imagine a different kind of community and national self-understanding. This book therefore emphasizes the confluence of intellectual aspiration, authorial activism, feminine identity, and national formation in these novels.

In chapter 1 of this book, "Race Mixture and the Representation of Indians in the United States and the Andes," I take a comparative approach to the representation of native peoples in novels by white authors in Ecuador (*Cumandá*), Peru (*Aves sin nido*), and the United States (*The Last of the Mohicans* by Cooper, *Hobomok* by Child, *Hope Leslie* by Sedgwick, *Ramona* by Jackson, and "Huck and Tom among the Indians" by Mark Twain). While clearly all the authors were influenced by such writers of the European Romantic tradition as Rousseau and Chateaubriand, Gustavo Pérez-Firmat notes that literatures of the Americas have more in common than their transoceanic indebtedness to European novels. My chapter concurs with his claim that "not enough has been said about . . . the intersections and tangencies among diverse literatures of the New World considered apart from their extrahemispheric antecedents and analogues" (2–3).

Therefore, in chapter 1 I aim to familiarize readers of U.S. literature with the Andean categories of *indianismo* and *indigenismo* to demonstrate how, when we speak of comparative literature of the Americas, similar literary works (here, white-authored novels about Indians) find distinct modes of critical discourse. White novelists, in both the North and the South, engage miscegenation themes in their imagining of Indians to serve nationalist aims: the portrayal of Indian-white sexual relations can determine a novel's thematic and political concerns. In this chapter I adapt methods of reading proposed by Edward Said and Pérez-Firmat: Said promotes "contrapuntal reading" that considers imperialism and resistance to it (66), and Pérez-Firmat's idea of "appositional" or "cheek-to-cheek" literary comparison suggests that scholars of U.S. literature might glean a new perspective on this body of writing by considering other hemispheric epistemologies. Further, I reflect on the use of the figure of the Indian to influence genre.

I consciously do not address miscegenation in U.S. antislavery narratives or fiction because this topic has been discussed at length by other critics. However, antebellum antimiscegenation discourse is discussed in chapter 2, "Temperance and Miscegenation in Walt Whitman's *Franklin Evans*." Aligned closely with Sollors's third explanatory category, the "paranoid" proslavery-racialist-fascist trajectory, Whitman's anti-alcohol novel presents the discourse of physical temperance as advocating racial temperance, so that warnings against imbibing, temptation, evil spirits, and debauchery (and in favor of abstinence) have a dual meaning. Just as incest and miscegenation themes often tidily enfold one another, the site of miscegenation in *Franklin Evans* envelops both temperance and racial reform. In this chapter I explore the multivalency of racial rhetoric to understand how Whitman employs purposefully flexible discursive strategies to link his dark and sensational Washingtonian message to dark and sensational miscegenation. Throughout the novel, an inebriated Evans uses drinking rhetoric to discuss sexuality, especially interracial sexuality. The novel thereby advocates racial temperance by showing the danger and folly in committing miscegenation.

Antislavery narratives in the Americas are represented by chapter 3, "Cuban Slave Fiction: Race Mixture in *Sab*," which moves the discussion to a comparative analysis of black and white sexual mixing in a Caribbean context. The chapter focuses on *Sab*, an antislavery novel that uses the trope of miscegenation to critique the Cuban slavocracy system. The novel enacts what I term somatized heteroglossia: competing corporeal discourses of race literally embody a double-voiced discourse. Although *Sab* has many points of comparison with Harriet Beecher Stowe's novel *Uncle Tom's Cabin*, it dares to present a miscegenous love story and a lament for a slave's debased subjectivity. Confusing family bonds with human bondage, *Sab* articulates the threat of bodies merging in transgressive miscegenous desire.

In chapter 4 I discuss U.S. Reconstruction and analyze how theories of hybridism in the plant world, as opposed to the animal world, can be employed to reconfigure mixed-race women as deserving of respect, dignity, and national citizenship. Entitled "Floral Counterdiscourse: Miscegenation, Ecofeminism, and Hybridity in Lydia Maria Child's *Romance of the Republic*," the chapter demonstrates how Child uses the conventional nineteenth-century language of flowers as an uplifting counterdiscourse to challenge Reconstruction prejudice against African Americans and mixed-race people. I provide a historical context by discussing contemporary theories of hybridity, gardening manuals, floral handbooks, floral poetry anthologies, floral dictionaries, the language of flowers from the nineteenth century, and the role of hybridizing plants in cultivating a new nation. Child's documented interest in gardening attests to her familiarity with botanical concepts of hybridism, and she attempts to elevate the denigrated status of her light-skinned black heroines by endowing them with flowers' "purity" and "innocence," virtues usually reserved exclusively for white women. Thus Child rewrites race prejudice by merging the discourse of race with the discourse of nature to interrogate what is "natural" about postbellum racial ideology. Miscegenation in the novel appears as a "natural" phenomenon, as natural as cross-breeding flowers to produce a more lovely and valued hybrid.

In chapter 5, "The White Blackbird: Miscegenation, Genre, and the Tragic Mulatta in Howells, Harper, and the Babes of Romance," I construct a literary genealogy that situates William Dean Howells, a major figure of U.S. literary realism, in the middle of a call-and-response literary conversation with popular women writers about race, gender, and genre. Since Howells correlated racial questions with realism, his only novel that treats intermarriage, *An Imperative Duty*, offered him an opportunity to deploy his presumably objective, scientific, realist knowledge about race to challenge romantic miscegenation plots found in Margret Holmes Bates's *Chamber over the Gate* and Alice Morris Buckner's *Towards the Gulf: A Romance of Louisiana*, two novels that he had recently read and reviewed. Central to both women's novels is the figure of the tragic mulatta, a woman raised as white who finds out that she descends from African ancestry and consequently dies. I argue that the tragic mulatta stereotype endures as a stock figure of romanticism and sentimentality so fraught with signification that she resists scientific discourse and thus defies Howells's goal of representing the figure according to the tenets of realism.

In her novel *Iola Leroy*, the African American poet, novelist, and orator Frances Ellen Watkins Harper cunningly recasts the tragic mulatta stereotype both to critique Howells's project and to represent the potential of black womanhood. Knowledge of Bates's and Buckner's works can change critical conversation about the influence of women writers on Howells, the understanding of the racialized woman's role in his fiction, and his conception of the link between the romantic mulatta and realist representation. Similarly, Harper takes issue with Howells's supposed ironic sophistication about race, and in *Iola Leroy* she rewrites many of his views to show how miscegenation is at once a novelistic and a national problem.

If, as Karen Sánchez-Eppler argues, "narrative formulas index cultural obsessions" ("Temperance" 60), then the fictions I discuss over the following chapters indeed index an obsession with race mixture in the Americas, for many of the fictions lean on specific formulas. Formula fiction, by definition, adheres to set patterns of plot, language, and character. Comparing popular formula fiction with highbrow, serious "literature," Beth Young argues that formula fiction "has been accused by academics and non-academics alike of being inferior in quality to literature, with plots, cardboard characters, and themes that either indulge in escapism or uncritically reinforce the status quo" (x). Formulaic plots often served reform movements very well: the U.S. temperance movement found formulas particularly advantageous for advocating sobriety. As David S. Reynolds and

I argue in the introduction to *The Serpent in the Cup: Temperance in American Literature*, "Although there were many, many stories about the battle with the bottle, they mainly followed formulaic conventions. Each retelling of the same basic story ingrained American literature with temperance imagery" (3). Whitman's *Franklin Evans* for example, conforms to temperance and proslavery formulas and thus reinforces prevailing white supremacist values.

Yet, as the fictions I examine demonstrate, sticking to a pattern can be simultaneously conservative and subversive. For example, the indianist novels discussed in chapter 1 work with the familiar formulas of the pure, pious heroine and the noble savage (a blueprint Gómez de Avellaneda follows in *Sab*). The authors present potentially subversive visions of mixed-race marriages in the Americas, but then generally end their works on a conservative note that forecloses the possibility of racial heterogeneity and laments the formulaic passing of the "Vanishing Americans." Chapters 4 and 5 demonstrate authors' serious wrangling with racialized formulas in a seditious attempt to overcome them. In both *A Romance of the Republic* and *An Imperative Duty* Child and Howells, respectively, subversively challenge the tragic mulatta stereotype by marrying their mixed-race heroines to respectable white suitors. Yet, as I demonstrate, even such dissenting views collapse into conformist visions as the authors' attempts to reconstruct narrative formulas fails.

Interest in pan-American literature has been steadily growing, and several essay collections have been published in the last few years that extend the normative boundaries of traditional critical dialogues. This book narrows the focus of pan-American studies by addressing the impact of literary treatments of nineteenth-century race mixture in a hemispheric context. While many critics today examine the general significance of race to literature, I claim a limited focus by pushing critics to think more closely about the mixture of races and by moving U.S. literature out of its insularity and into a wider hemispheric context. Clearly no ossified pan-American aesthetic exists, and I never attempt to assign a coherent hemispheric identity. Nevertheless, I hope that when readers close this book they have a wider sense of racial hybridity's significance to national and literary identity in the nineteenth-century Americas.

1

Race Mixture and the Representation of Indians in the United States and the Andes

Miscegenation in national literature repeats as a hemispheric theme across the Americas, for many U.S. and Latin American novels figure Indian-white mixing. To many intellectuals both northern and southern, a newly formed nation implied and necessitated a new national literature. For example, in an 1815 issue of the *North American Review*, William Channing lamented "the barrenness of American literature viz. the dependence of Americans on English literature, and their consequent negligence of the exertion of their own intellectual powers" (314). In 1821, John Gorham Palfrey wrote, "Whoever in this country first attains the rank of a first rate writer of fiction will lay his scene here. The wide field is ripe for the harvest, and scarce a sickle yet has touched it" (1). Both men believed that the United States had distinctive natural resources for novelists to draw upon: Puritans, dramatic landscapes, wilderness, and, most important, indigenous populations. Significantly, many early U.S. writers answered Channing's, Palfrey's, and others' nationalistic calls by penning fictions that prominently featured Native Americans. Even more significant is that many early white authors not only portrayed natives but also represented them in terms of sexual relations with colonists.[1] Linking a new body politic to the body human, these writers based literary sovereignty on Indian-white interracial mixing. We can draw a hemispheric literary parallel in the Andes region, where authors of the national novels of Ecuador and Peru, Juan León Mera in *Cumandá* (1879) and Clorinda Matto de Turner in *Aves sin nido* (1889), similarly explicitly turn to race mixture to elucidate national concerns. In Mera's evocation of his country's history and landscape and in Matto de Turner's contention that she is "making" Peruvian literature, both authors choose to frame their plots with anxiety about interracial sexual mixing.

In discussing the portrayal of natives in white-authored fiction, Latin American literary scholars, particularly of Andean literature, have identified two distinct genres, *indianismo* and *indigenismo*, and have developed a vocabulary to discuss them. *Indianismo* and *indigenismo* describe social as well as literary movements in nineteenth- and twentieth-century Spanish American literature, respectively. *Indianismo*, concerned with the portrayal of passive, uncivilized natives in an exotic, erotically charged natural setting, is often aligned with nineteenth-century romanticism and romanticized notions of the Other. Examples of *indianista* novels include José Martiniano de Alencar's *O Guarani* (Brazil, 1857) and his *Iracema* (1865), Manuel de Jesús Galván's *Enriquillo* (Dominican Republic, 1879), Mera's *Cumandá*, and Juan Zorilla de San Martín's *Tabaré* (Uruguay, 1886). *Indigenismo* is inspired by different cultural contexts and different attitudes toward Otherness. Associated with twentieth-century realism, *indigenismo* can be characterized as a socially progressive movement that exposes white and mestizo exploitation of Indians and advocates their eventual liberation. Examples of *indigenista* novels include Matto de Turner's *Aves sin nido*, Alcides Arguedas's *Raza de bronce* (Bolivia, 1919), Jorge Icaza's *Huasipungo* (Ecuador, 1934), Gregorio López y Fuentes's *El indio* (1935), Ciro Alegría's *El mundo es ancho y ajeno* (Peru, 1941), and possibly José María Argueda's *Yawar fiesta* (Peru, 1940).

With these classifications, Latin American scholars have developed an accepted taxonomy by which to distinguish the various modes of representing indigenous peoples (Peter J. Gold; Rosemberg; Rodríguez-Luis).[2] In marked contrast, scholars of U.S. literature do not have such categories; critical discourse grapples with ways to talk about nineteenth-century writings about Indians.[3] In other words, the many U.S. novels dealing with Indians are not distinguished by the *ways* they represent natives. Instead, such novels retain their primary classification of romance, frontier novel, sentimental fiction, and so forth and are only secondarily referred to as writings about Indians. Captivity narratives constitute a separate genre because they are actual autobiographical accounts, and westerns are differentiated by their emphasis not on Indians, but on masculine adventure, violence, guns, horses, the gold rush, the western landscape, railroads, sheriffs, and saloons. Lucy Maddox suggests that if Indians appear in a work of fiction, then it is usually classified as a romance (telephone conversation).[4] The blossoming field of Native American literature in the United States, in which Indians write about themselves, is, of course, quite distinct from the appropriation and representation of Indians by whites. Maddox agrees that critics have a literary blind spot and cannot recognize the substantial body of writings about Indians. However, Maddox herself does not distinguish between different *types* of representation of natives: she construes all novels as socially and ideologically similar. Further, Maddox is more interested in the political and cultural representation of the Indian figure than in the representation of Indian-white sexual mixing (*Removals*). The lack of ways to describe differing white-authored representations of natives suggests that critics of U.S. literature have not found such classification useful. In fact, until the critical boom in interest in such novels as Lydia Maria Child's *Hobomok* (1824) and Catharine Maria Sedgwick's *Hope Leslie* (1827),[5] scholars often assumed that few nineteenth-century authors were interested in the political and cultural dynamics of Indian-white relationships and that Cooper stands as the only significant writer in this area (Maddox, *Removals* 6).

Even though critics of nineteenth-century U.S. literature have no vocabulary to describe Indians' representations, the period from the 1820s to the 1880s nonetheless witnessed a shift in the novelistic representation of Native Americans and their sexual relations with whites. For example, Child in *Hobomok*, Cooper in *The Last of the Mohicans* (1826), Sedgwick in *Hope Leslie*, and other early novelists simultaneously portray the Indians romantically, as "noble savages" to be pitied or feared by whites, and tragically, as a doomed race fated to genocide through assimilation. Later in the century, however, particularly once federal Indian removal policies were underway, writers cast the figure of the Indian differently. For example, as we shall see, Helen Hunt Jackson in *Ramona* (1886) protests the continued exploitation of southern California Indians by the U.S. government. Twain in "Huck Finn and Tom Sawyer among the Indians" (1886) portrays the Sioux as debased and corrupt rapists.

Because Andean literature has a vocabulary specific to novelistic portrayals of Indians, an examination of *indianista* and *indigenista* literature, especially in light of U.S. novels about Indians, can be useful for demonstrating the significance of miscegenation to any national literature. In this chapter, I intend to familiarize scholars of U.S. literature with the Andean categories of *indianismo* and *indigenismo* to demonstrate how, when we speak of comparative literature of the Americas, similar literary concerns (here, white-authored novels about Indians) find various modes of critical discourse. Pérez-Firmat endorses the idea of "appositional" or "cheek-to-cheek" literary comparison that places "works side by side without postulating causal connections" so that "confluence takes precedence over influence and causal links, even when they exist, are deemed less relevant than formal or thematic continuities" (4). Using this idea of appositional literary comparison, I wish to suggest that New World studies scholars might gain a new perspective on white-authored novels about Indians by considering other hemispheric epistemologies.[6] I am not recommending that we squeeze U.S. literature into borrowed categories; rather, I am proposing that Latin American models of organizing discourses may challenge received conceptions of U.S. literary heritage. By viewing *Cumandá* alongside *The Last of the Mohicans* and *Hope Leslie* and then turning to *Aves sin nido* juxtaposed with *Ramona* and "Huck and Tom," we can see how all these fictions consciously articulate significant issues regarding the centrality and shifting representation of native-white sexual mixing. In such fictions, historical, political, and literary concerns pivot around the anxiety about interracial sex, suggesting that in both the United States and the Andes, the portrayal of Indian-white sexual relations influences a novel's thematic and national concerns.

Nineteenth-century U.S. fiction also conveyed anxiety about race mixture in slave narratives, slave novels, and proslavery romances. Although racial anxieties were displaced primarily onto Indians in Ecuador and Peru, such anxieties were displaced onto both Indians and blacks in the United States. Yet, reform movements in the United States that inspired Indian and slave reform fiction were separated by fissures of time and politics. True, José Martí linked the "Indian question" with the "Negro question" in his "composite figure of Stowe-and-Jackson [that] links the world-famous North American abolitionist with the nationally prominent spokeswoman for the Indian cause, bringing together what are in the United States the distinctly separate reform movements of the Negro and the Indian" (Gillman, "*Ramona*" 92). Nevertheless, although a comparative examination of race-reform fiction concerning U.S. slaves and Native Americans is beyond the scope of this book, a reexamination of genre borders and portrayals of Indians can point scholars to a pan-American dialogue on indigenous otherness. As Spanish imperialism waned in nineteenth-century Latin America, Anglo domination and expansionism rose in the United States, thus different literary takes on the fictional representation of Indians under Ibero-Catholic colonialism and Anglo-Protestant imperialism emerged.

Although I have briefly mentioned the categories *indianismo* and *indigenismo*, I would like to elaborate on them a bit to better adapt them for U.S. modes of representing Indians.[7] The romantic, sentimental *indianismo* literary movement derived from French Enlightenment thinkers who were popular throughout South America, especially Michel Montaigne in "Des Cannibals" and Voltaire, Guillaume Thomas François Raynal, and Jean-Françoise Marmontel (particularly in *Les Incas*). Rousseau's ideas about the inherent goodness of humanity if uncorrupted by civilization, and the "noble savage" state of humans before the rise of social organization, led to a literary valorization of nature and Indians in their exotic, "pure" state. Chateaubriand, an influential intermediary between natives and Western literature, provided a model for all subsequent *indianista* writing in his *Atala* (1801). Johann Gottfried von Herder's romantic racialism and the German Romantics—Georg Wilhelm Friedrich Hegel, Friedrich von Schlegel, and Johann Wolfgang van Goethe—also influenced views of the Indians. With their emphasis on the return to local color and nature, the German Romantics recognized the appeal of the Americas' wilderness and savages (Sacoto 24–32).[8] Finally, Cooper also inspired the genre; Mera, for example, acknowledges Cooper in his preface to *Cumandá*.

Indigenismo aligns more with realism and socialism; it was influenced by anticlericalism, scientific positivism, faith in progress, and was later buoyed by Marxism (Muñoz 72, 74). Drawing a distinction between the two genres, Aída Cometta Manzoni argues that la literatura indianista se ocupa del indio en forma superficial, sin compenetrarse de su problema, sin estudiar su psicología, sin fundirse con su idiosincrasia. La literatura indigenista, en cambio, trata de llegar a la realidad del indio y ponerse en contacto con él. Habla de sus luchas, de su miseria, de su dolor, expone su situación angustiosa; defiende sus derechos; clama por su redención.

[*Indianista* literature is superficially concerned with the Indian, without penetrating his problems, without studying his psychology, without understanding his idiosyncrasies. *Indigenista* literature, on the other hand, tries to approach the reality of the Indian and come into contact with him. It deals with his struggles, his misery, his pain; it exposes his anguishing situation, defends his rights, cries out for his vindication.] (20)[9]

Indigenista writers, mainly urban-educated and reasonably knowledgeable about the Indian majority (Pratt, "Women, Literature, and National Brotherhood" 61), studied the social, economic, and political conditions of native peoples in an attempt to understand their worldviews and problems. They also looked back to the pre-Columbian world to reinterpret the conquest and national history and thereby destroy the myth of the romantic Indian (Muñoz 102). Overall, *indigenista* novels are revisionary, have a distinct political platform, contain bits of native language, feature recognizable stereotyped characters, and support violent remedies for the Indians' plight (Echevarría 290). Evelio Echevarría goes so far as to claim a unique position in world literature for *indigenismo* as a genre written by whites on behalf of an oppressed minority. He maintains that few abolitionist novels can match the zeal with which *indigenista* novels rally for Indian liberation (289).

The answers to the Indian problem suggested in *indigenista* novels tend to fall into two categories: what Muñoz calls the liberal solution and the socialist solution. The liberal solution to Indian oppression resulted in the destruction of Indian culture: recognizing that those who exploited Indians would never favor charitable education and equality, liberals advocated rapid industrialization and modernization, a capitalist system intolerant of native communal, quasi-feudal social and commercial structures. Under this plan a dictator figure favorably carried out such destruction without affecting middle-class interests or investments (138–39). The socialist solution favored *mestizaje*: interracial mixing with whites so that Indian race and culture would lose distinct identity, on the theory that mestizos would inevitably adopt the dominant white culture and reject Indian identity as inferior. José Carlos Mariátegui rejects this theory with a blistering condemnation: "To expect that the Indian will be emancipated through a steady crossing of the aboriginal race with white immigrants is an anti-sociological naiveté that could only occur to the primitive mentality of an importer of merino sheep" (Urquidi 25). Involuntary on the part of Indians, *mestizaje* usually appears in novels as a white man's rape of an Indian woman. But like *indianismo*, *indigenista* novels, written by whites, appealed to the urban reading public, not to the natives themselves. Nevertheless, while *indigenista* novels glorify Indians' salvation, inevitably the native is denied a future as an Indian. *Indigenismo* as a genre dwindled around 1960 when novelistic innovations by the "boom" writers superseded interest in Indians.

Mera's Cumandá *and* Cooper's Last of the Mohicans

Writing in the genre now known as *indianismo*, Juan León Mera (1832–94) penned the pioneering fiction of Ecuador, *Cumandá; o, Un drama entre salvajes* (Cumandá; or, A drama among savages), published in 1879. Mera studied the local Quechua language and incorporated Indian themes into his poetry, fiction, and criticism. He considered himself a lifelong supporter of Ecuador's native population, both as a writer and as a governmental worker. In the novel, Mera details the geography and panoramic scenery of his beloved country to create an evocative local color resembling an exotic regionalism. He chose to write about primitive jungle natives, not the sierra natives of his adulthood, and set the novel seventy years back in time to 1808, twenty-two years before Ecuador achieved independence. Like Child, Cooper, Sedgwick, and Jackson in the United States, Mera situates his story in a mythic, simple past as if to plumb the depths of national history to find room for his reinterpretation of it. By setting their novels back in time, these authors evaded the reality of contemporary Indians' unfavorable conditions. Like some U.S. authors, Mera projects onto his Indian characters an aura of mysticism and stereotyped uncivilized exoticism.[10]

The idyllic, remote setting of *Cumandá*, however, might have another political purpose besides allowing Mera to recast history in his own image: the distant corner of Ecuador housing his novel's inhabitants may represent the border territory constantly in dispute with Peru. Situating a national novel in contested land suggests reappropriating and reclaiming that land as part of one's history and national identity. Instead of disengaging him from contemporary politics, such a move on Mera's part would place him in dialogue with political struggle and give *Cumandá* a nationalist agenda. Further, Mera's government affiliation illustrates Fernando Unzueta's point that outside of Latin America, "while government officials may participate in public discussions, the public sphere is independent from the state.... Nevertheless, in Latin America, partly because of censorship, but mostly on account of the close relationship between power and the letter ... such a separation has not been necessarily clear" (23). In other words, because in nineteenth-century Latin America a man of letters was often a man of government, the nationalism of *Cumandá* stems from the correlation between the rise of the public sphere and Mera's official status. Geoff Eley notes that "the emergence of nationality (that is, the growth of a public for nationalist discourse) was simultaneously the emergence of a public sphere" (296). Therefore, according to Unzueta, such "overdetermination is particularly relevant in the Latin American context, where most 'literary' organizations, discursive projects, and institutions have specific political and national agendas" (23).

Significantly, Mera openly acknowledged his debt to Cooper and Chateaubriand: "Bien sé que insignes escritors, como Chateaubriand y Cooper, han desenvuelto las escenas de sus novelas entre salvajes hordas y a la sombra de las selvas de América, que han pintando con inimitable pincel [I well know that distinguished writers such as Chateaubriand and Cooper have set the scenes in their novels among bands of savages and the shadows of the American jungles, which they have painted with inimitable brushstrokes]" (40). *Cumandá* parallels *The Last of the Mohicans* in many places, most notably in the cruelty of Magua and Tongana, the numerous episodes of danger and narrow escapes, the flights through the woods, the taking of prisoners, the rescues, the final scenes in which Indian and white mourn together over the body of a woman, the idealization of natives that nonetheless denies the purity of their unbaptized souls, and the insistence that society cannot accommodate a mixed-race marriage that unites white and Indian families. If the leading *indianista* novelist points to Cooper as his inspiration, then perhaps we can likewise view Cooper as writing in the *indianista* vein. For example, both novelists project onto their Indian characters an aura of romanticism and exoticism, while simultaneously glamorizing natives as living in a sentimental and nostalgic lost innocence. Again, I am not recommending that we force Cooper into an imported category, but perhaps by viewing his work among Andean categories we can better understand the movement from romanticized Indian representations by Cooper, Child, and Sedgwick to more realistic ones by Matto de Turner, Jackson, and Twain.

Although critics reviewed *Cumandá* favorably, few extensively addressed one of the novel's central concerns: interracial mixing.[11] Most essays address Mera's treatment of nature, romance, characterization, and incest. Recapitulating the foundational myth of the European conqueror Hernán Cortés claiming the native princess la Malinche, *Cumandá* obsesses over race and lineage, particularly in the descriptions of the eponymous heroine's skin, remarkably white for an Indian. For example, Mera writes that in Cumandá, "predomina en su limpia tez la pálida blancura del marfil [her clean skin strongly featured the pale whiteness of ivory]" (54). Mera no doubt had in mind here Cooper's descriptions of Alice Munro's whiteness as well as Cora Munro's darker skin in *The Last of the Mohicans*. Cooper casts Cora's skin as "not brown, but it rather appeared charged with the color of the rich blood, that seemed ready to burst its bounds" (19). The description of the rich-colored skin, along with Cora's dark eyes and hair, immediately alerts the reader to a stereotyped racial taint. As the dark heroine in a Fiedleresque scheme, Cora represents "corrupted woman, stained even before birth with the blackness of the primitive and passionate" (Fiedler 206), making her vital, strong, and unmarriageable to a white man. Similarly, Hawkeye reflects the novel's anxiety about racial mixing by insisting he is of a pure lineage. More than a dozen times he claims he is "a man without a cross." While some critics (Slotkin, *Regeneration*; Robinson) suggest that Hawkeye refers to his lack of Christian faith, it seems more likely that readers of the period would understand the implied discourse of race—that he has no cross to bear.[12]

Leslie Fiedler calls *The Last of the Mohicans*' miscegenation plot the secret theme of the novel, but it hardly seems secret since Cooper emphasizes its centrality by placing the revelation of Cora's mulatta background in chapter 16 in a novel with thirty-three chapters. Cooper reveals Cora's racial identity in the exact center of the novel, so it thereby serves as a fulcrum for the novel's action. *Cumandá* similarly demonstrates an obsession with race in its lament that the heroine's only fault is her resemblance to the hated whites, in the forbidden interracial romance between Cumandá and the missionary's son Carlos, and in the fatal ending, in which the Indian and her white lover discover they are siblings. Cumandá is fully white after all; kidnapped in an Indian raid as an infant and presumed dead by her family, she grew up in the household of chief Tongana as his daughter.

Cooper belabors the moments of potential miscegenation: to Magua's first offer of marriage (104), Cora replies that dying would be easier than marrying him and asks, "'Is life to be purchased at such a sacrifice?'" (109). The second time Magua offers marriage, he extends to her his hand, covered with the blood of a white man (177). Shirley Samuels draws a parallel between this mixture of white blood and red skin and the idea of miscegenation between Cora and Magua and interprets Magua's offer as a choice between physical and racial violence ("Generation through Violence" 103). The third time the two discuss marriage, Cooper draws a distinction between race as lineage and race as color. Tamenund orders Cora, "'A great warrior takes thee to wife. Go—thy race will not end'" (313). Although the Indian implies that Cora's genes, not whiteness, will survive, she sees the offer in terms of racial contamination: "'Better, a thousand times it should,' exclaimed the horror-struck Cora, 'than meet with such a degradation'" (313). And, in the final conflation of miscegenation and death, Magua forces Cora to choose between "the wigwam and the knife" (337). Seeing both as fatal, Cora cannot decide, and, raising her eyes and hands toward heaven, says, "'I am thine! do with me as thou seest best!'" It is unclear to whom she speaks—God or Magua. Both have the power to determine her fate, but Magua repeats his command to choose, as if he were the one being addressed. Cora's inability or unwillingness to make a distinction between miscegenation and death results in her being killed. In Cooper's vision, death is preferable to miscegenation.

Yet Magua understands Cora to be white, and in many ways she narratively functions as a white woman. Elise Lemire calls Cora's choice of death over marriage to Magua "the classic sacrifice of the white virgin" (44). Her preference for a white lover further serves to cast Cora as a white woman. Uncas's attraction to Cora and Duncan Heyward's to Alice perhaps signify the men's perception of their preferred women as *racially* more suited to their masculine designs. Although Nina Baym argues that Uncas chooses the sister who needs less protection from (white) society, she needs less only because her racial mixture already places her outside white society. Likewise, Duncan chooses Alice not just because her "weakness is her strength, inspiring men like Duncan, the representative of Anglo-American civilization, to fight for her" (29) but also because her whiteness allows her to be fought over. Lemire investigates Cora's shifting racial identity: that "Cora functions in the narrative as white sometimes and black other times explains, on the one hand, how she justifies the destruction of the Indians who want to mix with her—and, on the other, how she clears the way for Duncan to marry not this most attractive and outspoken woman but Munro's younger daughter whose passivity and pure white blood better suit her for the role of exchange object between the two men" (45).

In figuring miscegenation as a white man's desire for a seemingly Indian woman, Mera reverses Cooper's Indian man/white woman formula. Cora and Cumandá both exude an aura of sexual otherness that makes them attractive to a man of a different race. Cooper casts Magua's lust for Cora as repulsive and degrading, while Carlos and Cumandá share a chaste and ennobling love. Both these North and South American early novelists, however, demonstrate the failure of the literary imagination to accommodate race mixture. Like Cooper, Mera may be suggesting that racial affinity inheres as a powerful determinant in sexual attraction and hence that miscegenation is unnatural. Cooper hints that Alice attracts Duncan and that Cora attracts Magua because of racial affinity; that is, Duncan prefers Alice to her sister because he gravitates toward her unmixed whiteness. Similarly, Magua "senses" that Cora's mixed heritage removes her from sexual circulation among white society; her already mixed blood invites further mixture. Following his predecessor, Mera ascribes his hero and heroine's mutual attraction to their ability to "detect" their shared whiteness and shared parentage, in both a filial and a racial sense. By choosing Cumandá, Carlos instinctively chooses whiteness, thereby signaling that miscegenation is not as natural as racial homogeneity and that, like the case of Magua and Cora, thoughts of transgressing the color line, even if unconsummated, meet with death. Further, Carlos's recognition in Cumandá of an inherently good, sympathetic, and Christian soul makes it obvious to the reader that she is somehow more white than native. As we will see later, this ability to "detect" race surfaces also in *Ramona*, in which the discovery of the heroine's Indian ancestry accounts for her attraction to the Indian Alessandro.

The anxiety about racial integration in the novel proves unwarranted, for, after a series of unlikely events, the lovers Carlos and Cumandá find out that they are brother and sister. The anxiety about violating a blood taboo nonetheless still exists in *Cumandá*, but in a different form. More than the dread of miscegenation, the prohibition against incest keeps the would-be lovers apart. To dissuade readers from concluding the worst, the novel insists that Carlos and Cumandá's love has been chaste and fraternal. For example, Carlos claims that their affection for each other is so pure that it could have been ordained only by angels. By sanitizing their love, Mera deflects the incestuous tension (Sommer, *Foundational* 218). The incest plot provides a convenient reason why the lovers cannot marry and obviates forcing Mera or the reader to make a moral decision about the interracial romance. Incest, often a novelistic device to produce dread or show corruption, here rescues Mera from imagining miscegenation and produces a pseudo-happy ending: father, brother, and sister are reunited, but Cumandá is then killed and Carlos dies of grief. As we will see, Matto de Turner opted for the same resolution in *Aves sin nido*: the narrative unease with miscegenation is quelled by a convenient incest plot that obviates an authorial moral or political stance. The plots of *Cumandá* and *Aves sin nido* may remind many Latin Americanists of Gómez de Avellaneda's representation of *mestizaje* in an Afro-Caribbean context, especially in *Sab*. In that novel, more than ownership links the white Carlota with her slave Sab; the narrative strongly suggests that the two are first cousins. Sab's love for his mistress Carlota crosses the bloodline twice: exogamously he loves a racial other and endogamously he loves his cousin.[13]

Sommer finds a significant overlap between nationalistic histories and love stories. She seeks to address "*why* eroticism and nationalism become figures for each other in modernizing fiction" and then "*how* the rhetorical relationship between heterosexual passion and hegemonic states functions as a mutual allegory, as if each discourse were grounded in the allegedly stable other" (*Foundational* 31). Miscegenation stands as a powerful unifying force, and the prohibition against it often strengthens the erotic interest in Latin American novels. Referring to the theories that intermarriage elevates Latin America's Indians, Sommer suggests that "miscegenation was the road to racial perdition in Europe, but it was the way of redemption in Latin America, a way of annihilating difference and constructing a deeply horizontal, fraternal dream of national identity" (39). When the romance becomes thwarted, she argues, readers long for a political order in which such a love is possible. In *Cumandá* the romance fails; no erotic politics exist to portend racial integration or national consolidation. By the novel's conclusion, the love between Cumandá and Carlos offers society not redemption but sorrow at their deaths. Whether prohibitive or redemptive, race mixture does not occur in Mera's novel, thereby offering a critique of a racist society.

The Last of the Mohicans and *Cumandá* discursively engage political concerns about the role of Indian-white sexual alliances and thus signal rhetorically the centrality of racial heterogeneity to national identity. Cooper, the literary grandfather of *Cumandá*, did not concern himself with discrimination in his Leatherstocking series. Race mixture in *The Last of the Mohicans* proves undesirable, and Cora and Uncas die to preserve a legacy of unmixed whiteness for those who will dominate the United States. Departing from Cooper's vision, Mera welcomes Carlos's longing for the Indian maiden but, in creating an incest plot, offers a twist. According to Mera's schema, racism does not prevent Carlos from uniting his white heritage with Cumandá's Indian family, but incest does. For Mera, incest provides an alibi: an incestuous relationship is forbidden and thereby obviates further discussion about miscegenation. In fact, one could argue that Mera uses incest to naturalize the failure or impossibility of race mixture. Imagine how different *The Last of the Mohicans* would be if Cora and Uncas were kept apart not by racial prejudice but by incest —say, for example, if Major Munro had dallied with a native woman and fathered Uncas. A revelation of incest, the ending Mera chose and Cooper did not even consider, highlights what Cooper seems to avoid: familiarity and compatibility among peoples through racial heterogeneity. If *The Last of the Mohicans* could be identified as *indi-*

anista, as exemplified by its literary heir *Cumandá*, then two of Cooper's female contemporaries likewise wrote novels in which miscegenation plots cultivate *indianista* themes.

Race Mixture and Indianismo in Child's Hobomok *and Sedgwick's* Hope Leslie

In 1824, one year after the Monroe Doctrine's assertion of independence from Europe, twenty-two-year-old Lydia Maria Child answered Channing's and Palfrey's calls to found a national literature by writing her first novel. Set in the years between 1629 and 1633, *Hobomok* tells the story of the Puritan settler Mary Conant, who defies her father by marrying the Wampanoag Hobomok and having a child with him. Unlike the systematic pushing of Indians further west, Mary's intermarriage introduces the possibility of mixed-race progeny and assimilation. Child's novel departs from the "perennial heroic triad—the captive, the hunter, and the savage" (Slotkin, *Regeneration* 86), for while Hobomok represents the "savage," Mary is not a captive, nor does the novel contain a hunter in the mythic sense. Despite this divergence from the Anglo-American paradigm of frontier novels, Child's vision of natives aligns her with the *indianismo* genre. With miscegenation figured as a liberating fantasy and with no true understanding of natives' lives, Child's novel ends in a vision of whiteness and in complicity with the official rhetoric of Indian annihilation.

Scholars often read *Hobomok* as a novel concerned more with male-female relations than with Indian-white relations since Mary Conant chooses her own husband, changes the views of her father and community, and links women's and Indians' inferior status. While it is important to acknowledge gendered power differentials and the role of women in a male-dominated wilderness setting, it is equally important to recognize the significance of miscegenation in determining Mary's feminist victory and in marking the text as distinctly U.S. in origin. Mary commits herself bodily to a Native American while Child commits herself to refashioning early U.S. history in terms of racial miscibility. Conflating gender and race, *Hobomok* suggests that gendered power structures among whites falter when a white woman is willing to step outside the confines of patriarchy to take a dark lover.

By living among the "savages" in Hobomok's teepee, Mary leaves "civilization" without leaving domesticity, for she still plays the role of dutiful wife and mother; instead of making an errand into the wilderness, she brings the Indian into the home. As a U.S. writer, Child broke with English tradition by writing about Indians; as a U.S. woman writer, she ruptured social convention by creating a white female character who has a sexual romance with a dark other. *Hobomok* demonstrates that frontier fiction does not have to be only a male genre and that women writers had an important role in imagining the landscape, the limits of white civilization, the natives, and, most important for this study, Indian-white sexual relations.

For Mary, race mixture serves as an act of independence, of breaking away from a paternalistic power, mirroring the colonies' break with England. Child presents the three principal women characters—Mary, her mother, and her best friend, Sally—as a continuum of varying views of marriage and female autonomy. Mary prefers to marry Charles Brown, of whom her father disapproves because Charles is Episcopalian, not Calvinist. For advice Mary turns to her mother, who feels torn between obeying her husband and seeing her daughter happy.

The novel also compares Mary with Sally, who receives and rejects marriage proposals from two suitors and instead virtually proposes marriage to the man of her choice. Sally represents a midpoint between Mrs. Conant and Mary in terms of her willingness to express her thoughts about her marriage options. Whereas Mrs. Conant fears to voice her opinion, let alone act on it, Sally wisely avoids an undesirable suitor by assuming the masculine role of pursuer. Despite this, she chooses someone "safe," someone sure to earn the approval of her family and church. Although Sally defies convention, she does not defy her community. Mary, on the other end of the spectrum, proposes marriage to an Indian and suffers social ostracism. Of course, a white man could more easily have sexual relations with an Indian: in Child's story "A Legend of the Falls of St. Anthony," a white man marries a Sioux woman, knowing he could "dissolve the bond at any moment, with as little loss of reputation as if it were a *liaison* in Paris" (205).

Distraught after she receives news that her (white) lover has died in a shipwreck, Mary believes that only Hobomok loves her and that destiny binds them. In a scene unprecedented in U.S. literature, the white heroine says to the Wampanoag: " 'I will be your wife, Hobomok, if you love me' " (*Hobomok* 121). Mary hesitates when Hobomok takes her from Naumkeak (now Salem) to Plymouth, but evidently she loves him. At their Indian marriage ceremony, among his people, Mary swears, " 'I love him better than any body living' " (125) and after a short time confesses that " 'every day I live with that kind, noble-hearted creature, the better I love him' " (137). In these scenes Child draws upon the myth of the noble savage as inherently good, uncorrupted, and therefore deserving of a white woman's love. The heroine acknowledges the appeal of the return to the wilderness and embraces its emblem, Hobomok, as her lover. For these reasons, *Hobomok* shows similarities to Andean *indianista* novels. Furthermore, Child's representation of natives concurs with Mera's use of Indians to foster a nascent national literature. Child published *Hobomok* anonymously, signing it only "by an American" to emphasize its national, rather than personal, significance and to hide her gender. *Hobomok* begins with a preface narrated by a man named Frederic who wonders why anyone would attempt to write a novel " 'when Waverly is galloping over hill and dale. . . . Even American ground is occupied. "The Spy" is lurking in every closet,—the mind is every where supplied with "Pioneers" on the land, and is soon likely to be with "Pilots" on the deep' " (3). Child's technique of acknowledging Scott and Cooper's preeminence affords her an opportunity to offer, in the voice of an enfranchised male persona, her humble reasons for writing a competing novel as well as her critique of their literary history.

After the short preface, *Hobomok* begins in the first-person voice of Frederic's friend, who declares his national pride and simultaneously announces the novel's concern with national identity and glory: "I never view the thriving villages of New England, which speak so forcibly to the heart, of happiness and prosperity, without feeling a glow of national pride, as I say, 'this is my own, my native land' " (5). This exuberant patriotic pride then segues into the novel, thus drawing a link between national identity and its expression in fiction. The narrating voice intersplices his ancestor's manuscript with his own comments, taking the liberty of paraphrasing the Puritan's words since they are "antiquated and almost unintelligible" (7). With this condescending jab at a revered historical record, Child rewrites history as a fantasy novel of part-time and temporary miscegenation. Not until later in her life would Child develop a firm commitment to abolishing race prejudice and aiding disenfranchised Indians, blacks, and women.

Sedgwick in *Hope Leslie* also alludes to Cooper by reversing his plot in several ways. Like *The Last of the Mohicans*, Sedgwick's novel also concerns two sisters, but one succeeds in marrying a Native American. Sedgwick revises Cooper's story by imagining the strong Indian figure as a woman as well as by rewriting Cooper's rescue plot so that the Indian woman needs to be saved. Most significantly, Sedgwick rewrites Cooper by imagining interracial harmony through miscegenation. Sedgwick's vision more closely aligns with Child's in its liberal view of interracial sex, though, like Child's, her novel ends up Cooperlike with the disappearance of the Indians.

Like Child, Sedgwick returns to the founding myths of the Puritan white United States for the setting of *Hope Leslie* and offers an alternative to the received histories.[14] Iconoclastically, and perhaps in a nod to Cooper, she suggests in her preface that Native American chroniclers would depict their own people more justly than white writers could. Whereas Cooper declares in his introduction that he offers a corrective to the frivolous imaginings of his predecessors, Sedgwick distances herself from claims to historical accuracy, stating that her purpose in writing the novel is "to illustrate not the history, but the character of the times" while nonetheless alluding to actual events and people (5). Since Sedgwick considers the Puritans able recorders of colonial history but unsatisfactory accountants of colonial "character," she mixes fact with fiction, inventing what she found lacking. By filling gaps in the Puritan record, Child and Sedgwick participate in revisionist history by imagining expanded women's roles, native-white sympathy, and interracial desire and marriage. Sedgwick regards her novel as part of a project to steep U.S. literature in the country's distinctive history, for she concludes her preface by writing that "the ambition of the writer would be fully gratified if, by this work, any of our young countrymen should be stimulated to investigate the early history of their native land" (6). Race mixture, therefore, plays a key role in piquing interest in the foundations of the country's history and with imbuing the novel with a romantic, national sensibility—indeed, with an *indianista* sensibility.

Also like Child, Sedgwick believes the colonists' relationship with the Indians proved of prime importance, but she creates the first strong Indian female in U.S. literature, Magawisca, who also possesses a solid sense of national duty. Since Sedgwick did not know Native Americans personally, she derived her information on the Pequods from New England histories. Sedgwick establishes a miscegenation plot in *Hope Leslie* but forecloses the possibility of an enduring interracial romance and instead redirects her white hero toward an upwardly mobile society life while the beloved Indian disappears. Sedgwick does let one mixed-race couple survive: Hope's sister Faith, captured by the Pequods as a very young child, marries Magawisca's brother, Onceco. But since these characters remain minor and circulate outside domesticity, they disappear, childless, into the wilderness.

As with so many nineteenth-century novels, the plot of *Hope Leslie* works to marry off the heroine to a suitable hero. The Pequod Magawisca acts as a shadow heroine to Hope and also holds reciprocated affections for the hero, Everell. With these two women, plus Esther Downing, vying for Everell's attentions, Sedgwick reverses the usual marriage plot structure—here, women pursue the hero who must choose among his "suitors." The cross-racial desire structures the novel to suggest Hope for Everell's wife and exclude Magawisca and Esther. Like the women in *Hobomok*, those in *Hope Leslie* can be positioned on a continuum: Magawisca, Everell's first love, appears too Indian for the white hero; Esther, lacking affection for Indians, presents as too white. Hope, however, suitably hybridizes Magawisca and Esther in that her white skin melds with strong Indian sympathies and connections. Like Esther she represents whiteness and its attendant values of formal education and family status, but her independence and sense of adventure link her more strongly to Magawisca. Most important, though, Hope feels a deep affinity for Magawisca: their mothers are buried in the same cemetery, and, reversing *The Last of the Mohicans*, Hope engineers Magawisca's rescue from prison after Everell's attempt fails.

Hope and Magawisca claim another link as sisters-in-law. Hope's younger sister, Faith, abducted in a Pequod raid, married Magawisca's brother, Oneco. Magawisca eventually arranges a meeting between Hope and Faith, two sisters who have not seen each other for many years. Initially Hope rejoices in seeing Faith approaching by canoe, but her elation instantly turns to despair when she observes her sister's Pequod clothing and her attachment to Oneco: "At this first assurance, that she really beheld this loved, lost sister, Hope uttered a scream of joy; but when, at a second glance, she saw her in her savage attire, fondly leaning on Oneco's shoulder, her heart died within her; a sickening feeling came over her, an unthought-of revolting of nature; and instead of obeying the first impulse, and springing forward to clasp her in her arms, she retreated to the cliff, leaned her head against it, averted her eyes, and pressed her hand on her heart, as if she would have bound down her rebel feelings" (227).

Sedgwick presents the reunion as a wrenching encounter, again equating intermarriage with death, for Hope feels as if her heart has died. Race mixture here belies a "revolting of nature," and Hope clearly cannot accept it, no matter how much she cares for Magawisca. The authorial voice sympathizes with Hope's—and presumably the reader's—disapproval of the marriage. But by the end of the novel, the authorial voice condones the intermarriage through the mouth of Magawisca and castigates Hope and the reader for having opposed it. Magawisca also scolds Hope and the reader for thinking that Faith could ever return to white society: "Both virtue and duty . . . bind your sister to Oneco. She hath been married according to our simple modes, and persuaded by a Romish father, as she came from Christian blood, to observe the rites of their law. When she flies from you, as she will, mourn not over her, Hope Leslie—the wild flower would perish in your gardens—it is like a native home to her—and she will sing as gaily again as the bird that hath found its mate" (331–32).

Radical for its time, this scene insists that Faith belongs with her Pequod husband, and, even more significantly, that such an association does not degrade her. Hope reluctantly accepts her sister's fate, thereby extending her ties to the native world. By acknowledging Magawisca as her sister-in-law, Hope links herself to the native woman that society will never let Everell possess. The tension of miscegenation diverts onto Hope, racially white but culturally hybrid.

Coinciding with President Andrew Jackson's major efforts to remove southern Indians and the era's subsequent belief that the native population was doomed, the conclusions of *Hobomok*, *The Last of the Mohicans*, and *Hope Leslie* portray the ultimate imaginative failure of miscegenation and reinforce the belief that Indian annihilation or removal was inevitable. The Indian Removal Act, debated while these novels were being written and passed in 1830, thus connects novelistic assumptions about race and miscegenation with the project of nation building: the endings of *Hobomok, The Last of the Mohicans,* and *Hope Leslie* accord with popular sentiment and official policy, for they know that the Indians will move west and disappear. By looking to the past, to a period before major wars were fought between whites and Indians, before the U.S. government began active campaigns to push the Indians westward, Child, Cooper, and Sedgwick avert their consciences and persuasive powers from contemporary Indian injustices. Set in romantic pasts of lush wildernesses and pioneering spirits, their novels did nothing to alert U.S. readers to the contemporary plight of Native Americans. Not until later in their careers did Sedgwick endorse the abolitionist movement and Child become an outspoken activist on behalf of Indians and blacks, articulating her ideas more forcefully than she did in *Hobomok. Cumandá, The Last of the Mohicans, Hobomok,* and *Hope Leslie* discursively engage political concerns about the role of Indian-white sexual alliances in society, thus signaling rhetorically the centrality of miscegenation to national identity. If Mera, Cooper, Child, and Sedgwick use the fear of miscegenation and its repression to usher in nationhood, they portray Indians exotically and erotically and in no way do their novels contain elements of social realism or progressive reform. Therefore, these novels could be said to share traits with the *indianista* genre that preclude elements associated with the *indigenista* movement. In moving from Mera, Cooper, Child, and Sedgwick to Matto de Turner, Jackson, and Twain, we can detect a shift in white-authored representations of natives from the first quarter of the nineteenth century to the last quarter. Racial miscibility will prove key in determining the constraints of such representation.

Indigenismo *in Peru and the United States*

Clorinda Matto de Turner (1852–1909), a leading literary figure of nineteenth-century Peru, derives her literary and cultural status not from a Mera-styled *indianismo* but from the biting realist social commentary in her novels, especially in *Aves sin nido* (Birds without a nest), a novel that plays an important role in the evolution of Peru's literature.[15] *Aves sin nido* contains some elements aligning it with nineteenth-century romanticism, yet its portrayal of Indians' miserable living conditions and its critique of clerical abuse suggest a twentieth-century realist political sensibility. Critics have not failed to note the novel's fusion of romanticism and realism. For example, Wilfrido Corral considers Matto de Turner's transitional role as one that marks "la progresión hacia una nueva definición de civilización y barbarie [the progression toward a new definition of civilization and barbarism]" (399). Furthermore, John S. Brushwood notes that *Aves sin nido* "reveals the fundamentally romantic proclivity of the author and, at the same time, suggests her awareness (less than complete) of naturalism" (19). Yet although critics discuss the novel's fusion of literary movements, they overlook the significance of this genre miscegenation to the novel's articulation of racial miscegenation.

Aves sin nido tells the story of life in Kíllac, a fictional town in the Peruvian Andes, and the abusive "trinidad embrutecedora" (brutalizing trinity) of the judge, the governor, and the priest, who exploit the Indians. The novel details numerous manipulative ways in which the whites cheat the Indians and keep them in dire poverty. When the *cacique* threatens the Indians Marcela Yupanqui and Juan Yupanqui, Marcela turns in desperation to Lucía Marín, a rich white woman who takes pity on Marcela and gives her money to pay off her crushing debt. The corrupt governor and his cohorts try to kill Lucía and her husband, Fernando, to prevent their assisting the Indians; Marcela and Juan die defending their benefactors. While dying, Marcela reveals to Lucía a secret about the birth of Margarita, one of her two daughters. Readers do not learn the secret until the end of the novel. Lucía and Fernando take in the Indian couple's two girls and raise them as their own. Manuel, the governor's son, falls in love with Margarita, but Lucía and Fernando try to prevent Margarita from loving the son of her parents' killer. Manuel alleviates the Maríns' concern by telling them that the governor really is not his father. When the Maríns agree to the marriage, Manuel announces that his real father is the bishop don Pedro Mirando y Clara, who had raped his mother. Lucía reveals Marcela's tragic secret: Margarita's true father is this same bishop, who also raped Marcela. Manuel and Margarita share a father. As in *Cumandá*, the thwarted miscegenous love in this novel critiques a racist society while at the same time restoring family ties.

Matto de Turner pursued a lifelong interest in Indians' affairs and considered herself an activist for and supporter of their cause. In her preface to *Aves sin nido* she writes, "Amo con amor de ternura a la raza indígena [I love the indigenous race with tenderness]" and announces that she wrote the novel with "la idea de mejorar la condición de los pueblos chicos del Perú [the idea of improving the condition of the small towns of Peru]" (37–38), nearly the same reason Helen Hunt Jackson gives for writing *Ramona* (Banning 201–2). Matto de Turner charges the act of writing with the zeal of nationalism: she claims that her purpose in authoring the novel is "recordando que en el país existen hermanos que sufren, explotados en la noche de la ignorancia, martirizados en esas tinieblas que piden luz; señalando puntos de no escasa importancia para los progresos nacionales; y *haciendo* a la vez, literatura peruana [remembering that in this country many brothers suffer, exploited in the night of ignorance, martyred in the shadows that cry out for light; marking points of not little importance for national progress; and at the same time, *making* Peruvian literature]" (38).

Matto de Turner sees her craft as "making" Peruvian literature by writing about the downtrodden Indians. That is, representing and speaking for the Indians embodies the essence of the national literary heritage. Further, *Aves sin nido* represents the downtrodden lower class. The nineteenth-century Latin American novel that portrays the lower classes recognizes, according to Unzueta, that "its target audience, in addition to the generic and supposedly universal 'man' ('hombre'), has been broadened to include women and members of all social classes (including the 'menos cultas' [less cultured])" (27). Matto de Turner's campaign to awaken public consciousness cannot be separated from her novel's literary genre because, as a realist genre, *indigenismo* uses verisimilitude to probe and criticize Indian existence in Peru. To achieve verisimilitude the novel must, photographlike, reflect to readers both the joys and the ills of society to be prescriptive and corrective. As she also writes in the novel's preface, "La novela tiene que ser la fotographía que estereotipe los vicios y las virtudes de un pueblo, con la consiguiente moraleja correctiva para aquellos y el homenaje de admiración para éstas [The novel must be a photograph that stereotypes the vices and virtues of the people, with the consequent corrective moral for the former and an homage of admiration for the latter]" (38).

As in *Cumandá*, the incest plot in Matto de Turner's novel overwhelms the race mixture plot. But *Aves sin nido* differs remarkably from *Cumandá* because at no point in the novel does the interracial love affair present conflict. Whereas both Cumandá's and Carlos's parents discourage their mixed romance, neither the Maríns nor Manuel's mother protests Margarita's Indian bloodline. As representatives of society, the Maríns and Manuel's mother demonstrate the willingness of the general populace to accept race mixture, so its failure stands as a critique of systemic discrimination and clerical abuse. Although Matto de Turner's authorial voice does not comment either way on the lovers' racial suitability, it is clear that the foiled romance here serves as a nascent reform movement. According to Sommer, readers of *Aves sin nido* mark with tears and sympathy their sorrow at the lovers' frustration and are thereby sensitized and inspired to long for national unity and consolidation. Linking the body human with the body politic, the failure of erotic incorporation instigates the desire for partisan incorporation.

On the surface, Manuel and Margarita face a problem similar to that confronting Cumandá and Carlos: sexual tension between siblings of different races. Perhaps Peter Brooks best articulates the novelistic tension between the dual anxieties of miscegenation and incest. Brooks labels incest "that which overassimilates, denies difference, creates too much sameness," whereas miscegenation he defines as the "mixture of blood, the very trace of difference: that which overdifferentiates, creates too much difference" (308). But Brooks's pairing of miscegenation with difference may be misleading. The narrative anxiety about miscegenation reflects fears that the races may not be inherently different—interracial attraction presumes the humanity and sameness of the other. Miscegenous desire levels difference and hierarchy and therefore assimilates. In *Cumandá* and *Aves sin nido*, interracial love creates and acknowledges correspondence and compatibility between the races. Similarly, since cultures fear incestuous unions because of their potential to produce genetic deformities, incest can create monstrous difference and is thus prohibited.

The novelistic tension in *Cumandá* pulls in the seemingly opposite directions of miscegenation and incest, but here the antipodal taboos of too much sameness and too much difference collapse. The love interest in *Cumandá* cannot sustain the numerous paradoxes and becomes impossible. But in Matto de Turner's schema, no anxiety derives from miscegenation; all the tension comes from the possibility of incest. Again, as in *Cumandá*, the incest plot complicates authorial intention. Whereas Cooper, Child, and Sedgwick unambiguously portray frustrated miscegenous desire and reasons for racial segregation, Matto de Turner does not have to account for a viable cross-racial relationship. Although Manuel and Margarita desire each other, the reader does not have to formulate a moral judgment about their possible union. As does Mera, Matto de Turner uses incest as an alibi to naturalize the impossibility of race mixture. The reader can mourn the lovers' separation but celebrate restored family ties. *Aves sin nido* would be bolder had Matto de Turner depicted a consummated interracial marriage, yet she instead chose to condemn discrimination without anticipating a brighter future.

Racial Heterogeneity in Ramona

While *The Last of the Mohicans*, *Hobomok*, and *Hope Leslie* seem in many ways to correspond to the Andean *indianista* genre, as illustrated by Cooper's heir Mera, Helen Hunt Jackson's *Ramona* (1884) and Mark Twain's unfinished fragment "Huck and Tom among the Indians" (1884) have much in common with the *indigenista* movement. Jackson and Twain wrote *Ramona* and "Among the Indians" while questions of white westward movement and Indian policy were being actively debated. Written in the same year, *Ramona* and "Among the Indians" share some traits: both receive their titles from the central characters, orphans raised by guardians, and in both the protagonists flee the settled United States with a member of a persecuted race. However, although both authors represent the United States "as an intolerant and intolerable society" (Ziff 224), each has a specific agenda in replicating those very injustices he or she decries. Jackson and Twain share unquestioned assumptions about the inevitability of U.S. government encroachment into Indian territory in the West, but they do not share attitudes toward Indians and Indian-white sexual mixing. Jackson and Twain portray native-white race mixture in ways that differ greatly from those used by Cooper, Child, and Sedgwick, and we can better understand these differences if we see the shift in time from early to late in the century as a shift in genre from *indianismo* to *indigenismo*.

The "Indian question" split the eastern and western United States, and perhaps geography accounts for the varied representation of natives on either coast. For example, many easterners, having witnessed their Indian populations pushed west, upheld the noble savage stereotype and formed societies to save their "red brothers." Urban blacks lived in much closer proximity to eastern whites, and blacks' presumed permanence in U.S. society motivated white writers to represent them, rather than Indians, in fiction. Emerson's and Thoreau's resistance to the Indian Removal Act constitutes an exception to this generalization, while Robert S. Levine connects these concerns to the rise of urban reform movements from 1830 to 1860 (147–48). Western settlers, in contrast, still attacked by Indians who resisted their colonizing efforts, were less apt to accept the myth of Cooper's noble savage. Indeed, the name "Cooper" and "Cooper's Indians" became pejorative code words for easterners' romanticized and sentimental views of Indians. Post–Removal Act policy subordinated Indian interests to whites' demands for more land. With the western expansion of Manifest Destiny, victory in the Mexican War that added territory, and the beginning of the California gold rush in 1848, white settlers regularly encroached upon Indian lands.

Jackson and Twain held opposing opinions regarding Indians and the Indian question. In her book *A Century of Dishonor* (1881) and in her official capacity as special commissioner of Indian affairs in 1882, Jackson rallied for the Indian cause. Twain's feelings toward the Indians could not have been more opposed to Jackson's. In the most famous example of his antipathy, his hateful essay "The Noble Red Man" (1870), Twain refers to Indians as, among other things, the "scum of the earth" (444). Moreover, Twain equated being a "disciple of Cooper" with being "a worshiper of the red man" and, influenced by Cooper, believed he "had been overestimating the red man while viewing him through the mellow moonshine of romance" (*Roughing It* 83). In contrast, though antagonistic to Indians, Twain held some sympathies for blacks, as exemplified by his portrayal of Jim in *Adventures of Huckleberry Finn*.

Written well after Native Americans were pushed west, *Ramona* criticizes social and cultural prejudices against racial amalgamation and shows the abuse that Indians, especially Indian women, received at the hands of whites. Jackson assumes the inevitability of U.S. government encroachment and puts Indian-white miscegenation to political use by influencing readers' emotions and prejudices with it. Miscegenation themes articulate a struggle for control over two territories: the territory of the (white) female body and the geographical territory of the United States. Amy Kaplan notes that "the woman of mixed race preserves the forgotten history of the nation's westward expansion" ("Nation, Region, and Empire" 261); similarly, Indians, Mexicans, and whites clash over Ramona's body in a battle to determine the future of the nation.

In an 1883 letter, Jackson wrote, "I am going to write a novel, in which will be set forth some Indian experiences in a way to move people's hearts. . . . People will read a novel when they will not read serious books" (qtd. in Banning 200). Jackson considered *Ramona* a spoonful of sugar that sweetened her politics and hoped that the reader "would have swallowed a big dose of information on the Indian question without knowing it" (qtd. in Mathes 77). Jackson modeled *Ramona* after *Uncle Tom's Cabin*: "If I can do one-hundredth part for the Indians as Mrs. Stowe did for the Negroes, I will be thankful" (qtd. in Banning 201–2).

Despite its popular success, *Ramona* did not do for the Indians what *Uncle Tom's Cabin* did for slaves. Alessandro's character can be held partly responsible for the view of the novel as romantic. Not an average Indian, as Uncle Tom represented the typical slave, Alessandro instead acted like a highborn Mexican with a Christian sensibility. Even Ramona hardly considered him an Indian. Moreover, the romantic ending of the novel undermines Jackson's political intent. Had Ramona lived and died in misery and squalor, then perhaps the novel would have dramatized the injustices toward Indians more powerfully (Mathes 84). With the happy resolution, the reader rejoices in Ramona's good fortune and second marriage, and the tragedy of Alessandro is relegated to the forgotten past.

Furthermore, Jackson refrained from making Ramona fully Indian. Jackson's conception of the trajectory of U.S. history and her understanding of her audience mandated that Ramona be of mixed blood and that she be forced to think about race when deciding to marry. Unlike Mary Conant in *Hobomok* and Faith Leslie in *Hope Leslie*, white heroines who radically solve the Indian problem by marrying one, Ramona cannot represent a white heroine who uses her whiteness to challenge contemporary racial convictions. She grows up belonging to the Mexican part of Jackson's tripartite division of the United States. The characters reflect a clear hierarchy of race, with white at the top and Indian at the bottom. Throughout the novel Jackson works against this order by portraying the white settlers, other than Aunt Ri and her family, as depraved and unrepentant and the Mexicans and Indians as respectable and heroic. But Jackson still casts a vote against the Indians in favor of the aristocratic Mexicans, who, by virtue of their formal education and wealth, function as whites. Because of Ramona's mysterious natal circumstances, race announces itself early as a central concern of the novel. Ramona herself does not know the secret of her parentage, and the narrating voice informs the reader well before Ramona finds out. Ramona's Scottish father, shamed by his baby's Native American mother, abducts Ramona and entrusts her to his Mexican former lover. Born of an Indian and an Anglo, yet raised as a Mexican, Ramona represents a fleshly racial democracy, embodying the conjunction of three competing ethnicities.

The indeterminacy of the heroine's blood forces her to circulate among the competing races to determine not just her future but also the nation's. By marrying Alessandro first and then her adopted brother Felipe and having children with both, Ramona passes on a mixed-race legacy to her Indian and Mexican children. The closure of Ramona's marriage to Felipe and their move to Mexico distracts readers from the very injustices Jackson is trying to portray. The novel concludes by linking Indian disappearance to women's bodies, for Alessandro is remembered in the mind of his widow and in the body of his mixed-race daughter, also named Ramona. Like little Hobomok, the two Ramonas embody assimilation—they never come to know their mothers' Indian identity (Gutiérrez-Jones 63). The bodies of Ramona, mother and daughter, fleshly witnesses to native existence, disappear in the westward push of an expanding country. In writing such a sentimental story, Jackson hoped to change readers' consciousness about natives by revising whites' attitudes and prejudices. This social-action agenda distinguishes Jackson's representation of Indians from that of Mera, Cooper, Child, and Sedgwick and aligns her with the realist vindication platform of *indigenismo*, especially in the way that genre "se llena de indignación y convoca a la rebeldía en nombre de la justicia [is full of indignation and calls for rebellion in the name of justice]" (Sánchez 28). Twain similarly attempts to represent natives "realistically" to encourage his political stance but, as we shall see, his aims and outcomes differ greatly from Jackson's.

"Huck Finn and Tom Sawyer among the Indians"

Jackson and Twain have similar backgrounds: both spent considerable time among the Indians, Jackson as a special commissioner and Twain as a traveler on the Oregon Trail, which he wrote about in *Roughing It* (1872); in 1884 both wrote stories about Indian-white relations set several decades earlier. The authors' visions and politics, however, could not be more opposed.

According to a letter Twain wrote to William Dean Howells in July 1884, two months after *Ramona* was serialized in the *Christian Union*, he was writing "Among the Indians." The two authors had met five years earlier at the same birthday party for Oliver Wendell Holmes where Jackson met Stowe. As a man of letters, Twain was likely aware of *Ramona*'s runaway success, if not of Jackson's earlier work *A Century of Dishonor* (1881), but little did Twain know at the time that *Ramona* would outsell *Huckleberry Finn* (Ziff 225). Twain intended "Among the Indians" to be a humorous satire of the pervasive contemporary idealization of Indians by describing Indians "realistically." Twain's droll idea of realism produced negative characterizations of the Indians; the story thereby revealed what Walter Blair calls "a development like those which gave several of his earlier books a unifying theme—a change from romantic belief to disillusionment" (82). Wayne R. Kime may be alluding to *Ramona* when he claims that "Among the Indians" could "plausibly be viewed as an aborted experiment at bringing a measure of reality to the convention-ridden escapism that characterized the cheap fiction of his day" (331). If Twain wrote against clichéd, escapist "cheap fiction," he may have had *Ramona* in mind because he bashes many principles on which that novel is based.

Jackson's intent with *Ramona* was to raise awareness of the Indians' plight and kindle moral outrage at their abhorrent treatment. Twain, in contrast, portrays Indians as debased murderers, liars, and beggars in *Roughing It* and as a threat against women's bodies in *Tom Sawyer*, in which Injun Joe conspires to tie up the widow Douglas in bed and slash her face as revenge for the public flogging her husband had ordered him to undergo years before. Twain also pokes fun at Cooper's romantic and noble savages: after the Sioux massacre of the Mills family, Huck asks Tom, " 'Where did you learn about the Injuns —how noble they was, and all that?' " Silent for a moment, Tom shamefully answers, " 'Cooper's novels' " (*"Huck Finn"* 50). While Jackson, in addition to portraying the Indians favorably, criticizes U.S. government policy that grants land to white homesteaders but disregards Indian claims, Twain's fragment uncritically portrays the inevitability of the white westward momentum.

Jackson's romanticism and Twain's realism clash most fiercely over women's bodies and sexual relations with Indian men. Jackson idealizes Alessandro and uses his marriage to Ramona in an attempt to elevate the reader's opinion of the mission Indians. Twain's Sioux, in contrast, abduct and rape Peggy Mills, thereby giving the reader cause to hate the Indians. Just as Ramona's body represents the mixing of whites, Indians, and Mexicans and just as her fate articulates the battle for the land, so too does Peggy resemble the territories contested by whites and Indians. As the white settlers stake claims, the Sioux literally "stake" Peggy as their claim. The fragment suggests that the four stakes found in the ground were used to tie Peggy up during the rape. The fragment breaks off as Brace Johnson, Peggy's beau, plans to rescue Peggy—with Huck and Tom's help—and reclaim her, just as he will then stake a claim in Oregon.

Jackson and Twain agree on one point: interracial sex is disagreeable. To solve the dilemma of how to represent Indians as noble beings worthy of a white woman's love without actually portraying a white woman loving an Indian, Jackson envisions Ramona as a halfbreed. Ramona's Indian blood makes her an appropriate mate for Alessandro, while her whiteness suggests Alessandro's innate merit. Because Twain also considered Indian-white sex offensive, he represents miscegenation—configured as the rape of a white woman by an Indian man—as the ultimate sign of Indian depravity. But the prospect of rape was so abhorrent that Twain could not finish writing his story.

Twain started crafting "Among the Indians" while *Adventures of Huckleberry Finn* was in page proof, intending the sequel to be a story of disillusionment, with miscegenation as the final act that turns both his characters and his readers against the Indians. As the sequel to *Adventures of Huckleberry Finn*, "Among the Indians" deconstructs the myth of frontier expansion that its predecessor celebrates: there is nothing noble about an Indian who violates white female sexuality and demonstrates the white man's inability to protect her.

While Huck, Tom, and Jim search for adventure, Peggy keeps a dirk with which to commit suicide should Indians capture her. Sweetly naive, she does not understand why Brace insists she is better off dead than captive. Peggy reveals to Huck that she asked Brace for an explanation and that she " 'teased him to tell me, but he wouldn't. He kept trying to get me to promise, but I laughed him off, every time, and told him if he was so anxious to get rid of me he must tell me *why* I must kill myself, and then maybe I would promise. At last he said he *couldn't* tell me' " (44). The probability of rape and miscegenation causes Brace so much anxiety that he is unable to continue, a metanarrative reflection of Twain's own problem. Both Twain and Brace prefer silence to articulating miscegenation, which is literally unspeakable in the story.

Brace, who, like Hawkeye, has spent time among the natives,[16] explains the fear of Indian rape to Huck, but only in terms of the desirability of its alternative, death. After the Indian raid and massacre, Brace desperately insists that Peggy has killed herself. Confused, Huck asks Brace why he hopes Peggy is dead, but the reader does not learn Brace's answer. Huck reports only, "He explained it to me, and then it was all clear" (54). The unspeakable horror generates a sequence of further silences and cover-ups. Huck finds Peggy's dirk and hides it to sustain Brace's delusion that Peggy is dead. Huck and Tom also pretend to find and bury Peggy's body, preferring deception to the truth of rape. Tom at first refuses to fake Peggy's burial, compelling Huck to explain his reasoning: "So it looked like I'd got to tell him why I reckoned it would be better, all around, for Brace to think we found her and buried her, and at last I come out with it, and then Tom was satisfied" (59). To distance Huck from the act of speaking about rape, Twain does not use verbs such as "explain," "tell," "relate," "reveal," or "say." Huck simply "comes out with it," as though narrative agency was beyond his control: the unspoken speaks for itself instead. Neither Huck nor Tom expresses any concern or anxiety upon discovering the bloody piece of Peggy's dress and her footprint or when they learn about the near certainty of her rape. Kime speculates that "Twain may have wished to represent Huck as incapable of reacting to the heroine's plight as a mature person would, but this is not the impression given by his narrative. The impression is rather that he was unable or unwilling as an author to address explicitly the subject of rape" (330). As we will see, Twain's hesitation to write about rape, miscegenation, and the female body reflects his confusion about the genre contours of his story.

Race Mixture as Cannibalism

If "Huck Finn and Tom Sawyer among the Indians" meditates on the fear of Indian-white intercourse, it also expresses anxiety about nonsexual Indian-white merging via communal eating and cannibalism. Eating, like sex, is a taking of the other into the body, a sensual converging, an incorporation with an emphasis on corpus. The Roman Catholic doctrine of communion maintains that at the moment of consecration the wafer and the wine transubstantiate into the body and the blood of Christ. To Hulme, "of course the Christian communion consists in eating the flesh of man and there should be no difficulty, at least for believers, in calling it an act of cannibalism— if, that is, 'cannibalism' were to be defined simply as the eating of human flesh" (84). Hulme goes on to provide a careful reading of the difference between anthropophagy (the eating of human flesh) and cannibalism, which refers to a discourse of otherness. The French word *consommer* means both to consume and to consummate, linking eating and intercourse as capable of incorporating one body into another. Eating and kissing, notes Maggie Kilgour, "are obviously both oral activities, and at an extreme level of intensity the erotic and aggressive sides of incorporation cannot be differentiated, so that it becomes difficult to tell at what point the desire for consummation turns into the desire for consumption" (7–8).

Richard Slotkin links cannibalism to miscegenation when he notes that for the white hunter, "the traditional revulsion against cannibalism was heightened by the horror implicit in the idea of sexual marriage with the wilderness" (*Regeneration* 125). In "Among the Indians," Twain juxtaposes fear of rape ("sexual marriage with the wilderness") with eating, partially blaming Peggy's rape on the Mills family's willingness to share food with the Indians. In the fragment, unnatural social mixing leads to perverse sexual mixing. Miscegenation and communal eating intimately dissolve the boundary between white and Indian.

Tom first senses that something is wrong after the Indians finish eating dinner with the Mills family. He notices that the Sioux do not smoke a pipe, indicating that the meal is not over, that peace has not been attained. Tom is right, for the slaughter and abduction take place right after the meal. During the hellish night, Huck wanders around frightened. His first thought the next morning is of food: "When daylight come, I didn't dast to stir, at first, being afraid; but I got so hungry I had to" (48). Huck and Tom search for food amid the wreckage, again linking rape, death, and eating: "We scratched around for something to eat, but didn't find it, everything being burnt" (48). Finally, Tom describes to Huck the horrific way the Indians treated the Mills boys' bodies "and he told me how else they had *served* the bodies, which was horrible" (48; emphasis added). The word "served" strengthens the image of the Mills family as the ending of the Sioux's meal, with Peggy's rape as the dessert. Twain's juxtaposition of eating and rape, acts of interracial communion, clearly establishes his distaste for Indian-white comingling.

Miscegenation and Genre

"Among the Indians" breaks off as Brace, Huck, and Tom resume their search for Peggy. Brace disguises himself as a crazed medicine man by sewing dead bugs and lizards to his clothes in the hope that the Sioux will not kill a lunatic. In 1890, Twain considered changing the plot so that Tom dresses up as the crazed naturalist to infiltrate the Sioux camp, for he wrote, "Tom muss den Medicine man spielen" (*Notes* 594). Twain most likely ran into trouble here, for the momentum of the narrative would lead to finding Peggy, battered and raped. It would be difficult to end "Among the Indians" as *Ramona* ends, with the hero rescuing and marrying the untainted heroine. Ramona's time among the Indians is portrayed as innocent and nostalgic, not cruel and debasing. Blair problematically suggests that "Twain might have achieved a happy ending, to be sure, by having his characters discover that the stakes had been used for another purpose—for the torture of male captives or for the torture of a female captive by a squaw" (91). Deflecting Peggy's fate onto another character hardly seems a "happy" solution.

Kime and Blair both maintain that Twain abandoned the story because he found rape and miscegenation too horrific to narrate. Kime contends that Twain worked himself into a double bind, for to portray Indian cruelty, he had to debase his heroine: "Here Twain fronted the problem he found insoluble: that his young heroine— generous, confiding, womanly, yet virginal—was the embodiment of an ideal which he himself worshiped.... The narrative framework he had created to explode false ideas about Indian character was forcing him into a task of authorship he was unwilling to complete" (331). Similarly, Blair asserts that, "unable to write frankly about rape, yet convinced that realism demanded he do so, Mark Twain abandoned the story" (272).

Yet Twain's silence about rape may be different from his characters' silence. Brace cannot bring himself to speak of Peggy's violation, but Twain probably could. Twain was not known to be prudish and probably was capable of writing about rape. But Twain faced the genre question of how to include rape in a comic story. The direction of the narrative suggests that Twain realized his audience would find the subject abhorrent. Therefore, Twain likely put down his pen not because he was discomfited by the topic but because he could not extricate himself from the formal, genre problem of mixing humor and rape. Since rape is no laughing matter, the miscegenation theme in "Among the Indians" influences its genre contours; rape and miscegenation tilt the genre of "Among the Indians" from comedy to melodrama. Similarly, genre concerns determine deployment of interracial mixing. Twain's aim in writing the fragment (an urban-educated intellectual using realism to convey true native conditions and debunk the romantic myth of the noble savage) corresponds to *indigenismo*'s purpose in that Twain pokes fun at Cooper to deflate the popular image of the noble Indian. But Twain cannot be classified as an *indigenista* writer because although his aims are revisionary and he maintains a political agenda, he does not attempt to understand natives or to champion their vindication. Realism for Twain is not a tool of Indian racial uplift when interracial sex is implied, but rather his use of realism's claims to verisimilitude demonstrates what Robert Berkhofer terms the "vitriolic racism of literary realism" (105).

Race mixture gives *Ramona* an exotic and romantic glow; the illicit interracial sex piques the reader's interest and imbues the story with a U.S. exoticism. In "Among the Indians," however, miscegenation as rape turns realism dark. Twain figures rape as the ultimate realist, if racist, device, even more potent a weapon than satire.

For all their differences, these nineteenth-century U.S. novels share a theme: the inevitable disappearance of the Indians.[17] In the nineteenth century the myth of the Vanishing American became a well-established political and literary theme as government policy and novelistic representation echoed and further entrenched the other's assumptions that the native population would forfeit land to whites. Between 1789 and 1820, one hundred novels were published in the United States (Davidson viii); in the following ten-year period of 1824–34, forty novels about Indian disappearance alone appeared, establishing what Brian Dippie terms the "cult" of the Vanishing American (21).[18] When cast in historical terms, this myth makes disappearance seem a natural step in the march of progress. The widespread acceptance of the myth made it easier to blame the Indians for their own annihilation. Since the Indians were dying from disease and war, U.S. government officials thought it best to remove them to some distant place where they would be safe and thereby saved (Dippie 71). Thus, U.S. removal policies became noble rescue missions.

The myth of the Vanishing American acquires a different valency in the context of miscegenation because a character's disappearance offers an easy and a credible reason for an interracial relationship to end. Disappearance becomes a narratological device to allow authors to extricate themselves believably from controversial or difficult plots. Since nineteenth-century sensibility would abhor an enduring racially exogenous relationship, writers instead created mixed-race ties that ended and hence they did not appear to condone them. Readers at that time, familiar with the myth of the Vanishing American, readily accepted plots that dissolved interracial romance by having the Indian simply vanish. If miscegenation creates a narrative problem, disappearance resolves it by shaping a satisfactory closure. Cooper, Mera, Child, Sedgwick, Matto de Turner, Jackson, and Twain all portray Indians who, one way or another, disappear. No other ending for them is possible.

2

Temperance and Miscegenation in Whitman's Franklin Evans

How are miscegenation and genre linked in temperance fiction? While the previous chapter suggests that representations of Indian-white race mixture shape generic contours, this chapter examines the way black-white racial mixing affects the popular temperance fiction genre. Much, although certainly not all, antebellum temperance fiction enjoyed success by adhering to a formula: a young innocent, often a country boy who moves to the city in search of work and excitement, tastes alcohol for the first time and slides down the slippery slope to drunken degradation, poverty, and death. Yet in Walt Whitman's conventional temperance novel, *Franklin Evans; or, The Inebriate* (1842), that conventional formula is modified by a black-white sexual liaison. Just as Indian-white relations affect narratives in chapter 1, race mixing turns Whitman's novel dark and sensational and steers its ostensible anti-alcohol message in another direction.

In the "Introductory" to *Franklin Evans*, Whitman asserts that readers surely have "heard the histories of intemperate men," and he underscores the major theme of his novel: "The following chapters contain but the account of a young man, thrown by circumstances amid the vortex of dissipation—a country youth, who came to our great emporium to seek his fortune—and what befell him there" (126). Although the reader may infer from the reference to "intemperate men" and "dissipation" that the story is a temperance tract, Whitman does not claim that the novel exclusively treats alcoholism.

Although Whitman points in his "Introductory" to an anti-alcohol text, a careful examination of his rhetoric shows that he simultaneously points around or points beyond alcoholic temperance to suggest a subtext of racial temperance. Much of *Franklin Evans*'s moralistic message is conveyed by deliberately vague or flexible language, so that Whitman's prohibitionary rhetoric against drunkenness can likewise be read as antimiscegenation rhetoric. That alcohol and race come together in this novel so that one bespeaks the other suggests the profound ways that alcohol and race address the racialized body, mental and corporeal enslavement, and reform. This chapter will look at the discourse of temperance in *Franklin Evans* and observe that it redoubles as a discourse advocating racial temperance, such that exhortations in favor of abstinence and warnings against imbibing, temptation, inebriation, evil spirits, and debauchery have a dual meaning. To do so, this chapter will identify where Whitman deliberately plays with the plasticity of language to employ purposefully flexible rhetorical strategies that link his dark and sensational Washingtonian message to dark and sensational miscegenation. Whitman thus conflates drunkenness and miscegenation to promote abstinence from the linked immoral vices of alcohol and interracial sex.

Although Whitman later claimed that he wrote this temperance novel with the "help of a bottle of port" and that *Franklin Evans* was "damned rot—rot of the worst sort—not insincere, perhaps, but rot, nevertheless," it arguably stands as Whitman's best-selling work, selling some twenty thousand copies and earning him $75 (qtd. in Traubel 93). *Franklin Evans*'s "Introductory," laden with a lecturing tone, suggests that interracial sexual mixing, as well as sobriety, is a matter of morality. The opening paragraph states that the novel's "moral—for I flatter myself it has one, and one which it were well to engrave on the heart of each person who scans its pages—will be taught by its own incidents, and the current of the narrative" (126). As the "current of the narrative" flows, the "incidents" by which the moral will be "taught" culminate when Evans is so intoxicated that he marries a slave woman. This incident represents Evans's moral nadir and interracial sexual mixing becomes the novel's central moral cause.

To convey a moralistic message, Whitman reminds the reader in the "Introductory" that "earlier teachers of piety used parables and fables as the fit instruments where by they might convey to men the beauty of the system they professed" (127). Parables and fables, significantly, teach morals or lessons indirectly via a narrative. Often parables and fables entertain the reader or listener through the exploits of animals or nonhuman creatures yet convey an underlying message. Thus, parables and fables employ what can be termed a "dual discourse"—in which one discourse contains another—a strategy that Whitman adopts in *Franklin Evans*. Cynthia S. Jordan uses the term "second story" to refer to "promotional surface narratives [that] are constantly threatened by evidence of opposing views, and that evidence constitutes a rival second story" (xi). Although in *Franklin Evans* the second story advocating racial temperance works with, and does not threaten, the novel's "promotional surface narrative" of alcoholic temperance, Jordan's term nonetheless proves helpful for understanding Whitman's work.

Although some readers have noticed that *Franklin Evans* seems to have something other than alcohol as its main topic, none has explicitly identified or adequately investigated racial hybridity as the central theme. For example, Karen Sánchez-Eppler points out that since the Virginia chapters treating Evans's relationship with a black woman comprise one-third of the novel, "their prominence attests to something other than an interest in the ills of drink" (*Touching* 58). Michael Warner writes that "when he is talking about alcohol in *Franklin Evans* Whitman often seems to be thinking about something else" and that if "alcohol does not quite seem to be the subject here, still it is no accident that Whitman's first extended treatment of a dialectic between self-mastery and self-abandonment should occur in the form of temperance fiction." Warner goes on to discuss the role of temperance discourse as a "fantasy of stateless public association," thus demonstrating the pliability of temperance rhetoric (31).

David S. Reynolds also notes that *Franklin Evans* allowed Whitman the flexibility to dabble with a second story. Reynolds contends that *Franklin Evans* "helped sow the seeds for *Leaves of Grass*, because it showed Whitman experimenting with an ostensibly pure vehicle— temperance reform—to explore themes that veered quickly into the sensational and erotic" (*Walt* 95). Reynolds further comments that when Whitman reprinted the novel in his newspaper, the *Brooklyn Daily Eagle*, in 1846, he gave it a nontemperance title, *Fortunes of a Country-Boy; Incidents in Town—and His Adventures at the South* (96).[1]

Michael Moon makes the strongest case for Whitman's use of dual discourse by reading a homoerotic subtext into Whitman's "Child's Champion." Moon asserts that "Whitman exploits to a high degree the capacity of language for allowing the writer to encode one discourse within another. . . . Anti-onanist and male-homoerotic discourses are often encoded in temperance writing," and such writing "exerts an ambiguous appeal because it provocatively 'points beyond' the conventional moralism it ostensibly upholds toward a forbidden world which it in a sense takes as its 'real,' albeit deferred, subject" (43). This indeterminacy of language "allows writers to develop practices which exploit the ungroundable quality of language in order to allow them to treat proscribed subjects with relative impunity" (157). As an example, Moon argues that in the nineteenth century anti-alcohol discourse had become imbricated with anti-onanist discourse. During the first half of the 1830s, when Whitman was pubescent, discussion circulated that endorsed limiting and controlling male sexual activity, especially that of bachelors. Whitman's poetic sensibility gravitated, in contrast, toward expressing male bodily pleasure. At the time language discouraging masturbation echoed with language discouraging drunkenness: both vices polluted and destroyed the male constitution. Moon argues that " 'constitution,' 'law,' 'laws of nature,' 'power,' 'mastery,' 'enslavement,' 'violation,' 'defilement,' 'ruin,' 'rebellion,' 'revolution,'—the same vocabulary which informed the discourse of the constitutional crisis of the decades before the Civil War—also informed the anti-onanist and anti-alcohol 'crises' of the same period, years during which masturbation-phobic and alcohol-phobic discourse appeared in print in enormous quantities" (19).

Both the male purity movement and the temperance movement tried to influence the behavior of the droves of unmarried men who moved to cities in search of work. These young men generally lived in boarding houses, away from restrictive and rectifying home environments. Such transient and unsupervised young men found themselves susceptible to the big-city temptations, both sexual and alcoholic, of saloons, bars, musical drinking houses, and brothels. Vivian Pollak argues that Whitman urged "his young male readers to marry as soon as possible to escape the loneliness of boarding house life. The rootlessness of boarding house life is presumed to precipitate alcoholism" (50–51). Whitman thus could discuss alcoholism and other pleasures of the body by writing about boarding houses.[2] In the culture anti-alcoholism and anti-onanism functioned as prohibitionary discourses that warned against the pollution and destruction of the male constitution from drunkenness and sexual indulgence. Drinking became linked to masturbation since both were considered nonproductive, wasteful, excessive, and indulgent behaviors. Evans's euphemism for drinking, for example, is "the fatal habit" (130), a common term for masturbation in anti-onanist writing.

By the early nineteenth century, U.S. public opinion on besottedness began to evolve as the moral and economic advantages of sobriety became increasingly valued. Temperance became a powerful movement that relied on moral suasion, rather than governmental intervention, to convert drinkers into abstainers. Temperance reform expanded and led to the twentieth-century national ban on the liquor trade. The movement swept through the country, influencing all strata of society and convincing many to put down the bottle. This antiliquor campaign was a major avatar of sobriety and a national eagerness to restrict the ravages of intoxication.

Black Americans linked temperance to social acceptance; they believed sobriety and self-control could open the door to economic opportunity. In Julie Winch's study *Philadelphia's Black Elite*, she contends that "temperance had long been a concern of the elite, not only in Philadelphia but throughout the North. Since community leaders accepted the argument that they could secure civil rights if they proved to whites that they were capable of self-improvement, they advocated temperance in the belief that it would induce whites to look more favorably upon the black community" (148). According to Winch, the moral suasion method in 1842 induced 1,047 blacks and 120 whites to sign the temperance pledge. During this same period, however, Philadelphia's temperance leaders organized a parade of reformed alcoholics to march and celebrate West Indian emancipation—but race riots broke out (148–49). The conflation in *Franklin Evans* of rhetorics of antimiscegenation and temperance reflect such racial tensions. The white working class of Baltimore, Philadelphia, and New York resented blacks who worked for lower wages.[3] The black temperance movement, which successfully organized and motivated its members, threatened white economic dominance even further.[4] Whitman, a connoisseur of popular culture and movements, brings together drink and blackness in *Franklin Evans* to suggest that white men need to cultivate racial temperance.

Because alcoholism and efforts to combat it pervaded the antebellum United States, numerous writers espoused the temperance cause or responded to its images. An immense number of temperance novels and tales were published, many of which sold well, indicating the enormous popularity and cultural significance of reform. Recognizing the capability of temperance fiction to disseminate antialcohol propaganda to large numbers of readers, the American Temperance Union voted in 1836 to endorse the use of such literature to spread its message (Brown 201-3). By 1865, the National Temperance Society became a publisher of temperance fiction, thus assuring itself a public forum in the fight against intemperance.

The literary flowering between 1835 and 1860 commonly known as the American Renaissance produced two temperance best-sellers, George Cheever's *Deacon Giles' Distillery* (1835) and Timothy Shay Arthur's *Ten Nights in a Bar-Room* (1854). In addition, Nathaniel Hawthorne wrote a popular satiric temperance tale, "A Rill from a Town Pump" (1835), Edgar Allan Poe chillingly described alcohol's powers to induce depravity in "The Black Cat" (1843) and "The Cask of Amontillado" (1846), and temperance imagery made its way into various major works of the period, including *Narrative of the Life of Frederick Douglass* (1845), *Moby-Dick* (1851), *The Blithedale Romance* (1852), *Uncle Tom's Cabin* (1852), William Wells Brown's *Clotel* (1853), and Emily Dickinson's poems. Whitman, too, wrote other formulaic temperance pieces: "The Young Grimes" (1840), "Wild Frank's Return" (1841), "The Child and the Profligate" (1841), and "Reuben's Last Wish" (1842). Scores of lesser-known writers produced temperance novels, stories, poems, plays, and periodicals, yet none used temperance rhetoric to advance an antimiscegenation message, as Whitman does in *Franklin Evans*.

The period of the American Renaissance coincided with dramatic changes in the nation's temperance literature. Although there were many, many stories about the battle with the bottle, the early tracts usually followed formulaic conventions. Each retelling of the same basic story ingrained U.S. literature with temperance imagery. Often didactic, and sometimes insufferably so, temperance literature preached the values of sobriety and castigated the evils of drunkenness. The drinker in the typical story is often either an inexperienced young man like Franklin Evans who is seduced into the deceptively attractive life of drink or a miserable father who batters and impoverishes his family. In most stories, the first ill-fated taste of liquor leads inexorably to poverty and death. In contrast to the twentieth-century conception of alcoholism as a disease, nineteenth-century temperance stories understood inebriation as a sign of moral weakness and the drinker as the bearer of a moral defect. Temperance literature aimed, Scripture-like, to show drunkards their sinful ways and lead them to a life of sobriety, financial stability, and social prosperity. By swearing the temperance pledge, former drunkards testified to their newfound life of sobriety.

U.S. reformers used various strategies and discourses to combat intemperance. The evangelical, Washingtonian, and prohibitionist approaches to the problem used what Reynolds usefully terms, successively, conventional, sensational, and legalistic discourse ("Black Cats"). Conventional discourse, typified by some novels and by some sermons by evangelical preachers such as Lyman Beecher, featured relatively tame imagery and emphasized the moral and physical rewards of abstinence. Stressing the medical model, Benjamin Franklin and Dr. Benjamin Rush wrote about drink's ill effects on the mind and body.

Sensational discourse stemmed from the eighteenth century and was greatly intensified by the Washingtonians, a group of former drunkards who regularly held "experience meetings" during which they revealed details of their depraved lives before conversion to abstinence. Full of graphic descriptions of nightmarish adventures and domestic violence, this sensational discourse drew ever more people to the movement through its titillating confessions. Washingtonian tracts were often violent and lurid in rendering alcohol's ravages, and people eagerly read about and listened to the degeneracy and wickedness the works supposedly protested. The Washingtonian phase, which started in 1840 and extended in various forms until the early 1850s, was often egalitarian in spirit, imaginative in discourse, and riddled with contradictions and ambiguities that made it a fertile source of literary themes and images. *Franklin Evans* stands as an exemplar of this approach.

Although sensational discourse persisted into the Civil War period and beyond, it lost dominance in the mid-1850s to the legalistic discourse associated with the prohibitionist movement, which produced a series of state laws banning alcohol sales. Such laws presaged the advent of national prohibition in 1919 under the Volstead Act.

During this period temperance literature's prohibitionary rhetoric aligned it with other conservative moral reformist efforts, such as the male purity movement, that sought to limit individuals' actions. With its emphasis on constraint and control, the anti-alcohol crusade opposed the national mythology of the country: the American Revolution aimed to secure individual liberty and the Declaration of Independence assured freedom of choice. Thus the temperance movement's tenets sometimes conflicted with foundational U.S. identity.[5] For example, Whitman claimed that "man is the sovereign of his individual self" (Cmeil 212), yet he portrays Franklin Evans as a man who, influenced by alcohol, cannot control his self. Gretchen Murphy similarly argues that anti-alcohol discourse challenges the ur-myth of the self-made man, since temperance fiction shows the "insufficiency of domestic and self-possessive discourses to 'free' men from intemperance, and the essential 'enslavability' of the intemperate men who cannot maintain bodily mastery" (109).

In some senses, this conservative climate of self-moderation through discipline, humility, and self-restraint stood in contrast to the contemporaneous progressive reform movements of suffrage and abolition. In its emphasis on mastery of the self, the temperance movement appeared traditional and conservative when compared with the liberal and society-changing ambitions of the drive to enfranchise women and emancipate blacks. Whereas temperance fiction advocated the retraction of rights, the suffrage and abolition efforts championed the expansion of rights.

At the same time, however, temperance rhetoric did not contrast entirely with the rhetoric of women's and blacks' rights. Many prominent members of the Whig Party and its successor, the Republican Party, supported both antislavery and temperance; Lincoln was the most famous example of this dual allegiance. Many within abolitionist and feminist circles endorsed temperance. For abolitionists, the enslavement of southern blacks metaphorically paralleled the drunkard's enslavement to the bottle. For feminists, man's injustice against woman often figured as the image of the oppressed wife, such as Whitman's Margaret, brutalized by an intemperate husband from whom she could not escape.

Whether considered conservative or progressive, the discourses of temperance, suffrage, and abolition advance individual autonomy and middle-class esteem. As reform movements they all aspired to overhaul society and valued respectability. Temperance and abolition literature not only presented parallel versions of enslavement but also leaned on sensational discourse to attract attention. Just as such drink-related stories as *Franklin Evans* reveled in describing brutal fights and violent crimes, some slave narratives stirred interest with their lurid descriptions of naked slaves being cruelly beaten. Murphy argues that the "temperance genre's frequent depiction of a middle-class drunkard-protagonist upsets the raced and gendered conventions of domestic antebellum fiction, creating a narrative problem of a figuratively 'enslaved' white male" (97) such as Franklin Evans. Alcohol and slavery shared other pernicious ties: in some parts of the slave trade, rum was bartered for human chattel; also, slaves were needed to harvest sugar for distillation.

Just as oppression by white men affected women and blacks in separate but related ways, so too did alcoholism strike both. Although the female alcoholic remained largely invisible in temperance literature, alcoholism was very much a woman's concern: beholden to her husband for economic and physical support, a woman depended on having a sober and responsible spouse, a security Margaret certainly does not find in Franklin Evans. Tavern culture lured intemperate husbands away from domesticity and emptied their pockets of the money their wives needed to run a home. Numerous temperance stories, many written by women, contrast the ruin and loneliness of the drunkard's family with the bliss and strength of the temperate man's family.

It is also important to consider that many popular temperance authors did not restrict their work to tales of drunken rages and shattered homes. Many temperance workers, concerned that their men and boys might someday become drinkers, advocated sobriety and a vision of society in which all members engaged in productive, healthful activity. Drinkers were not welcome in fictional worlds that imagined a range of useful opportunities and occupations available to all citizens. A glance through collections of temperance tales, similar to gift books in the 1840s and 1850s, reveals many positive and moralistic stories that do not treat the theme of alcohol. For example, in the "Preface" to her popular collection *Water-Drops*, Lydia Sigourney asks, "Is abstinence from the intoxicating cup, the *whole* of temperance? Is it wise to pamper all the appetites, and then expect the entire subjugation of one? . . . Should not the whole of education teach the danger of self-indulgence, and the excellence of intellectual enjoyment?" (iv). Her collection of stories, poems, and essays demonstrates the value of being temperate in all appetites and the moral benefits to society and the self that result from general sobriety.[6]

In his "American Primer," written in the 1850s but not published until 1904 in the *Atlantic Monthly*, Whitman rallies for U.S. linguistic independence. He hopes that an "American" language would reflect and dignify its citizens and politics: "The Americans are going to be the most fluent and melodious voiced people in the world—and the most perfect users of words. Words follow character,—nativity, independence, individuality" (qtd. in Baron 115). In the mid-1850s, Whitman explicitly plays with drunken imagery by writing, "To drink to fulness of the nectar which Nature distills, is to be *intoxicated* with health. Drunkenness is the opposite of this" (*Notebooks* 2250; emphasis added). Is Whitman's elasticity with the word "intoxicated" part of a project to be "the most fluent and melodious voiced"? For him to set "intoxication" and "drunkenness" as opposing energies means that each word points beyond its surface meaning to a second meaning. Similarly, in the 1855 "Preface" to *Leaves of Grass*, Whitman mentions the "putrid veins of gluttons or rum drinkers" (*Collected Poetry* 21), suggesting that rum drinkers' blood could be tainted. Speaking of "putrid" veins also points beyond rum's poisoning qualities to the antebellum era's concern with tainted blood caused by race mixture.

In *Colonial Desire*, Robert J. C. Young discusses the racist scientific accounts of " 'promiscuous,' 'illicit intercourse,' and 'excessive debauchery' of a licentious primitive sexuality" (181). Interestingly, Young shows that the sexuality of Africans was considered "primitive" and that racial scientists considered African sexual practices as examples of "debauchery," a word used in *Franklin Evans* to allude to drink and prostitution. Evans meets an old man who warns him that "there will be a thousand vicious temptations besetting you on every side. . . . It is considered 'green' not to be up to all kinds of dissipation, and familiar with debauchery and intemperance" (145). The word "debauchery" in Whitman's novel implies the degradation that follows a drunkard, yet the word also points beyond, to a dual discourse of miscegenation as "excessive debauchery" with a "primitive" African. According to the temperance novel formula, a country boy recently arrived in the city is still "green" if he has not experienced drink and illicit sexual intercourse. But through the episode in which Evans, in a drunken stupor, marries the slave Margaret, Whitman molds temperance rhetoric so that it serves an antimiscegenation purpose.

Whitman likewise is deliberately vague when he writes that the story concerns a young man "thrown by circumstances amid the vortex of dissipation" (126). This being a temperance novel, we can assume the "vortex of dissipation" refers to the ruin that accompanies drinking to excess. The phrase, however, can have several meanings. The *Oxford English Dictionary* cites James Fordyce in 1766: "That whirl of dissipation, which like some mighty vortex, has swallowed up in a manner all conditions and characters." The dictionary entry also cites Maria Edgeworth in 1802 as writing, "I feel that I cannot be at ease in the vortex of dissipation." Susanna Rowson's use of the expression definitely sexualizes its meaning: the malcontent La Rue, unhappy with her life as a girl's schoolteacher, "wished to be released from what she deemed a slavery, and to return to that vortex of folly and dissipation which had once plunged her into the deepest misery" (57). Since Whitman specifies neither "all kinds of dissipation," nor debauchery, nor the "vortex of dissipation," the reader can fill in not only temperance but also drunkenness, miscegenation, prostitution, homosexuality, or any other vice of choice.

Throughout the novel, Evans links drinking rhetoric with sexuality. He calls drink "seductive," and in a musical drinking house with beautiful tunes and women, he "drank deeper than even the night before" (156). While drunk at the theater, Evans falls in love with an apparently beautiful actress who then turns out to be ugly and coarse. Drink muddles his perception and foreshadows his more serious problem of drunken lust for Margaret. Evans reports that he "imbibed" his ideas of marriage: "I had imbibed not a few of the pernicious notions which prevail among young men in our great American city, upon conjugal matters" (206).

Similarly, Evans sexualizes drink when he says, "There seems to be a kind of strange infatuation permanently settled over the faculties of those who indulge much in strong drink.... The mind becomes, to use an expressive word, *obfusticated*, and loses the power of judging quickly and with correctness. It seems, too, that the unhappy victim of intemperance cannot tell when he commits even the most egregious violations of rights; so muddied are his perceptions, and so darkened are all his powers of penetration" (206). This passage, deliberately placed in the context of interracial sex, suggests that drink muddles one's racial temperance; that is, drink loosens one's self-restraint or impulse to indulge sexually. Whitman's intemperate "unhappy victim" commits "egregious violations" of (white) "rights." A decade later, William Wells Brown explores similar themes in his 1853 novel, *Clotel; or, The President's Daughter*. Brown, Robert S. Levine argues, "shows how the lack of restraint on whites' 'enslaving appetite' for drink, power, and sexual gratification helps to perpetuate the enslavement of blacks in the South" (95). The last phrase of Whitman's "unhappy victim" passage in particular rings of an encoded discourse: "and so darkened are all his powers of penetration" suggests that the racially intemperate drunkard penetrates dark objects of affection.

Whitman even carefully coins a word to express the similar ways that drink and interracial sex cloud the mind. Karen Sánchez-Eppler points out that the word "fustigate" looms in Whitman's "obfusticate." According to the *Oxford English Dictionary*, "fustigate" means to cudgel or beat. Thus to describe inebriation with a word that, Sánchez-Eppler holds, "evokes the punitive beatings of slavery" (*Touching* 59) is to link drink and slavery via their bodily punishments. Again, casting drink and its results in terms of corporeal violations means that the discourse of temperance points to another kind of temperance.

The low point of Evans's adventures occurs when visiting his friend Bourne's Virginia plantation. Evans finds himself attracted to the slave Margaret: "I could not help being struck with her beauty, and the influence of liquor from the bottle by my side, by no means contributed to lessen my admiration" (205). Although Margaret attacks the lewd overseer, Phillips, with a farm instrument, Evans nonetheless decides that "my affection for the Creole had induced me to come to the determination of marrying her" (207). Bourne agrees to manumit Margaret as well as her younger brother, Louis, so that Evans would not have a slave for a relative. In his drunken stupor Evans marries Margaret. Instead of spending the wedding night with his wife, Evans drinks even more with Bourne: "I signalized this crowning act of all my drunken vagaries, that night, by quaffing bottle after bottle with the planter" (207).

In the morning, Evans wakes up with hate and disgust both at

Margaret and at himself: "I repented of my drunken rashness—for the marriage deserved no other name" (209). Marriage to a mulatta here can be explained only by drunkenness. And, significantly, drunkenness deludes Evans into marrying Margaret; if he had been sober, his only choice for interracial sexuality in this nineteenth-century world would have been rape. In other words, alcohol can confuse white men into exchanging their lust for a slave woman for the possessive desire of marriage.

But though spurned by her white suitor, Margaret is not the typical tragic mulatta—she does not die of heartbreak while her white lover seeks affection with a white woman. In later chapters, I will address how Lydia Maria Child, Frances Harper, and W. D. Howells uplift their light-skinned black women to an elevated status and refuse to cast them as tragic mulattas. Whitman instead scripts an alternative and misogynistic, though still melodramatic, ending to this episode: Margaret's reaction to Evans's disgust is rage. She does not conform to the weak, innocent, compassionate tragic mulatta prevalent in nineteenth-century literature because Whitman is not interested in awakening readers' sympathy and moving them toward egalitarian race reform. Instead, Margaret murders Evans's white mistress and then kills herself.[7] As expected in a temperance piece, Franklin Evans reforms his errant ways and Whitman concludes the novel with an uplifting vision extolling the virtues of temperance and linking it to the national destiny of the United States. Again Whitman uses indeterminate language that could refer to numerous vices: "A whole nation forsaking an evil mania, which has hitherto made it the mark of scorn to those who, coming from abroad, have noticed this one foul blot in contradistinction to all the other national good qualities—and turning a goodly portion of its mighty powers to the business of preventing others from forming the same habits" (238).

This dual discourse points beyond its apparent anti-alcohol message, for the "mark of scorn" that visitors from abroad denigrate is not specified. Obviously, alcohol affects not just U.S. citizens—visitors from abroad experience alcoholism in their own countries as well. The "mark of scorn" must somehow distinguish the United States from Europe. Because slavery allowed white masters virtually unimpeded access to their slave women, miscegenation could just as likely constitute the "mark of scorn," the "evil mania," and the "one foul blot" that stands in contrast to all-American white ideals. According to the logic of *Franklin Evans*, racial temperance as well as alcoholic temperance would prevent miscegenation. In the "Conclusion" to the novel, Whitman does specify alcohol when he invokes "the dominion of the Liquor Fiend" and the efforts of temperance societies (236). As in the "Introductory," Whitman summarizes his aims and morals, but the dangers seem to reach beyond mere drink: "In the story which has been narrated in the preceding pages, there is given but a faint idea of the dangers which surround our young men in this great city. On all sides, and at every step, some temptation assails them" (238). The conclusion to *Franklin Evans* serves as a call to moral action consistent with the temperance genre's moral reform function.

If *Franklin Evans* does indeed draw upon the established conventions of the temperance genre to employ a dual discourse that delivers an antimiscegenation message, where did Whitman stand on issues of race and slavery? If we look to his poetry, lines 189–98 of "Song of Myself" show the poet compassionately aiding a runaway slave, and later, in line 838, he says, "I am the hounded slave, I wince at the bite of the dogs." Yet Whitman, the embracer of all humanity, can also include those who keep and whip slaves: line 286 of "Song of Myself" reads, "As the wooly-pates hoe in the sugar field, the overseer views them from his saddle." And in lines 95–97 of "I Sing the Body Electric," Whitman writes, "A man's body at auction, / (For before the war I often go to the slave-mart and watch the sale,) / I help the auctioneer, the sloven does not half know his business." Harold Aspiz points out that Whitman "assumed that the evolutionary vanguard was white-skinned" and that Whitman kept among his papers an article "in which physiognomy, phrenology, and craniometry were used to prove the superiority of white Americans" (139).

Whitman expressed unpalatable views toward black-white mixture in a 6 May 1858 article for the *Brooklyn Daily Times* entitled "Prohibition of Colored Persons." He argues in favor of Oregon's constitution, which prohibits blacks from entering the state. He asks, "Who believes that the Whites and Blacks can ever amalgamate in America? Or who wishes it to happen? Nature has set an impassable seal against it. Besides, is not America for the Whites?" (qtd. in Freimarck and Rosenthal 47).[8] Whitman also was forced to resign as editor of the *Brooklyn Daily Eagle* in part because he strongly opposed the extension of slavery, which would have granted slave states too much power in the nation (Freimarck and Rosenthal 35).

Further, Whitman may have hated slavery, but he nonetheless held prejudicial views against blacks. According to Alan Trachtenberg, the "question is not whether Whitman was a racist. It's beyond debate that many of his random remarks were racist then just as they would be racist today. The more troubling question is the light this lurid feature of the Whitman landscape casts upon the meaning of equality, of democracy itself." Trachtenberg reminds readers that Whitman primarily identifies with white working-class men and suggests that Whitman's celebration of democracy may thus be a Jacksonian whites-only democracy. Whitman's surname itself derives from "white man" (127). The sympathy with the slave that Whitman demonstrates in "Song of Myself" represents the poet's antebellum concern for the black body in bondage, a concern that became less urgent after emancipation. As Ed Folsom argues, Whitman's "radical identification with blacks diminished when slavery ended and when the much more difficult era of assimilation and equal rights began" (93). Similarly, Betsy Erkkila confirms that "like Lincoln and the majority of the American people, [Whitman] was not fully prepared to integrate the black person into his vision of a free and equal America" (240).

In his ambitious study of the impact of slavery on Whitman's poetic development, Martin Klammer summarizes critical controversy over Whitman's racial attitudes as "contradictions between his conservative, prejudiced views as a journalist, rooted in the mainstream Northern attitudes of his day, and his visionary, egalitarian ideas as a poet, inspired by the hope of a multiracial, inclusive America" (3). Klammer traces the stages of development in Whitman's thoughts about slavery as an institution, but not Whitman's personal responses toward African Americans. Klammer begins with Whitman's agitated treatment of blacks and slavery in *Franklin Evans* and concludes with a reading of the 1855 *Leaves of Grass* as an imaginatively new and vital poetic work that reinterprets the slave condition.

Klammer positions *Franklin Evans* as a derivative immature novel that borrows conventions from proslavery fiction and combines them with the genre demands of temperance fiction. Because Whitman's own ideas about race prejudice had not yet calcified, he borrowed from other sources, Klammer argues, so that as long as Whitman's "own racial attitudes reflect the racial prejudice of a mainstream segment of American culture, his discursive strategies will largely be the imitation of what he has seen and read" (10). According to Christopher Beach,

> Whitman's appropriation of the "mulatto wench" figure may tell us more about popular racial stereotyping of the time than it does about Whitman's personal beliefs. *Franklin Evans* was, after all, conceived and written within the conventions of a popular genre. . . . Anecdotal evidence does suggest, however, that Whitman had no personal fondness for blacks, and that he may indeed have shared the feeling of most white northerners at the time, composed of a benevolent desire to liberate and protect slaves on the one hand and a deep-seated distrust and even revulsion on the other. (87)

Although *Franklin Evans* starts out as a conventional temperance novel along the lines described thus far, the Virginia chapters of the novel then mimic what Klammer calls "pro-slavery rhetorical and fictional conventions," such as "the conversion experience, the plantation owner's fantasy, the 'virgin/whore' paradigm [and] the violent, emotional, and 'insane' black woman" (21). For example, Bourne's claims that slavery is benevolent and that his slaves happily abide by their status concurs with the pleasant image of slavery concocted by proslavery romancers. Although Evans does not articulate a "conversion" to the proslavery side, he nonetheless contentedly imagines himself as the owner of Bourne's plantation. The virgin/whore dichotomy most explicitly plays out in the character of Margaret and in the contrast between her and the white Mrs. Conway, to whom Franklin devotes his attentions after spurning Margaret. Margaret's turn to violence aligns with the proslavery tenet that blacks cannot handle their freedom. Pollak goes so far as to argue that Margaret kills her rival out of jealousy over skin color: "There is a sense, then, in which the light-skinned Margaret murders because she aspires to whiteness, which is associated in the novel with domesticity and with middle-class norms of erotic fidelity" (39). In so clearly borrowing from the proslavery genre, Whitman demonstrates an affinity with proslavery romancers and their racist beliefs.

Karen Sánchez-Eppler posits that "in miscegenation Whitman finds an extremely potent instance of mediation, a blatant demonstration that otherness can be reconciled, that opposites of black and white can meet and blend" (*Touching* 59). The sensationally brutal murder-suicide ending of *Franklin Evans*, however, seems instead to demonstrate a disgust and hatred of the black body, especially when it threatens to merge sexually with the white body. In no way does Whitman suggest the possibility of black-white intermarriage. Murphy's discussion of the conflation of proslavery and temperance genres also suggests Whitman's conjoining of races, but certainly not in a conciliatory gesture: "The threat of amalgamation follows from the use of the slave trope in Stowe's and Whitman's temperance fiction, and calls for a strategy to reinscribe self-mastery onto the 'enslaved' white male body" (110).

Franklin Evans does *not* "stand between" (to use the title of Sánchez-Eppler's Whitman chapter) binary opposites of black and white in a mediating capacity. Through both the proslavery and temperance genres, Whitman finds a way to express and literarily sanction antimiscegenation views. Later, as a mature poet in command of his powers, Whitman will revolutionarily transmute these ideas to express the merging and unity of diverse U.S. bodies. Although it can be quite difficult to pin down Whitman's views of race and miscegenation, his novel *Franklin Evans* exploits the indeterminacy and flexibility of language to advocate racial temperance in a liquor-temperance tract. Whitman conflates temperance and racial discourse to show that miscegenation, like alcohol, is a dark blot on the U.S. character and a threat to a healthy U.S. C/constitution.

3

Cuban Slave Fiction: Race Mixture in Sab

Although autobiographical slave narratives and fictions treating slavery, such as Whitman's *Franklin Evans*, are sometimes mistaken as indigenous only to the United States, they also emerged simultaneously and autochthonously in Cuba. In both the United States and Cuba, antislavery stories posed counterdiscourses to the national master narrative, thereby challenging institutionalized political and literary representation. For this reason, some critics compare the Cuban novel *Sab* (1841) by Gertrudis Gómez de Avellaneda with U.S. slave novels, especially Harriet Beecher Stowe's *Uncle Tom's Cabin* (serialized in 1851–52 and published in novel form in 1852), written a decade later.[1] *Sab* and *Uncle Tom's Cabin* share some concerns of interest to my study of race mixture in nineteenth-century fictions: the problem of women's status in male-dominated society, the attempt at resistance to authority, and, most significant for the discussion here, the racialized body's role in such resistance.[2]

Gómez de Avellaneda and Stowe voraciously read the Bible, Shakespeare, and European novels, and one can detect in *Sab* and *Uncle Tom's Cabin* the tremendous influence of Aphra Behn, Chateaubriand, and Victor Hugo. Like European Indianist novels, *Sab* features a romantic hero cast as an exotic Other of royal extraction (Sab's mother was an African princess) and was written in the Old World but set in the New World. In general, the noble native genre of Rousseau and Chateaubriand appears in Cuba in the form of antislavery novels (Gutiérrez de la Solana 303). Gómez de Avellaneda returned to this theme only in *Guatimozín, último emperador de Méjico*

(1846), a historical novel. Sab himself epitomizes the romantic protagonist: pure and noble in soul, sentimental, effusively emotional, and devoted to his beloved mistress, Carlota. Both *Sab* and *Uncle Tom's Cabin* reflect Romantic values: writing with grand emotion, the authors construct their eponymous male heroes as outcasts who are altruistic, sensitive, passionate, and passive. Their exoticism often resonates with the natural world and with women; indeed, both Sab and Uncle Tom are to some degree feminized. The heroes' essential goodness and inability to fit in with a corrupt society reflect their noble soul (Scott, "Introduction" xi; Ward; DelCampo; Guerra).

Critics compare *Sab* with *Uncle Tom's Cabin* not only because both hold antislavery ideals and portray loyal slaves with noble souls but also because both support feminist readings and because, as white women, Gómez de Avellaneda and Stowe entitle their novels after beloved dark men. The two women, however, wrote under vastly different circumstances (Stowe amid a rich midcentury abolitionist and feminist cultural context, Gómez de Avellaneda outside her own country and subjected to censorship) and, consequently, the two works differ greatly. For example, a love plot does not drive *Uncle Tom's Cabin*, but *Sab* is primarily a love story. The loving feelings exchanged among Stowe's characters include those between parents and children and Little Eva's innocent adoration of Uncle Tom. Gómez de Avellaneda, in contrast, pictures love to be adult, heterosexual, and miscegenous, a combination that would have undermined Stowe's purpose by offending her readers. In *Uncle Tom's Cabin*, miscegenation figures as rape (i.e., as Simon Legree's lascivious desire for Cassy or Emmeline) or as an event that transpired in the past to produce such mixed-race characters as Eliza and George Harris.

Further, *Uncle Tom's Cabin* derives much of its power from being a domestic novel filled with right-minded mothers. One thinks immediately of Eliza, Rachel Halliday, Emily Bird, and Cassy. In *Sab*, however, mothers are largely absent. Neither Sab, Carlota, Teresa, nor Enrique has a mother, although Sab adopts the indigenous Martina as his mother. Evelyn Picon Garfield notes that "en clara oposición a las madres ficticias cubanas, la madre blanca de *Uncle Tom's Cabin* cumple con la misión regeneradora y salvadora de una sociedad escindida por la esclavitud [in clear opposition to the fictive Cuban mothers, the white mother in *Uncle Tom's Cabin* fulfills a regenerative and salvific mission in a society torn apart by slavery]" (58–59).

Stowe herself was a mother of many children, while Gómez de Avellaneda birthed one child who died in infancy. With an absence of maternal figures, *Sab* cannot posit a strategy of domesticity, yet in its close linking of women's condition to that of slaves, the Cuban novel voices a more feminist agenda than does the New England novel. Finally, Stowe seems interested in providing documentary evidence of abuse of her sympathetic characters and positing an ardent Christian message, whereas Gómez de Avellaneda does not channel her message through religious imagery.

Although no reader doubts that *Uncle Tom's Cabin* registers both a vehement antislavery and an abolitionist call, *Sab* presents an interesting contrast, for it voices antislavery sentiments without necessarily urging abolition. One of Gómez de Avellaneda's biographers, Emilio Cotarelo y Mori, argues that *Sab* cannot be compared with Stowe's novel: "Algunos han querido dar a esta obra carácter abolicionista semejante al de *La Cabaña de Tom*, de Enriqueta Beecher Stowe. No hay nada de protesta contra la esclavitud, más que el hecho de admitir en el héroe el impedimento de aspirar a su dicha [Some have wanted to consider this work abolitionist, like *Uncle Tom's Cabin* by Harriet Beecher Stowe. But there is no protest against slavery except the fact of recognizing the hero's inability to achieve happiness]" (75). Ivan A. Schulman concurs that *Sab* and other early Cuban antislavery novels do not express abolitionist intent, but he believes that "they do set a mood, perhaps too lachrymose, and undertake a morally inspired social analysis, critical of a major economic institution in a period in which prosperity still dominated the slave system" (364). Nara Araujo points out that the abolitionist message is muted because "no hay odio contra el dueño [there is no hatred of the slave owner]" (46). Yet Shirley M. Jackson claims that Sab "bitterly protests the injustices of Cuban society" (88), and Jill Ann Netchinsky discusses the novel at length as an antislavery work.

Although abolitionist novels in the United States enjoyed a wide readership and participated actively in forming a national consensus against slavery, the same kinds of stories were censored in the Spanish colony of Cuba in an attempt to maintain the slave economy. In the United States, abolitionists penned antislavery stories. In Cuba, however, anti-abolitionist sugarocracy slave owners wrote against slave society in their fictions.

Although the theme of hybrid racial identity may abound in slave novels from both North and South America, Cuban slave fiction sharply distinguishes itself: because of Cuba's colonial status, all Cubans could conceive of themselves as slaves to Spain, and possibly to England, as Gómez de Avellaneda cautions. While white U.S. writers were themselves free, Cuban writers could insert themselves in the place of their slave protagonists. The Cuban slave novel conjoins racial liberation with creole political liberation in a way unimaginable in U.S. fiction. Indeed, the "colonized subject shifts easily from brown to white to woman in Cuba" (Sommer letter), so that Cuba's incipient independence movement becomes inscribed in abolitionist and feminist writings. Further, Cuban abolitionist pieces often articulate a powerful contradiction: the repressive racialist state based on the slave-dependent sugarocracy nonetheless fostered a powerful church that preferred interracial marriage to cohabitation.

Sab articulates a corporeal and political anxiety about miscegenation at once familiar to readers of U.S. literature and yet compellingly dissonant and in some ways more radical than *Uncle Tom's Cabin*. In his fleshly identity and carnal desires, Sab contests the very system that forces a cleavage between his "white" soul and mixed-race body. Sab's body represents the discourse of master and slave, one imposed upon the other in what can be termed somatized heteroglossia.

The History of Cuban Antislavery Literature

The Cuban antislavery genre was promoted by Domingo Del Monte (1804–53), a Venezuelan-born planter described by Vera M. Kutzinski as "a retired sugar baron turned reformer and patron of the arts" (18). Del Monte led a prestigious literary circle in Matanzas in 1834 but moved it to Havana the following year. Similarly, much of Stowe's early encouragement came from salons that provided her with literary training and an audience. Desiring gradual change in race relations, Del Monte and his colleagues "placed their faith in literature, especially in antislavery narratives, as an instrument of social change" (18). Del Monte's group of liberal intellectuals disdained romanticism, advocating realism to advance political causes contrary to Spanish colonial rule. Morally opposed to the dehumanizing slave trade but not in favor of the immediate abolition of slavery, Del Monte formed a working relationship with Richard Madden, the British consul in Havana and an ardent abolitionist. In the first half of the nineteenth century, England was the most active power in eliminating slavery, and Madden hoped to collaborate with Del Monte in collecting a portfolio of antislavery works to attest to the prevailing conditions in Cuba. Cuban slaveholders resisted Del Monte's alliance with Madden, whom they viewed as an extension of British colonial power (Sommer, *Foundational* 133). Del Monte's group also was opposed by Spanish imperial authors: "El gobierno de Madrid opuso toda la resistencia que pudo, porque creyó que la agricultura de las colonia perecería sin el comercio de negros [The government of Madrid opposed all the resistance it could because it believed that colonial agriculture would collapse without the traffic in slaves]" (Saco 229).

Del Monte had read Victor Hugo's novel *Bug-Jargal* (1826)[3] about a slave uprising in St. Domingue (now Haiti) and commissioned his associates to write antislavery novels. In 1836 the fugitive slave Juan Francisco Manzano, a published poet, read his poem "Mis treinta años" in Del Monte's literary salon. With Del Monte's assistance, Manzano wrote his way out of slavery: in 1837 Del Monte's group purchased Manzano from bondage in exchange for the slave's written autobiography. Madden translated Manzano's "Apuntes autobiográficos" as "Life of the Negro Poet." Another salon member, Anselmo Suárez y Romero, made grammatical corrections. Madden published the manuscript, along with some of Manzano's poems and some of Madden's own antislavery poems, in London in 1840 for the General Anti-slavery Convention under the title *Poems by a Slave in the Island of Cuba*. The manuscript of Suárez y Romero's revisions disappeared, and for almost one hundred years the only available version was Madden's translation. Manzano's original manuscript eventually surfaced in the Cuban national archives and was published in Cuba under the title *Autobiografía* in 1937.

Influenced by his own editing of Manzano's life story, Suárez y Romero wrote the first Cuban antislavery novel, *Francisco: El ingenio; o, Las delicias del campo* (Francisco: The sugar mill; or, The delights of the country) in 1839. Again Del Monte's influence stands out: Suárez y Romero wrote a letter to Del Monte in 1839 requesting that his mentor assess "the defects of my novel . . . to correct those errors which lend themselves to correction" and to "consider my novel yours and dispose of it as you wish" (qtd. in Schulman 357), but because of colonial censorship, it was not published until 1880. In fact, the Cuban political machinery censored all early antislavery novels, forcing authors to seek publication abroad. Just as Manzano's and Suárez y Romano's works faced censorial disapproval, Gómez de Avellaneda's *Sab*, banned in Cuba, was published in Spain in 1841, making it the first abolitionist novel to be published in Spanish. Cuba finally allowed *Sab* to be published in 1883, when it appeared in the Havana magazine *El museo*. Antonio Zambrana wrote and published *El negro Francisco* (1875) in Santiago de Chile, where he solicited support for Cuban independence. Another Cuban author, Félix Tanco y Bosmeniel, composed *Escenas de la vida privada en la isla de Cuba* and *Petrona y Rosalía* in 1838, but these remained unpublished until 1925. His "Un niño en la Habana" (1837) disappeared in the Biblioteca Nacional de Madrid until 1986. Cirilo Villaverde published a short version of his antislavery novel *Cecilia Valdés* in 1839, but the complete novel did not see publication until 1882 in New York City. Francisco Calcagno penned *Romualdo, uno de tantos*, in 1869 but could not publish it until 1891.[4] All these novels, with the exception of *Sab*, received Del Monte's sponsorship. Gómez de Avellaneda, separated by geography and gender, stood apart from the Havana literary circle. Unlike these other works, her antislavery effort was written entirely by her hand (Scott, "Introduction" xxi).[5]

Written in defiance of censorship and arguing against the institutionalized system of slavery, these antislavery works were quite revolutionary in this period of Cuba's history (although Spain abolished slavery in 1880, it did not disappear from Cuba until 1886). In general, the narratives represent blacks and slaves as individuals, as subjects with feelings and emotions, not as objects indifferent to their condition of bondage. Often the stories suggest that the slave owner was himself enslaved by a colonial power and that achieving his own political independence was dependent upon, even preconditioned by, emancipating his slaves (Barreda 52). Yet like Del Monte's, none of these novels actively champions abolition. A major irony of these novels is that the authors wrote them for their own small circle and were aware of the need for change but hesitant to instigate it at the expense of their material comfort. In fact, Suárez y Romero wrote *Francisco* while in charge of his family's sugar plantation (Fivel-

Démoret 7–8).⁶ According to Kutzinski, "while the majority of Cuba's criollo elite would agree in principle that slavery was incompatible with the cause of national independence, economic considerations superseded moral concerns until well into the second half of the nineteenth century" (18). Del Monte, Tanco y Bosmeniel, and Suárez y Romero, all slave owners, did not believe in emancipation, either of slaves or of themselves as colonial subjects under Spanish rule. As Schulman observes, "The aim of the antislavery writers, given their ties with the economic interests of the plantation owners, was a gradual, forward-looking and humanitarian policy of limiting the growth of slaves through the enforcement of the slave traffic treaties" (359). Because Del Monte's literary circle opposed immediate emancipation, censorship appeared to work in the authors' favor: they could use their pens to protest the evils of a slave society, but censorship prevented their critiques from being too widely disseminated.

Despite their different origins *Sab* and *Cecilia Valdés* in particular have numerous points of contact: these two Cuban antislavery novels were written within two years of each other, both were censored, both portray impossible cross-racial sexual desire (in *Cecilia Valdés* the mulatto figure is a woman, in *Sab* it is a man), both condemn the Cuban slavocracy system, and both demonstrate the close link between slavery and family ties. The eponymous heroine of *Cecilia Valdés*, a mulatta, falls in love with the white Leonardo Gamboa, who turns out to be her half brother. The incest plot that *Sab*, *Aves sin nido*, and *Cumandá* resist finds full expression in Villaverde's hand: Cecilia and Leonardo have a child together. Because *Cecilia Valdés* has been treated extensively elsewhere (see Sommer, *Foundational*; González; Benigno Sánchez-Eppler; Kaye; Holland), I will focus on *Sab* and explore its thematization of racial heterogeneity.

Gómez de Avellaneda and the Novel

Born in 1814 in the central Cuban town of Puerto Príncipe (now Camaguey), where the major economic product was not sugar but cattle, Gertrudis Gómez de Avellaneda received a superior education. The Cuban poet José María Heredia served as her tutor and undoubtedly influenced her poetry, in which she began demonstrating talent early in life. Gómez de Avellaneda's father owned slaves, thus she was raised with "the fervent Cuban nationalism that characterized a Creole class resentful of Spanish colonial policy" and educated with "a particularly Cuban brand of liberalism that had through bitter historical experience become critical of the hypocrisy of Spain's liberal government towards its colonies" (Kirkpatrick, "Toward" 135). Nonetheless, part of Gómez de Avellaneda's education seemed to involve instruction in being a slave owner accustomed to the manual labor of slaves. For example, in her *Autobiography*, Gómez de Avellaneda compares her education in Cuba with that of her relatives in Spain:

> The education which young ladies receive in Cuba is so different from that in Galicia that a woman of my country, even one of the middle class, would think it degrading to perform some duties which in Galicia even the most socially prominent women look on as an obligation of their sex. My stepfather's female relatives therefore maintained that I was good for nothing because I didn't know how to iron or cook or knit socks; because I didn't wash dishes nor make beds nor sweep my room. According to them, I needed twenty maids and assumed the airs of a princess. (*"Sab" and "Autobiography"* 17)

The reason Gómez de Avellaneda, "one of the middle class" in Cuba, would find it "degrading" to "iron or cook or knit socks" as do her Spanish relatives is that she has been educated into the ways of slavery and the presence of slaves. Thus we can see Gómez de Avellaneda oscillating between critiquing the slavocracy system yet benefiting from the labor-saving comfort it afforded her.

Anxiety about a slave uprising abounds in *Sab*, perhaps because of Cubans' memory of the 1791 uprising in St. Domingue (now Haiti and the Dominican Republic) and of the 1838 slave insurrection in nearby Trinidad. Fearing that slave insurrection might spread to Cuba, Gómez de Avellaneda's mother and stepfather moved the family to Europe in 1836, a year after Del Monte established his salon in the Cuban capital. While most biographers (Cotarelo y Mori, Figarola Caneda, and Bravo-Villasante) focus on Gómez de Avellaneda's heterosexual love affairs, Janet Gold emphasizes the importance to her work of her early female friendships with Rosa Carmona and her cousin Elena Arteaga, a claim readily confirmed by reading her *Autobiography*. Despite her marginalization, Gómez de Avellaneda managed to become one of Spain's most important playwrights and poets. Although she wrote six full-length novels, her dramas brought her the most popular and critical successes, and she received numerous literary prizes. In 1853 she bid for a seat in the Royal Spanish Academy but because she was a woman and therefore banned in principle, her efforts failed. One supporter told her, "In my judgment, almost all of us are worth less that you; but, nevertheless, because of the question of gender (and talent should not have any), we supporters must bear the sorrow of not counting you among our academicians for now" (qtd. in Scott, "Introduction" xvi).

Although Gómez de Avellaneda famously rejected marriage proposals, she was married and widowed twice. Her second husband, Colonel Domingo Verdugo, was posted to Cuba in 1859, and this trip afforded the famous literary personality the opportunity to return, a star, to her homeland. She received a massive celebratory welcome and a "crowning" in the capital as a major Cuban figure. During what was supposed to be a six-year stay in Cuba, she wrote numerous novels and dramas and founded and edited a journal, *Album cubano*, becoming the only woman to do so in Cuba at that time (Scott, "Introduction" xvii).[7] When her husband died in Cuba, Gómez de Avellaneda returned to Spain in 1864, where she actively wrote and edited her works until her death in Madrid of diabetes in 1873.

About the composition of Sab, Gómez de Avellaneda wrote that "en ratos de ocio escribía desaliñadamente el *Sab* que comenzé en Lisboa, el año de 1838 y concluí en Sevilla en 1839 [in leisure moments I lazily wrote *Sab*, which I began in Lisbon in 1838 and finished in Seville in 1839]" (qtd. in Cotarelo y Mori 429). Unlike writers in Del Monte's group, Gómez de Avellaneda did not pen her antislavery story while witnessing daily the human toll of bondage, nor did she try to counter slavery's ills from within the country. As an expatriate, Gómez de Avellaneda's *cubanía*, or Cuban authentic identity, could be questioned. Therefore, at several points in the novel, Gómez de Avellaneda seems to try to claim an "insider" identity. For example, the first time the reader meets Sab, he is singing a native Cuban song known only to those who have heard islanders sing it (DelCampo 171). The opening chapters invoke such local birds as the cao, guacamaya, and tomeguín. Further, much of the novel meditates on the injustice of Cuban financial and commercial transactions. Netchinsky affirms Gómez de Avellaneda's project of steeping her novel in

Cuban feeling: "By virtue of its reflections of the island's economic conflicts, character types, landscapes and legends, *Sab* celebrates Cuban identity as whole-heartedly as it condemns slavery; thus, Gómez de Avellaneda's first novel is significant in the formation of an independent Cuban literary nationality" (200). Yet while the novel celebrates Cuban identity, it also explores alienation from that sense of inclusiveness—Sab's skin color prevents him from fully belonging.

Because Gómez de Avellaneda wrote *Sab* soon after her departure from Cuba, where her family had been slaveholders, she has been faulted for writing while in voluntary exile and therefore for not speaking as a colonial living under an imposed regime. Admittedly, Gómez de Avellaneda's devotion to poetry and to the theater scene in Spain indicates that the antislavery cause did not rank as her highest priority. Though scholars claim Gómez de Avellaneda insisted on "touting her love for Cuba and her affinity with writers like Heredia," she also "did not spend her life counting the hours of Cuba's misfortune, but rather writing her work and searching for suitable accommodations for her theater" (Montes-Huidobro 234). And because she wrote in a foreign country, she had the advantage of being able to publish her novel, an opportunity unavailable to Del Monte's salon members.

Yet these same reasons for faulting her can also count in her favor. Writing outside Cuba and Del Monte's circle, Gómez de Avellaneda came to the antislavery theme without support, patronage, or commission. Furthermore, whereas Del Monte's society attacked the abuses of slavery, Gómez de Avellaneda wrote a more penetrating critique of racist ideology and the institution of slavery itself. Although she did not participate in Cuba's movement for independence, she extended her argument to rally against all kinds of persecution, including the subjugation of women. One critic commends her analysis of white tyranny: "Avellaneda criticizes the suicidal myopia of a society that breeds hatred through systematic oppression; she thus established the causal relationship between white oppression and black aggression conveniently glossed over by [other antislavery writers]" (Fivel-Démoret 9–10). Her outspoken themes and formidable intellect inspired one male critic to remark, "Es mucho hombre esta mujer [This woman is very much a man]" (qtd. in Miller 202).

The Madrid literati approved of *Sab*, and respected journals published favorable reviews. Some reviewers praised the novel's romantic passion but ignored its social protest. For example, *El conservador* of Madrid ran the following review on 23 January 1842: "No es *Sab* una novela española, ni menos inglesa o francesa. *Sab* es una novela americana, como su autora. . . . El carácter y la pasión de Sab, que es toda la novela, están descrito con un pincel de fuego [*Sab* is not a Spanish novel, any more than it is English or French. *Sab* is an American novel, as is its author. . . . The character and passion of Sab, which are throughout the novel, are written with a brush of fire]" (qtd. in Cruz 102). In another review, the critic taunts Gómez de Avellaneda for attempting to critique social issues novelistically and views her condescendingly because she is a woman and a colonial. As Susan Kirkpatrick maintains, "The exoticism of her colonial origin, like the difference of her gender, was double-edged: both attracted and pleased, not to say titillated, attention, but at the same time they were regarded as marks of inferiority in relation to the norm" (*Las Románticas* 161).

Although Spanish readers found much to praise in *Sab*, the Cuban censors prevented its receiving an island audience. Gómez de Avellaneda's brother, however, tried to bring copies of *Sab* to Cuba, which suggests that the author desired Cuban readers (Williams 86). Both *Sab* and Gómez de Avellaneda's second novel, *Dos mujeres* (1842), which focused on women's status in marriage, "in 1844 were denied entrance at Customs in Santiago de Cuba by Hilario de Cisneros, the Censor Regio de la Imprenta. His decree of exclusion stated that the first 'contained a doctrine subversive to the system of slavery in the island and contrary to morals and good customs, and the second . . . was immersed in immoral doctrines'" (362). According to Araujo, 1844 was a year of "violenta represión esclavista y tensa situación política [violent slave repression and tense political situation]" (44). The Cuban public could not read *Sab* until 1883, when the magazine *El museo* published it in Havana.

Cuban officials were not the only ones who suppressed the publication or distribution of *Sab*; later in life, Gómez de Avellaneda seems to have censored herself. While still a resident of Spain, Gómez de Avellaneda edited her complete works, published from 1869 to 1871, and purposefully omitted both *Sab* and *Dos mujeres*. Lorna Valerie Williams suggests three possible reasons Gómez de Avellaneda left her first two novels out of her *Obras literarias* that "range from the mercenary (that Avellaneda wanted to retain the lucrative Cuban market for her works), to the aesthetic (that the mature writer considered this youthful work unrepresentative of her literary accomplishments), to the ideological (that the author yielded to the recommendations of her relatives and/or religious advisers in an attempt to blunt the liberationist threat of her work)" (87). Kirkpatrick rejects the aesthetic hypothesis because Gómez de Avellaneda consistently preferred to revise her poetry rather than discard it. Instead, Kirkpatrick believes that Gómez de Avellaneda omitted the novels because in 1869 they still could not circulate in Cuba. Including them in a larger volume would prohibit the accompanying "acceptable" works from being published. Therefore, Kirkpatrick concludes, "the selection of works for the definitive edition was a form of self-censorship, aimed at making the *Obras* palatable to the largest possible public" ("Toward" 134).

Reading Race Mixture in Sab

What about *Sab* is so subversive that it merited censorship by both Cuban officials and Gómez de Avellaneda herself? *Sab* tells the story of a loyal, sensitive, and intelligent slave in love with his mistress, Carlota. Kindred spirits, they grow up together. Carlota, however, loves the greedy Englishman Enrique Otway, who wants to marry Carlota only for her money. Carlota's orphaned cousin, Teresa, secretly loves Enrique and divulges her clandestine passion only to Sab, who understands what it means to suffer from unrequited love. When Carlota loses her fortune, Enrique decides to abandon her. Sab saves his mistress by giving her a winning lottery ticket that restores her wealth and returns the avaricious Enrique to her. At the hour of Carlota and Enrique's marriage, Sab dies of a broken heart and Teresa decides to spend the rest of her life in a convent. After many years of being trapped in a miserable marriage, Carlota reads a letter from Sab, which Teresa had been keeping, in which he discloses his feelings for his mistress, and Carlota realizes that she was truly loved by a venerable soul.

Sab is a subversive character because he is the only slave in Cuban literature to love his white mistress. Mary Cruz situates Gómez de Avellaneda's boldness in imagining a woman "de la raza dominante [quien] reconozca en el hombre esclavo condiciones admirables y lo halle digno de ser amado. Para la mentalidad de su tiempo, muy especialmente en Cuba, donde el caso inverso era regla—solapada, naturalment—, esta osadía de la Avellaneda debió parecer monstruosa [of the dominant race who recognizes admirable qualities in a slave and finds him worthy of being loved. For her time, especially in Cuba, where the inverse case was the norm, discreetly, Avellaneda's boldness must have seemed monstrous]" (42). Most Latin American novels that feature miscegenation describe it as "a loving or eroticized version of the white man's burden. They describe an active lover who is both male and white (the liberal bourgeoisie) and the yielding object of his galvanizing attention who is often a mulatta (the masses to be incorporated in a hegemonic project)" (Sommer, *Foundational* 125).

With the exception of *Sab*, in all Cuban antislavery stories, as in most U.S. slave narratives, the white master satisfies his lust for a black or mulatto woman only to abandon her later. Gómez de Avellaneda reverses the usual terms of exploitation to create a more polemic love interest. As a lover and a slave Sab is a threat to white aristocracy through his desire for Carlota and his attractiveness to Teresa. Plots involving the white master's power over the black female slave reflect the extent of institutionalized rape in the slavocracy. Verena Martínez-Alier points out that, "significantly, those who wanted to draw attention to the dangers of interracial marriage often talked only of coloured men wanting to marry white women, although in reality the reverse was more common" (117). Martínez-Alier suggests that the combination of a black man with a white woman was more taboo because lineage could more easily be traced through, and thereby corrupted by, women. To prevent illegitimate children, women's honor had to be more tightly circumscribed than men's. Because illegitimate children were the responsibility of the mother, a "man's sexual conduct was of less social consequence. Hence, hypergenation, that is, procreation between upper-class men and lower-class women, could be tolerated and did not constitute a menace to group integrity" (118).

The slave's love for his white mistress drives the novel, even though Sab knows that his race and condition of bondage will prevent his love from being reciprocated. Identifying himself with Othello, Sab sees a literary model for his love: "Un día Carlota leyó un drama en el cual encontré por fin a una noble doncella que amaba a un africano, y me sentí transportado de placer y orgullo [One day Carlota read a play where I found for the first time a noble woman who loved an African, and I felt transported with pleasure and pride]" (277). Yet Sab realizes that slavery constitutes an unbreachable gulf that distinguishes his plight from Othello's.[8] He laments, "Tú no te alimentaste jamás con el pan de la servidumbre, ni se dobló tu soberbia frente delante de un dueño. Tu amada no vio en tus manos triunfantes la señal de los hierros" "[You never ate from the bread of servitude, nor did you ever bow your proud brow in front of a master. Your beloved never saw the mark of irons on your triumphant hands]" (277–78).

Pulled apart by competing corporeal discourses of race, Sab represents what can be termed somatized heteroglossia. Literalized in his mulatto skin, Sab embodies double-voiced discourse: he descends from both master and slave, his fleshly identity comprises opposing languages of power, class, race, and world meanings (Bakhtin 344). When writing of double discourse Bakhtin refers to language in novelistic prose, but his terms can also apply to racial identity, because identity takes place within language. The commingling of races that produced Sab and his mulatto skin can be seen as a Bakhtinian hybrid construction:

> What we are calling a hybrid construction is an utterance that belongs, by its grammatical (syntactic) and compositional markers, to a single speaker, but that actually contains mixed within it two utterances, two speech manners, two styles, two "languages," two semantic and axiological belief systems. We repeat, there is no formal—compositional and syntactic—boundary between these utterances, styles, languages, belief systems. . . . It frequently happens that even one and the same word will belong simultaneously to two languages, two belief systems that intersect in a hybrid construction—and, consequently, the word has two contradictory meanings, two accents. (304–5)

Bakhtin's theories of the hybridity of language teach readers to regard some of Sab's statements in a different light. For example, Sab's spoken Spanish is educated and flawless, apparently not hybrid. Yet when he speaks such words as *libertad* (liberty), *poder* (power), and *amor* (love), Sab dialogically refers to a larger political context. Sab's one body belongs to two different systems, giving his identity two "accents." But the race mixture between Sab's parents, which took place before the time of the narrative, does not bestow upon Sab a socially recognized hybrid identity; instead, slave society deems Sab one of the owned and not owner of himself.

Bakhtin defines a hybrid construction as seamless, as lacking boundaries. Sab feels a part of both sides of the racial divide, confirming Antonio Benítez Rojo's contention that "mestizaje is nothing more than a concentration of differences" (26). Throughout the novel, Gómez de Avellaneda specifically refers to Sab as "el mulato," not "el negro." In its indefinite, cryptic features, the mulatto body attests to the cross-racial desire that must be repressed to justify the master/slave dichotomy. The mulatto's countenance epidermalizes the dread of interracial compatibility, and his body voices "anxieties about racial mixing as a threat to a political order dependent on physiognomy as reliable index of class differences. The mulatt[o], then, measures the extent to which what appeared to be previously fixed sexual, social, and racial hierarchies within that political order are no longer stable—no longer reliably (that is, physiognomically) marked" (Kutzinski 27). Antislavery fiction in the Americas somatizes heteroglossia, especially onto mixed-race bodies, and thereby creates a corporeal witness to and protest of institutionalized bondage.

Although Sab's skin tone seamlessly mixes black and white, society flattens his duality into a single slave identity. Sab's miscegenous desire for Carlota endangers the slavocracy because it threatens to repeat Sab's embodied double discourse. That is, the love of a slave for his mistress fractures the monologism of hierarchy that created and sustains slavery's justification. The slave system cannot allow Carlota, emblematic of white elitism and white property, to open herself and her status to racial hybridity. By giving herself to Sab, Carlota would voluntarily replicate the hybridization that is usually effected only through rape.

Sab's syncretic standing spreads throughout the novel via his character zone. Bakhtin writes that a "character in a novel always has, as we have said, a zone of his own, his own sphere of influence on the authorial context surrounding him, a sphere that extends—and quite often far—beyond the boundaries of the direct discourse allotted to him" (320). The discourse surrounding Sab's liminal position between his slave ancestry and his free ancestry extends to the discourse of women's unfortunate status in nineteenth-century Cuba. In an emotional letter to Teresa, Sab compares his condition as a slave with that of women in bondage to their husbands:

> ¡Oh, las mujeres!, ¡pobres y ciegas víctimas! Como los esclavos, ellas arrastran pacientemente su cadena y bajan la cabeza bajo el yugo de las leyes humanas. Sin otra guía que su corazón ignorante y crédulo eligen un dueño para toda la vida. El esclavo, al menos, puede cambiar de amo, puede esperar que juntando oro comprará algún día su libertad: pero la mujer, cuando levanta sus manos enflaquecidas y su frente ultrajada, para pedir libertad oye al monstruo de voz sepulcral que le grita en la tumba. (280–81)

> [Oh, women, poor and blind victims! Like slaves, they patiently drag a chain and lower their heads under the yoke of human laws. With no guide other than their naive and believing heart, they choose a master for life. The slave at least can change owners and can hope to save enough money to one day buy his liberty; but a wife, when she raises her emaciated hands and worn brow to ask for freedom, hears a monstrous deathly voice that shouts, "In the grave."] (Gómez de Avellaneda, *"Sab" and "Autobiography"* 144–45)

Feminist dialogicians would find that Sab's letter exemplifies the cultural resistance that dialogism makes possible (Bauer and McKinstry). Gómez de Avellaneda refracts society's power structure stylistically: she protests women's lack of rights in the voice of a slave who also condemns society. Sommer finds this protest particularly compelling because Gómez de Avellaneda identifies with a slave through their common act of writing (*Foundational* 114–15). The two use their pens to subvert the ruling ideologies that restrain them.

Significant to antislavery novels in the Americas is the threat or already consummated act of miscegenation, usually rape and concubinage between the white master and his female slave. Although Cecilia Valdés, the heroine of Villaverde's devastating critique of Cuban slavocracy, is not a slave, she is first exploited and then abandoned at the whim of her white lover, who is also her half brother. Often harsh assessments by antislavery narratives use the miscegenation trope to somatize the problems of slavery with slaves' black bodies. If the slave's body, bent under the burden of manual labor, scarred with lashes, and indelibly marked by blackness, is the basis of the slave system and stories about it, then the slave's body is also fundamental to narrative signification. The story of slavery can be told by the movement of black bodies through space and time, since blacks were transportable objects that could be rearranged, placed, and displaced at the master's will.

Supervised by an overseer and circumscribed by the master's family, the black body comes into dangerously close contact with white bodies. The threat of bodies merging in transgressive desire, and the subsequent anxiety about the dissolution or recasting of hierarchical difference, fuels antislavery stories. Political and economic justifications of slavery cannot contain the risk of interracial sexual encounters. Whether brought about through mutual desire or through rape, miscegenation stands as a pervasive theme in most stories about slavery. Miscegenation often confuses family bonds with human bondage because the master's sexual exploitation of his female slaves creates progeny that is also property. A slave's ownership of his or her own body is complicated when that very body is a commercial entity legally owned by another. Because the slave's body is created by the nation's economic, political, and social ideology, and because the slave is part of the master's figurative or literal family, Franz Fanon notes that "there is no disproportion between the life of the family and the life of the nation" (142).

Similarly, "antislavery fiction's focus on miscegenation evades the difficulties of representing blackness by casting the racial problematics of slavery into the terms of sexual oppression" (Sánchez-Eppler, *Touching* 246). Because the female slave can be exploited for her childbearing labor as well as for her physical labor, her body becomes the paramount site of oppression. The institutionalization of exploitation and rape of the female slave led to generations of mixed-race children. As are U.S. writers, Cuban writers have been interested in these children of miscegenation and particularly in the children of what one critic calls "ambiguous racial origin" (Kutzinski 21).

More than just ownership link Carlota and her slave; although not stated outright, the narrative strongly suggests that the two are first cousins. When Enrique tells Carlota that he thinks Sab is related to her, she replies, "'Así lo pienso yo también, porque mi padre le ha tratado siempre con particular distinción, y aun ha dejado traslucir a la familia que tiene motivos poderosos para creerle hijo de su difunto hermano don Luis [I thought so as well, because my father always treated him specially, and he has even hinted to the family that he has strong reasons to believe him the son of his dead brother Luis]'" (149).⁹ These hints at Sab's parentage also hint at the interracial rape and/or concubinage endemic to slavery. Since Sab's mother descended from royalty ("princesa en su país, fue vendida en éste como esclava [a princess in her own country, she was sold as a slave in this country]" [131]) but did not marry Carlota's uncle, she was undoubtedly exploited as don Luis's slave. Sab's love for Carlota crosses the bloodline twice: exogamously he loves a racial other and endogomously he loves his cousin.

In story after story, these transracial violations inevitably turn out to be incestuous. Because of confounded bloodlines, conclusive relatedness is often impossible to define. Numerous nineteenth-century Spanish American novels portray brother-sister incest as a tragic result of unknown and unclaimed parentage, implicating a corrupt society in the perpetuation of this sexual taboo. Incestuous desire in *Aves sin nido* results from white exploitation of the Andean natives. Cirilo Villaverde pushes incest to its extreme in *Cecilia Valdés* when the eponymous heroine and her brother, Leonardo Gamboa, actually have a child together. Antislavery stories such as these enfold and enmesh romance within the parameters of the family because bondage and family bonds are often one and the same. In most stories, including *Sab*, incest occurs or threatens to occur because an exploitive father fails to pass on his surname or the universal law that prohibits incest, which Jacques Lacan calls the Name-of-the-Father. The sense of moral bankruptcy produced by incestuous situations, and the damage it inflicts on the family, serves to gauge the ills of society: "By situating antislavery discourse within an idealized domestic setting these stories purport to offer moral and emotional standards by which to measure, and through which to correct, the evils of slavery. The problem is that these standards are implicated in the values and structures of authority and profit they seek to criticize" (Sánchez-Eppler, "Bodily Bonds" 249).

Sab's impossible love for Carlota, intended to be pure and sublime in the noble Romantic tradition, nonetheless represents a threat to the very foundation of sugarocracy and white hegemony and thus cannot avoid being represented in the novel in terms of violence and threats. The slave loves his mistress so fiercely that his love assumes the patina of savagery. For example, when Sab first confesses his love for Carlota to Teresa, Teresa becomes suspicious and assumes Sab wants to warn her of an impending slave uprising. She asks him, " '¿Me habrás llamado a este sitio para descubrirme algún proyecto de conjuración de los negros? ¿Qué peligro nos amenaza? ¿Serás tú uno de los . . . ? [Did you call me here to warn me of some conspiracy among the blacks? What danger threatens us? Are you one of the . . . ?]' " (220). Ironically, Teresa thinks Sab wants to inform her of a slave insurrection that endangers the family, when actually only one slave threatens the family by overthrowing racial ideology through his love. Sab does admit, however, that the slaves do not need much incitement to revolt: " 'Acaso sólo necesitan para romperla, oír una voz que les grite: "¡sois hombres!" pero esa voz no será la mía, podéis creerlo [All they need to break free is to hear a voice shout "you are men!," but this voice will not be mine, rest assured]' " (220). Garfield finds a similarity between Sab's boiling anger and that of George Harris in *Uncle Tom's Cabin* when he brandishes a gun against whites but then relinquishes it (64). Stowe, however, does not tie her antislavery message to eroticism.

Both Gómez de Avellaneda and Stowe tread a fine line in representing their heroes' masculinity: on the one hand, as antislavery advocates the writers have a stake in demonstrating the inviolable and noble spirit of their men. On the other hand, neither author dares present to her readership a dark-skinned man harboring masculine violence. In summarizing the Cuban antislavery hero, Richard L. Jackson argues, "An apparent acceptance of blackness as inferior is projected even in these novels as they dwell at length on the negative qualities of the black man whom they are especially prone to portray as docile, tranquil, resigned to his fate, and lacking in a rebellious spirit" (22). Williams also finds Sab emasculated: because Sab's labor as a worker is not linked to the productivity of the sugar plantation (he does not work in the fields nor do we see him in his prescribed job as an overseer but rather see him as a mail carrier, tour guide, or food server), Williams suggests that Gómez de Avellaneda thus "assimilates the slave's domain to that of the women in the novel" and that the "condition of that assimilation is the suppression of all signs of sexual prowess in the hero" (94). Further, Sab's close ties to his pony suggest a possible animal nature, but one nonetheless tamed and servile.

But the scene in which Sab confesses to Teresa his miscegenous love for Carlota demonstrates, and then suppresses, Sab's insurrectionary potential. Although the novel makes no reference to contemporary slave uprisings (Millones-Figueroa 85), Sab harbors such passionate erotic fantasies about Carlota that his overwhelming desire erupts into criminal thought. Since society will not let him love Carlota freely, he dreams about taking her by force: "Arrebatar a Carlota de los brazos de su padre, arrancarla de esa sociedad que se interpone entre los dos, huir a los desiertos llevando en mis brazos a ese ángel de inocencia y de amor [To snatch Carlota from the arms of her father, to tear her away from the society that separates us, to flee to the wilderness carrying in my arms this angel of innocence and love]" (223). Sab confesses that his frustrated love has caused him to consider whether "bañarme en sangre de blancos; hollar con mis pies sus cadáveres y sus leyes y perecer yo mismo entre sus ruinas, con tal de llevar a Carlota a mi sepulcro: porque la vida o la muerte, el cielo o el infierno . . . todo era igual para mí si ella estaba conmigo [to bathe myself in whites' blood; to tread on their corpses and laws and perish among their ruins, as long as I can carry Carlota to my grave: because life or death, heaven or hell . . . it is all the same if she is with me]" (223). Sab's fevered passion shows both the iniquity of a society that prohibits cross-racial love and the danger to society of letting a slave love his mistress. That is, while Sab's unending suffering constitutes a critique of slavocracy, his threat of violence against whites reinforces the system of separation and justifies the fear that caused Gómez de Avellaneda's family to flee Cuba. Because Sab's love for Carlota is so intense that it transcends the division between life and death, race mixture must be revered for its sublime eroticism but feared for its lethal potential.

This incestuous attraction between first cousins shows that love and lust cross racial lines and that people understood to be racial Others are compelling, enticing, and desirable to one another. In *Sab*, interracial attraction is not limited to the eponymous hero and Carlota; an affinity also exists between Sab and Carlota's illegitimate cousin, Teresa. Sab and Teresa, both outcasts because of their "improper" blood pedigrees, suffer from unrequited love that positions each of them in a love triangle: Sab loves Carlota and Teresa loves Carlota's fiancé, Enrique. In a secretive midnight discussion, Teresa comes to realize how much she and Sab have in common and how much she admires him. In one of the most radical moments in the novel, Teresa recognizes Sab's humanity and sees him for the first time without the filter of race or class:

> Teresa temblaba, y una sensación extraordinaria se apoderó entonces de su corazón: olvidaba el color y la clase de Sab; veía sus ojos llenos del fuego que le devoraba; oía su acento que salía del corazón trémulo, ardiente, penetrante. . . . Parecióle también que ella era capaz de amar del mismo modo y que un corazón como el de Sab era aquel que el suyo necesitaba.
>
> [Teresa trembled, and an extraordinary sensation overtook her heart: she forgot Sab's color and class; she saw his eyes full of fire that devoured him, she heard his voice that came from his pounding, burning, penetrating heart. . . . It also seemed that she was capable of loving in the same way and that a heart like Sab's was one that hers needed.] (223)

Sab laments his condition and his damnation in having to go through life unloved: "'Ninguna mujer puede amarme, ninguna querrá unir su suerte a la del pobre mulato [No woman can love me, none would want to join her future with that of a poor mulatto]'" (223). This confession affects Teresa deeply, and, in another daring scene, she offers herself to him: "'Aislados estamos los dos sobre la tierra y necesitamos igualmente compasión, amor, y felicidad. Déjame, pues, seguirte a remotos climas, al seno de los desiertos . . . ¡yo seré tu amiga, tu compañera, tu hermana! [Both of us are alone on the earth and equally in need of compassion, love, and happiness. Let me follow you to remote places, to the heart of the wilds. I will be your friend, your companion, your sister!]'" (223). Sab loves Carlota too deeply to accept another woman's passion, and the taboo against mixed-race love prevents Gómez de Avellaneda from allowing consummation. Gómez de Avellaneda skillfully extracts Sab and the reader from this scene—Sab is grateful for Teresa's benevolence, but declares himself unworthy of her selfless love.

Carlota, however, naive about her slave's erotic love for her, generously recognizes the worthy qualities in Sab that make him deserving of being loved. Extolling Sab's virtues, Carlota offends Enrique by comparing Sab with him: "'Su alma era tan noble, tan elevada como la tuya.' . . . Al oír estas palabras la mirada de Enrique, que había estado amorosamente clavada en los bellos ojos de su mujer, vaciló un tanto . . . como si su conciencia le hiciese penosa una comparación que sabía bien no era merecida ['He had a noble soul, as elevated as yours.' . . . Upon hearing these words, Enrique's gaze, which had been lovingly fixed on the beautiful eyes of his wife, wavered a bit, as if his mind made a painful comparison that he knew was not deserved]" (262). Enrique fears this association between his soul and that of a slave, for it presumes that Carlota could venerate her slave as she does her husband.

Another reason suggests why Enrique would be upset at being compared with Sab: he fears the recognition that they are both racial outcasts. In the novel's atmosphere of illegitimate blood, it is quite possible that yet another racial taint exists. The novel suggests that Enrique and his father, Jorge Otway, are Jewish and have tried to assimilate to mask their unacceptable lineage. As a Jew, being compared with someone of mixed race would be quite unsettling, since racial codes did not always consider Jews to be pure whites. As a Jew, Enrique would be as racially unfit as Sab to marry Carlota. For Carlota's family to permit such a marriage would be to introduce impurity into a system predicated on racial inequality and would erode the slavocracy's hierarchy of privilege.

Jorge, an Englishman, immigrated to the United States, where he was a peddler and moneylender (*buhonero* and *usurero*) before moving to Havana and then Puerto Príncipe (141–42) to build the family's wealth. Gómez de Avellaneda characterizes Jorge and Enrique in terms of their excessive interest in money, behavior coded as stereotypically Jewish. Mary Cruz identifies Otway as "un judío inglés [an English Jew]" (71) who is "la personificación del amor al dinero [the personification of the love of money]" (72). In the way that they scrutinize the land and its value to maximize their possessions and profits, Jorge and Enrique embody Mary Louise Pratt's "seeing-man"; that is, a "European male subject of European landscape discourse—he whose imperial eyes passively look out and possess" (7). Enrique marries Carlota purely for financial security, and much of life for the Otways can be reduced to commercial interest. To establish himself in the mercantile life of Cuba, Jorge converted to Roman Catholicism, although the novel does not specify his original religion: "Aunque el viejo Otway se hubiese declarado desde su establecimiento en Puerto Príncipe un verdadero católico, apostólico, romano, y educado a su hijo en los ritos de la misma iglesia, su apostasía no le había salvado del nombre del hereje [Although the elder Otway had declared himself a true Roman Catholic since arriving in Puerto Príncipe, and had educated his son in the rites of the same church, his apostasy had not saved him from being called a heretic]" (144).

Nina M. Scott translates *apostasía* ambiguously as "the abandonment of his former religion" (Gómez de Avellaneda, *"Sab" and "Autobiography"* 40), which also leaves room for Judaism. Furthermore, Carlota's family protests her marriage to Enrique because they remember that he used to be poor and that he is a convert: "No faltaban en ella [la familia] individuos que oponiéndose al enlace de Carlota con Enrique, fuesen menos inspirados por el desprecio al buhonero que por el horror al hereje [Some individuals in the family opposed the union of Carlota and Enrique, less influenced by the contempt for the peddler than by the fear of heresy]" (144). In other words, his former religion, not his avaricious aims, presents insurmountable difficulties for Carlota's family. Although the Otways' original religion remains unnamed, Sommer points out that Gómez de Avellaneda characterizes the English as "social parasites" perhaps because she did not approve of excessive English intervention in Cuba's struggle for freedom (*Foundational* 133). As Protestants, the English exemplify outsider status in colonial Catholic Cuba. Of course, the English can also be Jewish, as is the eponymous heroine of Jorge Isaac's novel *María*.

Yet Carlota loves Enrique and convinces her father to let the marriage take place. When Carlota's father loses his fortune, it becomes imperative that Carlota marry a protector. Enrique's money and class status compensate for his possibly "tainted" outsider blood, but Sab's winning lottery ticket can never buy the slave the whiteness needed for him to marry Carlota. Carlota soon realizes she is trapped in an unhappy marriage and becomes disconsolate when she recognizes she was loved deeply by one she could not love in return. Eventually, Carlota withdraws from society.

The taboo against interracial desire inheres as too great to transcend, and the narrative works to punish or contain Sab and Teresa, the transgressors who bear the taint of hybrid eroticism. The two originally transgress by being *hijos naturales*, or natural rather than legal offspring, which further means they are "cut out of the patriarchal system and left closer to nature" (Ward 36). Sab and Teresa serve as scapegoats that must be sacrificed to purge society of the miscegenous desire that circulates within it. Sab's and Teresa's bodies channel illicit lust by displacing transgressive desire from Carlota, who represents the future of the white landed aristocracy.

As a commodity to be exchanged, Carlota with her inheritance must pass from the care of her father to the care of a deserving husband, since she stands as property that passes from one protector to another. As a symbol of white property, Carlota can be exchanged only between white men. In discussing kinship ties and the exchange of women, Abdul R. JanMohamed distinguishes between consent and appropriation (108–9). In a racist society, a white woman such as Carlota can never be exchanged between a white man and a mulatto, let alone a slave. Such an exchange would signal the kinship and equality between the two families. Black women, however, were appropriated, not exchanged, by white men from black men. The white master who fathered Sab, for example, most likely deemed irrelevant Sab's mother's consent. The possible rape of Sab's mother subverts the paternal function and denies Sab a father figure and even his father's name.

Although implicated in miscegenous desire because she is the object of Sab's desire, Carlota safely marries off into whiteness. Yet she still suffers because she cannot distinguish Enrique's greed from Sab's earnest love for her. Racial prejudice prevents Carlota from identifying Sab as an ideal lover, as it would keep her from loving him even if she could recognize his virtues.

Instead of castigating all slaves for covetous wishes, Gómez de Avellaneda makes only Sab die in longing for his white mistress. Similarly, any hint of reciprocated love on Carlota's part is displaced onto Teresa, whose desire is contained by the only alternative to death—the convent. Enrique has at stake a new wife whose reciprocated admiration for a slave he does not want to consider, for it places him in the intolerable position of being compared with the slave. After Sab's death, the overseer delivers a letter that Sab wrote as he was dying. As Carlota's guardian, Enrique reads the letter, which contains a bracelet, woven of Carlota's hair and clasped with her portrait, which she had given to Teresa as a token of affection and which Teresa had given lovingly to Sab as a keepsake of his beloved Carlota. Teresa rightfully states that Sab wrote the letter to her and that she gave the bracelet to Sab, who was "la person quien he creído en este mundo más digna de mi afecto y estimación [the person in this world most worthy of my affection and esteem]" (260). At first it appears that the letter is for Carlota and that she must have given the bracelet to Sab, pointing to a possible liaison between the two. But the tension defuses when Teresa steps in to identify herself as the addressee of the letter and previous owner of the bracelet. Enrique recognizes the opportunity to emphasize the connection between Teresa and Sab and thus deflect any sentimental link away from Carlota and onto Teresa. He restates Teresa's words to accentuate her relationship to Sab: " 'Yo ignoraba que tuvieseis correspondencia con el mulato, y que os devolviese él una prenda que, según decís, sólo podíais ceder al hombre a quien quisieseis y estimaseis más [I didn't realize that you corresponded with the mulatto, and that he would return to you a gift that, as you said, you would only give to the man you most loved and esteemed]' " (260).

In the confusion, Carlota fails to comprehend what transpired, as if the idea of a cross-racial alliance were far removed from her sensibility. Enrique must explain to her, " 'Fácil es adivinar . . . Teresa amaba al mulato [It is easy to guess . . . Teresa loved the mulatto]' " (262). Carlota expresses shock at the possibility of miscegenation between Teresa and Sab: " '¡Amarle! . . . ¡Oh, no es posible! . . . ¡A él, a un esclavo! [She loves him! Oh, that's not possible! He is a slave!]' " (262). By recognizing Teresa's affection for Sab and charging Teresa with the love between Carlota and Sab, Enrique deflects the miscegenous desire away from his wife and onto her illegitimate cousin. Carlota remains morally and spiritually untainted because her illicit desire has been transferred to a woman who already has a marginal position in society. Teresa chooses to spend the rest of her life in a convent since she cannot marry Enrique, but Enrique interprets her action as an admission of guilt for secretly holding miscegenous desire.[10] Since Carlota never knew of Teresa's love for Enrique and since Enrique is the head of the household and thus speaks for his wife, his interpretation of Teresa's action becomes official. For committing the unforgivable sin of interracial love, the narrative demands that Sab die, that Carlota be exculpated, and that Teresa, the scapegoat, expiate her sin by denying earthly desire in a convent.

The novel concludes with the authorial voice declaring its inability to inform the reader of Carlota's fate. The narrator speculates that Enrique's wealth most likely led him to establish himself far from Puerto Príncipe but that perhaps Carlota lives in London. The very last line of the novel avoids implicating Cuba in Carlota's pain; instead, it suggests the shared misery of slavery and women's inferior status: "Pero cualquiera que sea su destino, y el país del mundo donde habite, ¿habrá podido olvidar la hija de los trópicos, al esclavo que descansa en una humilde sepultura bajo aquel hermoso cielo? [But whatever her destiny and the country of the world in which she lives, could the daughter of the tropics ever forget the slave who rests in a humble grave under that beautiful sky?]" (284). Since her whereabouts are unknown, Carlota could be any woman unable to escape the confines of society.

With this envoi, Gómez de Avellaneda identifies not with the buried slave but with her heroine: both are far from home, both are unhappy with the lot of women and slaves. Referring to this conclusion, many critics point out that much in *Sab* parallels Gómez de Avellaneda's autobiography. For example, Netchinsky identifies in the novel "the striking attention to landscape, the plot and character relations to the Romantic canon, the stirrings of feminist consciousness, the critique of Cuban society, the abolitionist intent" (201), all present in Gómez de Avellaneda's life. Sommer locates surprising parallels between the white, female, upper-class author and the mulatto, male, slave hero: Sab takes up his pen and through his letter ends the novel, Sab's love letter to Carlota echoes a love letter Gómez de Avellaneda wrote to her own unrequited love, and Sab pities both women and slaves for their oppression. Sommer notes that "the stunning thing about this self-portrait is that it identifies author with apparently helpless slave through their shared productive function, their literary labor conditioned in both by the need to subvert and to reconstruct" (*Foundational* 114–15). Even more striking, as Kirkpatrick points out, is that Gómez de Avellaneda, a middle-class white woman, "colonized" a slave's subjectivity to express her own anguish: "Gómez de Avellaneda was more fearful of openly representing female ambition and rebelliousness than she was of acknowledging the justice of Sab's anger with her own class and race" (*Las Románticas* 158–59). The figure of the mulatto and the theme of hybridity served Gómez de Avellaneda well as platforms for advocating change that would help her avoid Carlota's fate. Unlike Carlota, Gómez de Avellaneda turned her protest into a career and dared critique the system of slavery and women's subordination.

4

Floral Counterdiscourse: Miscegenation, Ecofeminism, and Hybridity in Lydia Maria Child's Romance of the Republic

One way that the eponymous slave hero of Gertrudis Gómez de Avellaneda's *Sab* shows his love for his slave mistress is through the lush garden he maintains for her. Knowing how much Carlota loves flowers, Sab "había cultivado, vecino a la casa de Bellavista, un pequeño y gracioso jardín hacia el cual se dirigió la doncella, luego que dio de comer a sus aves favoritas [had cultivated, next to the Bellavista house, a small and pleasing garden where the maiden would head when she wanted to feed her favorite birds]" (163). Gómez de Avellaneda describes the garden as "un cuadro perfecto [picture perfect]" (163) and one that Sab designed himself ("Sab no había consultado sino sus caprichos al formarle [Sab consulted only his whim when designing it]" [163]) to ensure it pleased Carlota: "Sab había reunido en aquel pequeño recinto todas las flores que más amaba Carlota [In that small enclosure, Sab gathered all the flowers that Carlota loved most]" (163). In this novel of reform, Gómez de Avellaneda eroticizes Sab's garden, and by using the chaste and beautiful green world of flowers as a mediating device between black and white, she aims to "naturalize" Sab's love for Carlota.

Similarly, Lydia Maria Child advocates race reform by taking advantage of the woman-as-garden convention in her fourth and last novel, *A Romance of the Republic* (1867). Child, however, uses horticultural associations to offer an uplifting floral counterdiscourse of botanical hybridity to counteract the postbellum prejudice that viewed African Americans and mixed-race peoples as animals. By choosing such botanical names for her mixed-race heroines as Rosabella and Flora Royal and by comparing them with valued and aesthetically pleasing flowers, Child raises questions about the natural and the social. In particular, Child uses hybrid flowers and language derived from contemporary botanical manuals to construct a philosophy of hybrid racial identity. In *A Romance of the Republic*, Child attempts to elevate black women's status by using horticulturally identified heroines and constructing a positive floral counterdiscourse that reclaims African American women's subjectivities as "pure" flowers. That is, Child merges the discourse of race with the discourse of flowers to interrogate what is "natural" about Reconstruction racial ideology. Yet, Child's creation falls short of utopia because she unwittingly equates black female agency with a flower's quiet passivity. Although at first glance it might appear that the discourse of race and the discourse of flowers are at cross-purposes, I will explore the discursive strategies of hybridity to yield a "green" analysis of Child's miscegenation plot.

In addition to her writings that aimed to elevate the status of African Americans, Child also tried to advance the rights of women and Native Americans in such works as *History of the Condition of Women, in Various Ages and Nations* (1835) and *Hobomok*. Slavery no longer existed in the United States when Child was writing *A Romance of the Republic*, so the novel does not resonate politically in quite the same way as *Sab*. Yet no less significantly, Child tried to reform postbellum society's persistent and vicious race prejudice via her fictions. Describing her motives in a letter to Robert Purvis, a Philadelphia black leader and founder of the American Anti-Slavery Society, she wrote, "In these days of novel-reading, I thought a Romance would take more hold of the public mind, than the most elaborate arguments; and having fought against Slavery, till the monster is *legally* dead, I was desirous to do what I could to undermine Prejudice" (*Selected Letters* 482–83). A versatile writer with numerous novelistic and narrative options, Child chose a romantic incest and miscegenation plot for *A Romance of the Republic* as her best weapon for overturning racial division.

Much criticism of *A Romance of the Republic* focuses on the role of race mixture in solving race problems and the critique of race and racism inherent in Child's baby-switching plot in which a white baby is raised as a slave while his black brother grows up in the master's house.[1] The main plot of *A Romance of the Republic* revolves around Rosa Royal and Flora Royal, two beautiful and accomplished young women who, when their father dies, find out that their long-dead mother had been a slave and that they are, therefore, mulattas and slaves. The dishonest Gerald Fitzgerald "marries" Rosa knowing full well that this legally unrecognized union with a mulatta could be broken at any time. Fitzgerald subsequently legitimately marries the white Lily Bell. Both women bear him sons at the same time. Rosa switches the infants so that her own son grows up in the white man's house unaware of his mixed-race heritage and later dies fighting in the Civil War. Rosa takes Lily's son and raises him as black. This boy, believing himself to be a light-skinned African American, eventually marries a dark black woman, Henriet. Meanwhile, Flora Royal marries her German suitor, Franz Blumenthal, and Rosa becomes a successful opera singer and marries her old friend the white Alfred King. The children of the two sisters become friends and the novel ends with a vision of a happy multiracial household.

Although critics have focused on black-white relations in the novel, they have not considered Child's use of botany and the relationship between gardening and racial constructions. For centuries women have been identified with flowers, beauty, and innocence, and Child trades in this currency. For example, when Alfred King, an eligible white suitor of the talented Royal sisters, first walks in the Royals' parlor, he exclaims, " 'This is the Temple of Flora. . . . Flowers everywhere! Natural flowers, artificial flowers, painted flowers, embroidered flowers, and human flowers excelling them all,'—glancing at the young ladies as he spoke" (5). In addition, Alan Bewell points out the "role that botany played in late eighteenth-century sexual theory, which arose directly from the traditional association of women with flowers. This identification went well beyond the anatomical analogy, explicit in the idea of sexual defloration, because women were consistently viewed as being linked, in ways that men were not, to the Realm of Flora" (135). Yet, as Claudette Sartiliot notes, flowers "appear as having no stable *topos*. In texts, as in the natural world, they are alive with stratagems, devoted to metamorphoses and mimicries: they can easily be turned into their opposites and thus express the feminine, the masculine, or both—they can even show the artificiality of their opposition" (4).

Child, however, flexes the plant language to create a floral counterdiscourse. In an essay on miscegenation and colonialism, Susan C. Greenfield argues that during this period "ideas about sexual normalcy underwrote constructions of national identity and imperial ambition" (216). In *A Romance of the Republic*, Child similarly tackles issues of sexual normalcy by linking female sexuality to flowers. Flowers literally are plants' sexual organs and in literature function as an "expression of transgressive erotic desire" (Stein 46). To name Rosa and Flora after flowers is thus to emphasize the sisters' sexuality and sexual currency in society as well as their "natural" state, here constituted as guileless and chaste. Since the women's racial identity in the novel is as important as their sexual identity, however, the language of flowers is grafted onto the language of race, especially in the idea of hybridity.

To discuss the cultural and social consequences of Child's merged discourses of nature, race, and hybridity, we can refer to Donna J. Haraway's claim that "bodies, including sexualized and racialized bodies, appear as objects of knowledge and sites of intervention" (*Simians* 134). Rosa's and Flora's bodies are initially presented to readers and to Alfred King as objects of knowledge that embody accomplishment and polished beauty befitting southern white gentility. With their trained voices, graceful and flirtatious manners, coiffed hair, and elegant dress, the sisters emblematize the class, race, and sexual status in which their father has "cultivated" or "bred" them. Rosa's and Flora's floral names link their cultivated status to the plant world, thereby questioning whether "cultivation" and "breeding" are biological processes or performances of social codes. Once the sisters' bodies become racialized, that is, once race and hybridity suddenly become an issue when their slave condition is revealed, then Rosa's and Flora's bodies become sites of intervention onto which Child can superimpose her reformist agenda of miscegenation and her moral critique of a racist society. At the same time, the limits of Child's floral counterdiscourse are revealed in her inability to imagine darker black women as contributors to cultural elevation.

Child's florigraphic intervention serves as a counterdiscourse to the prevailing Reconstruction rhetoric of hybridity that invoked animals and animality to discuss species, race, and black women's sexuality. For example, even the common term "mulatto" has a bestial origin: the *Oxford English Dictionary* defines "mulatto" as coming from the Spanish *mulo*, meaning "young mule, hence one of mixed race." Numerous theorists and racial scientists of the period looked to animals and animal sexuality as a way to discuss human reproduction and hybridity. In *The Origin of Species* (1859), Darwin included a chapter entitled "Hybridity" and cites examples of crossbreeding in the animal world (see Robert J. C. Young 11). Robert Knox wrote in *The Races of Men* (1850) that "naturalists have generally admitted that animals of the same species are fertile, reproducing their kind for ever; whilst on the contrary, if an animal be the product of two distinct species, the hybrid, more or less, was sure to perish or to become extinct" (qtd. in Robert J. C. Young 7–8). The U.S. craniologist S. G. Morton, most famous for his *Crania Americana* (1839), in which he theorized a link between cultural advancement and brain size, argued in his essay "Hybridity in Animals and Plants" (1847) that "since various species of animals are capable of producing together a prolific hybrid offspring, hybridity ceases to be a test of specific affiliation" (qtd. in Robert J. C. Young 131). W. F. Edwards based his theories of hybridity, published in 1829, on crossbred mice (see Robert J. C. Young 79). These examples of animal hybridity were then abstracted and applied to humans.

Racial scientists used animal discourse as a way to infer rules of human sexuality and thereby embossed human hybridity with a negative patina. About Darwin, Harriet Ritvo notes that "in the middle of his argument that species and varieties were indistinguishable, he consistently denominated the offspring of parents of different species as 'hybrids' while denigrating the offspring of parents of different varieties as 'mongrels'" (45–46), words later used to label humans of mixed-race descent. Further, Victorian animal breeders concerned with purity of lineage and pedigree in animals frequently denounced the mixing of bloodlines. Most telling, perhaps, is the concept of telegony, a belief widely accepted by nineteenth-century breeders and scientists that the sire of a female's first offspring would influence the biology of her subsequent offspring. Evidently in 1820 a chestnut mare of seven-eighths Arabian descent was bred with a quagga (defined in the *Oxford English Dictionary* as a "South African equine quadruped, related to the ass and zebra, but less fully striped than the latter"). Her first foal looked like both parents, but subsequent foals, sired by a black Arabian horse, nonetheless looked like the quagga. From this reported incident, as well as others, theories flourished predicated on containing and controlling female sexual activity (Ritvo 45–46).

Just as the discourse of animality appealed to racial scientists, it also appealed to many novelists, who incorporated bestial images in their fictions. For example, although George Washington Cable basically sympathizes with people of mixed-race heritage, he describes a mulatta as a "leopardess" in *The Grandissimes* (1880) (57). Thomas Dixon Jr., not at all sympathetic to interracial relations, describes Lydia Brown, the mulatta servant and mistress in his novel *The Clansman* (1905), as a "leopardess" and as endowed with an "animal beauty." When Lydia hears her master talk about his view of Reconstruction, her face "wore the mask of a sphinx" (100).

Since the normative discourse of hybridity was based on such animal imagery and suffused with negative connotations, Child needed a more positive discourse of breeding, cultivation, and natural production to serve her reformist impulses in *A Romance of the Republic*. Botanical metaphors personally resonated with her longstanding interest in gardening. For example, before her husband, David, departed on his speaking engagement on behalf of the Kansas Aid Committee, he tried to comfort Child, who was anxious as her father hovered between life and death, by protecting her beloved garden. Referring to these loving efforts, Child later wrote in a letter to him, "It almost made me cry to see how carefully you had arranged everything for my comfort before you went," especially the "bricks piled up to protect my flowers" (qtd. in Karcher, *First Woman* 401). After David's death, Child found comfort in her garden in Wayland, where she could recall David's voice "bidding a loving good morning to my flowers, as he used to do" (583).[2] Child's fondness for flowers and her interest in their language surface in some of her earlier works. For example, in her short story "The Quadroons" (1842), Child endows her mixed-race protagonist with a floral name, Rosalie. Child further links Rosalie to the plant world by frequently comparing her with a passion flower and remarking that her white lover, Edward, "fondly twined its [the passion flower's] sacred blossoms with the glossy ringlets of her raven hair" (91). In the first issue of her

Juvenile Miscellany, Child wrote "The Tulip and Tri-Colored Violet," a didactic essay with talking flowers who encourage girls to cultivate qualities that will make them "useful and cheerful companions, in preference to those, which fit them only to be the gay flutterers of an evening" (389-90).

In an era when public speech was not encouraged for women, flowers and what became known as the "language of flowers" offered an acceptable way for women to express numerous sentiments and interact with the "wild" outside the home. Lady Mary Wortley Montagu introduced the idea of the language of flowers to Europe through letters she sent from Turkey in the eighteenth century. By the nineteenth century, the language of flowers "presented a set of highly formalized lists of meanings together with a whole semiotic analysis of this language" (Goody 134). An association with flowers as well indicated a woman's religious virtue. As Susan Harris argues, "By the nineteenth century, the association of specific flowers with specific meanings had become a symbolic code, in large part reflecting liberal Protestantism's assumption that nature reflects God's intentions" (80). Through the language of flowers in *A Romance of the Republic*, Child taps into a sentimental, virtuous discourse to overturn sexual and racial norms. The cult of true womanhood did not permit women to venture forth into unmediated wilderness, but women could bring the wilds home into a domesticated, supervised, planned, fenced garden, could paint flower images, and could write sentimental poems about nature, activities that "positioned them as caretakers or teachers of nature's moral lessons" (Stein 25). The liminal space of agriculture and gardening has been described accurately as "an ambiguous conceptual position in American thought, belonging both to a green world of nature, a realm that exists independent of human control, and to a world defined by a human culture that dominates and influences nature" (Sarver 4). Women in this liminal space cultivated themselves as proper ladies while taming unruly nature.

Elizabeth Petrino summarizes the liminal zone of gardening as offering "two competing, though perhaps not contradictory, approaches to the natural world in nineteenth-century America: one scientific, rational, and exploratory, the other sentimental, aesthetic, and poetic" (133). This border zone between domesticity and the wild also afforded women access to an acceptable form of science education: botanical instruction. Young ladies mastered arranging, sending, and receiving flowers and learned plant biology and identification at the same time. Similarly, as Kathleen Gips argues, "this scientific aspect gave validity and a sense of purpose to naming flowers and translating their messages" (10). Even Almira H. Lincoln's academic tome, *Familiar Lectures on Botany*, the text Emily Dickinson studied, includes a floral dictionary. Lincoln notes in the introduction to the floral dictionary that, "besides the scientific relations which are to be observed in plants, flowers may also be regarded as emblematic of the affections of the heart and qualities of the intellect." She revises the meaning attached to some flowers, however, to influence girls' moral constitution: "In a few cases, alterations have been made, in order to introduce sentiments of a more refined and elevated character, than such as relate to mere personal attractions" (431).

Yet this liminal space between the scientific and the sentimental offered women a powerful cultural and rhetorical position in which to develop meaning and presented Child with a potent way to merge two discourses. The nineteenth-century poet Frances Sargent Osgood believes, as did many antebellum women, that flowers "utter in 'silent eloquence' a language better than writing" (*Poetry of Flowers* 23). Floral dictionaries, which proliferated in the middle third of the nineteenth century, list flowers and their many potential meanings. In fact, because meanings could vary, it was important that both sender and receiver of bouquets referred to the same dictionary. The numerous meanings attributed to flowers in no way limited women's choice in writing, but rather offered women expansive access to expression.

Literature *became* flowers in numerous anthologies of poetry whose titles evoke the green world. Child's reliance on horticultural metaphors to convey meaning in *A Romance of the Republic* places her in floral conversation with an extensive community and tradition of mainly antebellum women writers. Consider the following: Caroline Kirkland's *Poetry of the Flowers* (n.d.); Dorothea Dix's *Garland of Flora* (1829); Child's own collections *Garland of Juvenile Poems* (1836), *Flowers for Children* (first and second series in 1844 and third series in 1846), and *A New Flower for Children* (1856); Osgood's *Wreath of Wild Flowers from New England* (1838) and *The Floral Offering, a Token of Friendship* (1846); Grace Greenwood's *Greenwood Leaves* (1850); Sarah Josepha Hale's *Flora's Interpreter and Fortuna Flora* (1850); Fanny Fern's *Fern Leaves* (1853); Walt Whitman's *Leaves of Grass* (1855); and Lucy Hooper's *Lady's Book of Flowers and Poetry* (1858). Kirkland firmly believes that flowers, poetry, and women readers were linked, a connection Child maximizes in *A Romance of the Republic*. Speaking of flowers, Kirkland writes: "Universal is their hold on human sympathies; universal their language. Floral Poesy is, therefore, the most appropriate of all presents; and, in giving this title to a language of flowers, and a collection of charming poems on them, we believe we have not been guilty of a misnomer" (7). These titles reinforced the cultural links among flowers, poetry, and femininity. Hale indicates in her 1832 introduction to *Flora's Interpreter: or, The American Book of Flowers and Sentiments* that she hopes her collection "inspire[s] our Young Ladies to cultivate those virtues which can be truly represented by the fairest flowers" (1).

Gips explains that during the Victorian era, flowers were believed to embody human emotions and attributes, "so it seemed logical that they could also speak, using their own language" (26). Kirkland, as do many authors of books on flowers, goes on to detail this special language of verbalized flowers:

> When a flower is given, the pronoun *I* is understood by bending it to the right hand; *thou* by inclining it to the left.
> "Yes" is implied by touching the flower given with the lips.
> "No," by pinching off a petal, and casting it away.
> "I am" is expressed by a laurel-leaf twisted round the bouquet.
> "I have," by an ivy-leaf folded together.
> "I offer you," by a leaf of the Virginian Creeper.
> "To win"—a sprig of parsley in the bouquet.
> "May," or "I desire"—an ivy tendril round the bouquet. (221)

Although this language of flowers offered Child an already codified set of meanings to draw upon in her work, black women in nineteenth-century U.S. culture were not constructed as having a positive link to nature, so the language of flowers did not necessarily speak their desires. An awareness of the double standard in play when describing black and white women finds full expression in Harriet A. Jacobs, whose *Incidents in the Life of a Slave Girl* (1861) problematized the relationship between black women and nature. Child herself served as editor of Jacobs's *Incidents*, and the organic orientation of *A Romance of the Republic* must have been influenced by Child's familiarity with Jacobs's interrogation of the starkly differentiated images of nature associated with black and white womanhood.

For example, Jacobs states that black women "are considered of no value, unless they continually increase their owner's stock. They are put on a par with animals" (49). Yet she recognizes the connection between white women and garden imagery: "The fair child grew up to be a still fairer woman. From childhood to womanhood her pathway was blooming with flowers." A black girl, however, "was very beautiful; but the flowers and sunshine of love were not for her" (29). By calling attention to such a contrast, Jacobs seems to be critiquing readers' assumptions about metaphors racializing nature. When Jacobs flees from her master she initially flees into nature, but the landscape she hides in is no garden. Instead, she finds herself in a swamp where she is bitten by mosquitoes and a poisonous snake. Such descriptions of nature echo the stereotype linking untamed nature with black women's rampant sexuality. Further, as Ann Gelder points out, pastoral analogies in *Incidents* "conceal cultural violence with images of nature and culture in harmony, especially in descriptions of homely, cultivated vines around slaves' quarters" (255). Jacobs wrote for a white audience that was, as Vera Norwood argues, "threatened by the thought that women of color could take on the mantle of the cultured domesticity reserved for Euro-American women" (185). Further, the woman-as-garden metaphor did not work for female slaves because "to portray a slave at ease among the cultivated flowers of the ornamental garden would violate the stereotype of the black women as, by their nature, incapable of purity" (192).

Given these examples, it is extremely important to recognize Child's strategy in greening Rosa Royal's and Flora Royal's sexuality. By using botanical discourse to discuss race and hybridity, Child domesticates and cultivates proper white womanhood and sexuality for her mixed-race heroines. To this point slave women's sexuality had been compared with animals' sexuality and termed feral—the only sense in which it had been "naturalized." Child's florigraphic rhetoric replaces the debased figuration of nature she encountered when editing Jacobs's autobiography and effectively enacts what Stein labels the "ecofeminist axiom" that "questions of nature are always also deeply social concerns embedded within complex histories and that recourse to 'nature' has often been used to naturalize disturbing colonialist social arrangements" (146). Aware of this tactic, Child purposefully tries to "purify" black women by endowing them with floral graces usually reserved for white women.

Mrs. A. E. Johnson adopts a corresponding strategy in *The Hazeley Family* (1894): she portrays racially indeterminate characters, although she herself is African American and the novel seems aimed at a black middle-class readership. Barbara Christian hypothesizes that "to render her moral story about the qualities that young black respectable women—rather than stereotypical mammies or wenches—needed to keep their families intact and flourishing, Mrs. Johnson may have found it necessary to characterize her family in nonracial terms" (xxviii). Not only are Johnson's characters nonracial but also the heroine is named Flora and the novel incorporates many images of flowers, fruits, and vegetables. Christian points out that the novel's nature imagery is not associated with sexuality or reproduction but rather with "the naturalness of family and home and woman's place in it" (xxxiv). Thus, the floral discourse in *The Hazeley Family* may reinforce what the novel's deracialized discourse suggests: that black women are entitled to the same status of pure-as-flowers true womanhood as white women. Much later, Zora Neale Hurston makes a similar move in *Their Eyes Were Watching God* (1937) in her creation of Janie, a character, Norwood argues, "whose sexuality, by virtue of its expression through plant reproduction, was cleansed of disturbing connections with animal behavior. Janie's sensitive reading of the plants in her landscape also articulated African American plant lore and the importance of gardens in black women's lives" (192–93). *A Romance of the Republic* predates Johnson's and Hurston's novels by several decades but shares their revisionary agenda of rewriting black female sexuality.

Specifically, Child's choice of characters' names rewrites stereotyped bestial sexuality. Child names her characters after flowers to signal something about their comportment, virtue, values, and manner—in other words, their character. Referring to late-nineteenth-century novels concerned with race, Cathy Boeckmann argues that "the crucial and determining issue was not race per se but rather the implications and conclusions that could be drawn from the manifestations of racial character: the question of race had become a question of character" (15). The link between race and character is particularly salient for literary convention, because, as Boeckmann suggests, the "notion of character clearly straddles the conceptual worlds of science and literature. Character is a building block of literature, and it intrudes itself upon scientific discourse in the basic requirement that an assessment of character be *characterized*—whatever conclusions can be drawn about character have to be given shape in descriptive language. Therefore, an emphasis on inherited race character brought racial theory into a close relationship with literary notions about characterization" (15).

In *A Romance of the Republic*, Child tries to counter "scientific" knowledge about race through floral characterization. Thus, to do her characters justice, Child reveals her character's hybrid racial character by turning to the language of flowers. By relying on sentimental fiction's convention of stereotypes, Child taps into cultural agreement about flowers' symbolism and character and redresses negative scientific discourse on hybridity.

For example, for her principal heroine, Child chooses the name "Rosa" or "Rosabella," whose beauty Child describes as "superlative and peculiar" (3). Undoubtedly, in choosing this name, Child means for readers to sense Rosa's beauty, virtue, and loving and passionate nature because of the rose's association with love, carnality, and ardor and its status as the queen of flowers.[3] Perhaps Child also knew that the rose was one of the flowers most experimented with and hybridized. According to Samuel Bowne Parsons's popular tome *The Rose: Its History, Poetry, Culture, and Classification*, only 182 varieties of roses existed in 1814. Extensive hybridizing produced more than 4,500 varieties by the time his 1860 edition was published (182). Rosa Royal likewise is a hybrid: her father is white and her mother is a mixture of Spanish, French, and African descent. Although Rosa is legally a slave, Child goes to great lengths to convince her readers that Rosa is well bred and highly cultivated. Because Rosa's mixed race cannot immediately be identified and she passes as white, Child asserts Rosa's refined character through refined floral association.

Child's language of hybridity in *A Romance of the Republic* resonates with the Victorian vocabulary used to discuss hybridity in roses. For example, to describe the way the races mix to produce Rosa's lovely daughter, Child draws upon contemporary interest in cultivating hybrid plants: "Nature is very capricious in the varieties she produces by mixing flowers with each other. Sometimes the different tints of each are blended in a new color, compounded of both; sometimes one color is marked in distinct stripes or rings upon the other; and sometimes the separate hues are mottled and clouded" (302). Rosa's daughter inherits the best racial traits of both parents:

"She inherited her mother's tall, flexile form, and her long dark eyelashes, eyebrows, and hair; but she had her father's large blue eyes, and his rose-and-white complexion. The combination was peculiar, and very handsome" (302).

Child's description here echoes Parsons's explanation for the best way to achieve successful hybrid roses: "Those who intend to raise new roses from seed should select varieties differing as much as possible in color and habit.... These should be planted together in a rich soil, and as far as possible from any other roses. If there are among them any two varieties whose peculiarities it is desired to unite in a single plant, place these next to each other, and there may possibly be such an admixture of the pollen as will produce the desired result" (182–83). Parsons explains that the hybrid plant will nonetheless maintain some "peculiarities" (a word Child uses) of its parents: "It is a fact generally admitted by botanists, that all varieties of plants will generally produce from their seed plants entirely dissimilar, preserving perhaps some peculiarities of their parents, but differing in many essential particulars" (189). Because flowers are a plant's sexual organs, Parsons's descriptions of the hybridizing process seems to parallel human sexual behavior: "Linnaeus, with many subsequent authors, published observations tending to prove that, even in the natural state, new species were formed by two different plants, the pistil of one having been fecundated by the stamens of the other" (187). Both Child and Parsons employ the word "peculiar" to mean special or distinct characteristics, which accords with the *Oxford English Dictionary*'s definition of "one's own private property." But "peculiar" also reminds readers of the common term for southern slavery: the "peculiar institution." In Child's text, "peculiar" is positive and pleasingly exotic, thereby reversing negative racial stereotypes.

Child's co-option of horticultural hybridization imagery is instructive, if not prescriptive. Clearly she means to teach educated readers a new way of viewing race relations. The didactic dialogue she holds with readers echoes the pedantic dialogues found in Jane Haldimand Marcet's *Conversations on Vegetable Physiology* (1830), which teaches botany to young ladies through conversations between a Mrs. B and her students Emily and Caroline. Particularly notable is conversation 16, "On Grafting," in which Mrs. B explains the hybridizing art of grafting as "placing a portion of one plant in juxta-position with another, in such a manner that they shall unite and grow together." Caroline responds with, "This, then, is not a mode of multiplying plants, but of changing their nature" (198). Mrs. B adds, "The advantage of grafting consists in improving the quality, not augmenting the number, of plants. . . . The principal advantage of grafting consists in its affording an easy means of propagating individual plants, which have, either by cultivation or some casual circumstance, attained a high degree of perfection" (200).

Child's agenda of promoting racial equality and interracial marriage concurs with this botany manual that grafting or hybridizing results in "improving the quality" of the species. Here hybridity is a strength, not a method of degenerating a species or race. In finding such a positive model of species mixture, Child anchors her heroine's miscegenated heritage in the virtuous floral world and thus corrects the pejorative bestial rhetorics of hybridity.[4]

Flora Royal receives the nickname "Pensee Vivace," French and Italian for "spirited thought." According to floral dictionaries, pansies symbolized tender thoughts, as one would expect from the French origin of their name. Pansies are also called viola tricolors, heartsease, or johnny-jump-ups, a name Alfred King (who is linked to the green world by his name, an inversion of the variety of daffodil known as the King Alfred) modifies to "Jump-up-and-kiss-me" (5). To nickname a black woman "Pansy" is to link her to thought, if not to identify her as a thinker. The name "Flora" also serves as a general term for anything relating to flowers and amounts to calling the black woman "Everywoman." As well, the name "Flora" invokes the goddess Flora who rules over the plant world. Thus, Child radically modifies black women's standing by choosing a name that suggests a chaste and thinking girl who functions as a universal representative of black womanhood.

Rosa and Flora are clearly identified as flowers, as are their daughters Lila and Rosen, yet the status of the other flower-associated woman who lives in their house, the black servant Tulipa, is questioned. Throughout *A Romance of the Republic*, Rosa's and Flora's rank as flowers remains secure. Yet when Tulipa calls them to tea, Alfred asks, " 'Is *she* a flower too?' " Flora answers positively: " 'Yes, she's a flower, too. . . . We named her so because she always wears a red and yellow turban' " (6). In some ways, Alfred's question serves as the driving question of the narrative, for during the course of the novel,

Child tries to build a strong case that these women are as pristine and as good as flowers. According to law at the time, all three women—Rosa, Flora, and Tulipa—are slaves, so Child's choice of the name "Tulipa" for the only *visibly* black woman is particularly interesting. While the floral name "Tulipa" accords the servant a sense of beauty, virtue, and true womanhood, the associations of the tulip are quite different from those of the rose and raise provocative questions about Tulipa's sexual and racial status in the novel.

The tulip received its name, according to numerous floral dictionaries, from "tulipan," or "turban," a choice Osgood claims is based upon the "similarity of [the flower's] corolla to the superb head-dress of the barbarous Turks" (*Poetry of Flowers* 52). The red and yellow turban of the Royals' slave no doubt recalls the exotic Turkish headpiece. Mrs. E. W. Wirt writes that the "tulip has always been considered as the *rival of the rose*, displaying a more gorgeous and varied tinting of colors, to balance the superior fragrance of her compeer. The *Turks* regard this flower with so much favor, that in addition to their '*Feast of Roses*,' their '*Feast of Tulips*' is celebrated annually in the Grand Seignior's gardens, with a magnificence of splendor and pomp, that can only be compared to the fairy scenes of the Arabian Night's Tales" (69). Osgood similarly details the oriental fantasy of the feast of tulips in which the harem leader watches a slave dance: "In the center of the seraglio a splendid pavilion shaded the Grand Seignior, who negligently reclined on costly skins; while the lords of his court, habited in their richest attire, were seated at his feet to behold the dances of the lovely women of the court in all the luxurious display of their light and dazzling dresses. These sometimes encircled, and at others glided round the vases of tulips, whose beauty they sung. . . . Ah no! two poor slaves alone had troubled his heart" (*Poetry of Flowers* 53).

It is significant to quote these descriptions of the tulip in the seraglio at length because when Alfred King first enters the Royals' residence and comments on the "Temple of Flora," he seems to have entered a harem, complete with "poor slaves," although at this point in the novel the sisters do not know of their slave ancestry. The ornate decorations, musical background, perfume, and flower-drenched maidens surely conjure an exotic atmosphere appealing to an eligible young man. Rosa and Flora's father had first noticed their mother because of her dark, sensual beauty: "The irresistible attraction I felt toward her the first moment I saw her was doubtless the mere fascination of the senses" (19), an attraction befitting the stereotype of the mulatta's sexual availability. Since it is possible that Alfred King might similarly feel a sexual attraction to the sisters ensconced in their sensual floral temple, the haremlike nature of their home must be deflected onto Tulipa. If the tulip and the rose are sexual rivals and if the tulip elicits exotic, orientalizing, harem-type associations, then it seems that Child loads the darker black woman with sexual overtones, thus further sanitizing Rosa's and Flora's sexuality. The florigraphic rhetoric of names maintains Rosa's and Flora's pure womanhood while suggesting something else about Tulipa's.

Furthermore, the tulip was bred and hybridized extensively, and cultivated species commanded high prices during the economic frenzy of Holland's Tulipomania in the seventeenth century.[5] Wirt also mentions that the tulip has no calyx. In the section of her book devoted to explaining the seven parts of a flower, she defines the calyx as "the envelope in which, in most cases, the tender flower lies, for a time, concealed, as the green leaves of a rosebud, which cover the blossom, and burst as the flower opens" (11). This detailed description casts the calyx as that which conceals or protects the flower's sexual parts until the blossom is ready to open. As a bondswoman, Tulipa has no calyx; that is, as a slave she is assumed to have ready sexuality. She does not have a protector or concealer of her procreative parts. She rivals Rosa and Flora sexually in that, in her turban and in her slave identity, she absorbs negative connotations of the mulatta condition. In comparison with her, Rosa and Flora appear all the more virtuous and dramatize how pure white womanhood depends on the existence of debased black womanhood for contrast.

Of course, the character with the purest association is the white woman Lily Bell, the legal wife of Gerald Fitzgerald. Hooper writes that "we usually associate the idea of extreme whiteness with the Lily, so that it is common to express a pure white by comparison with the flower, as with snow" (93). Perhaps Child gave Lily her last name because Wirt describes the lily's corolla as "bell-shaped, smooth on the inside" (40). The character Lily is a verbalized flower in that she represents the purity of northern white womanhood that becomes debased through the institution of slavery. Child furthers her critique of a racist society by showing how slavery dirties white womanhood as emblematized by Lily—her husband fathers two baby boys at the same time, one by Lily and one by Rosa, babies that Rosa switches so that Rosa's mixed-race son grows up believing he is white, while Lily's biological son grows up thinking he is black.

Other characters have floral names as well. The name of Flora's adopted mother, Lila Delano, recalls the lilac (signaling first emotions of love and fastidiousness). Appropriately, Mrs. Delano always dresses in violet colors. Right-minded, Mrs. Delano overcomes race prejudice to love and cultivate Flora as her adopted daughter. As Carolyn L. Karcher points out, Mrs. Delano's surrogate mothering of Flora "as a metaphor for the integration process" is still fraught with problems because, "inescapably reproducing the built-in inequality of the parent-child relationship, it defines the white godmother as the adult and her black protegée as the child" (*First Woman* 522). Yet her name, "Lila," and her dressing in violet link her to the viola tricolor and to Pensee Vivace, Flora's nickname. Perhaps through the associations garnered through the green world, Child suggests that an affinity exists between the two women. Black and white women might aspire to the same goals and sensibilities and, although of different stations in life, might both be deserving of a respectable and virtuous name.

Flora nicknames her suitor, Franz Blumenthal, "Florimund." His name obviously links him to the restorative world of blooms and flowers. He likewise is a hybrid, albeit a cultural hybrid of German ancestry. As a white man willing to marry a woman of slave origin, he at first seems to be the perfect model for Child's utopian vision of intermarriage. Yet, as Karcher points out, he is "foreign-born—hence, free at the outset from American race prejudice (as Child believed was generally true of Europeans)—he does not represent a genuine solution" (522). Franz stands in contrast to the devious Gerald Fitzgerald, a character whose name noticeably lacks a connection to the green world. Further, with the word "Gerald" repeating in his first and last names, and with the name repeating in the next generation with his son, Gerald Fitzgerald Jr., Child suggests an endogamous race purity that borders on inbreeding. Gerald Fitzgerald's name also clearly marks him as Irish, perhaps even "black" Irish in contrast with the English-sounding names of the Royal sisters, one of whom marries a man named King. Gerald Senior then is doubly bad: his name points to his racist ideas of purity of lineage and he aspires to an English status his Irish name betrays.

Although Child attempts to value what the Royal sisters term the "olla podrida" (a miscellaneous Spanish stew) of mixed race, she fails in her representation of Henriet Falkner (274). Henriet is the mulatto wife of George Falkner, the switched baby Rosa raised as her own son. George "really" is white, the biological son of Lily Bell and Gerald Fitzgerald, but he grew up thinking he was the black son of a slave mother and hence he married a black woman. Susan Koppelman rightly points out that Child, in her 1842 short story "The Quadroons," was "the first white writer to grant black and racially mixed women the right to be 'ladies.' Child portrays the enslaved woman as partaking with grace and virtue in the life typically reserved for the mistress" (2). Yet Lyde Cullen Sizer criticizes Child for the reasons Koppelman praises her: Sizer argues that Child "retained a sense that New England white culture was preferable to all others: for blacks to enter white society as equals, they must become white.... White men still had their choice of women, black and white, and black women were allowed to be 'true women' by virtue of white desire to continue marking them as malleable, domestic, and passive" (254–56).

Sizer is right, for, quite disturbingly, Child makes no effort to suggest that Henriet could also be a flower. Henriet's lack of a floral name stands out quite noticeably. Alfred King indicates that he cannot integrate George Falkner into U.S. society because George's " 'having a colored wife would put obstructions in his way entirely beyond our power to remove' " (416). When Rosa asks Lily whether she thinks Henriet's daughter, and hence Lily's granddaughter, is pretty, Lily answers, " 'She might be pretty if the yellow could be washed off' " (422). In fact, the kindest comment Child can muster about Henriet is that she "proved good-natured and unassuming" (420) when taught skills and behavior befitting a proper freed woman. Child's interest in using florigraphic discourse to challenge postbellum racism collapses in her representation of Henriet. By so obviously abandoning the botanical vocabulary she had carefully cultivated with other characters, Child marks the dark black woman as undeserving of purity and innocence. Child's failure to portray Henriet as a verbalized flower compromises the novel's power and radical vision.

Similarly, Child's admirable goal of assigning stereotypical white women's qualities to black women can be seen as negative because the language of flowers relegates women to a passive, purely ornamental realm. Bewell points out the damaging potential of "the botanical analogy, as it leads women to value blushing ignorance, weakness, beauty, and sweetness as essential to their sex, while equating virtue and power . . . with their ability to please men" (137). Since hybrid flowers often were unable to reproduce, Bewell writes that "men have actually cultivated women for the same purpose as they have cultivated flowers: to increase their beauty at the expense of their fruitfulness" (138). The sterility of hybrid flowers may work in Child's favor, however, because slave women were "cultivated" for their status as breeders; therefore, "cultivating" black women for their beauty, without regard for their reproductive capabilities, elevates them.

Child's astute use of florigraphic rhetoric and theories of hybridity to revise national prejudice accords with the role of hybrid plants in nation building. A new industry developed among professional gardeners to collect, test, and hybridize new plants suitable for the untamed land of the United States. Plant breeders capitalized on the chance to create improved varieties of flowers and vegetables. Gardening magazines to support the new industry began to appear, including the *Magazine of Horticulture* (1835–69) and the *Horticulturist and Journal of Rural Art and Rural Taste* (1846–76). Agricultural and horticultural societies were first organized in the 1790s and proliferated nationwide by the 1870s (van Ravenswaay 7–11). Hybridizing new plants to suit the climate of the new nation resonates with nationalism, for this botanical exercise seeks to cultivate both soil and nation simultaneously. If a nation can be defined by its distinct flora and fauna, then surely making U.S. citizens goes hand in hand with making literary and natural production. Not all flowers could take root out West, so frontier settlers needed to cultivate sturdy hybrid plants and people who could populate the West and thrive. Child participates in a national project by similarly experimenting with hybridity. If flowers could speak their own language, and Victorians believed that flowers were the "alphabet of angels," then Child uses a horticultural language to spell out a new theory of race relations.

Child's national project of reforming race relations through florigraphic discourse parallels the subtle national agendas in contemporary floral dictionaries and poetry anthologies. For example, in her

1842 introduction to *Flora's Interpreter*, Hale knows her readers are familiar with English floral sentiments and therefore imagines a distinctly U.S. audience: "To the Youth of America I commit my books" (v). She writes that in her book, "there is nothing new attempted, except in the arrangement, and the introduction of American sentiments" and hopes that her collection "would promote a better acquaintance with the beauties of our own literature" (iii). In her 1850 edition, however, Hale includes a new introduction in which she writes that "the most important aim of the work was to select and incorporate with our love of nature and flowers the choicest and best specimens of American poetry." She acknowledges the overwhelming presence of British poets and injects a New World sensibility by asserting that "we have endeavored to place these truly classical specimens of the Old World literature in a new light, by linking them, as it were, with the hopes and loves of our 'own green forest land' " (iv). Similarly, Kirkland calls attention to a national agenda in her collection of poetry with an "Introduction by American Editor" (1). Hooper writes in her preface to *The Lady's Book of Flowers and Poetry* that "to the selections from our own native poets we turn with pride and pleasure" (3), and Dix hopes her *Garland of Flora* "might also display many pleasing traits of national manners" (1).

A Romance of the Republic participates in this national linking of literary production with floral cultivation by emphasizing hybridity and New World soil. Rosa develops her operatic career in Europe, achieves the status of wife in Europe, and could easily remain in Europe as a diva. Instead she patriotically chooses to return to the United States and face racial discrimination. Likewise, the Falkners end up temporarily running the Marseilles branch of the King family business, but we assume they will return to the United States. The novel's closing image, of a hybridized family enacting a patriotic tableau while singing "The Star-Spangled Banner," can only be Child's vote for a new mixed-race vision specific to the United States. Child suggests that hybridizing flowers is an aesthetically pleasing endeavor essential to cultivating a new nation and that, to hasten social reform, the discourse of race mixture can be fruitfully grafted onto the discourse of nature.

5

The White Blackbird: Miscegenation, Genre, and the Tragic Mulatta in Howells, Harper, and the Babes of Romance

Lydia Maria Child closes *A Romance of the Republic* with her mulatta heroine moving from Europe to the United States with her white husband. William Dean Howells also wrote a novel that addresses a white man's marriage to a mixed-race woman, but in that novel, *An Imperative Duty* (1891), the mixed-race couple cannot reside on this side of the Atlantic. Instead, Howells's character Rhoda Aldgate believes her racial taint would receive more acceptance in Italy. In *An Imperative Duty*, his only novel-length treatment of race mixture, Howells uses his preferred genre of realism to counter such novels as Child's, which he believed portrayed miscegenation too melodramatically.

Bristling at criticism of *The Rise of Silas Lapham* (1885) and faulting the previous generation of fiction typified by Dickens and Thackeray, Howells wrote on 24 January 1886 to a friend that he planned to defend his writing and promote the convictions of literary realism by "banging the babes of romance about" (*Selected Letters* 3:152). Couched in playful, if unsavory, banter, this comment strongly suggests Howells's anxieties about gender, genre, and his position in the literary marketplace. The type of fiction written by the "babes of romance" commanded the market, compelling Howells, James, and other male writers to craft "women's stories" to compete for the predominantly middle-class white female readership (Carby, *Reconstructing Woman-*

hood 72). Howells's comment clearly places romance writers in an infantilized and inferior position.[1]

Contrary to romance writers' view, Howells, the champion of realism, believed fiction should instruct and not just entertain. He found a way to "bang about" romance writers in *An Imperative Duty*: he challenged and rewrote their romantic worldview from his realist perspective, even though this put his work in the position of being rewritten, and by an African American woman writer at that.

Today the term "realism" remains quite slippery and comes freighted with conflict. Amy Kaplan usefully summarizes recent critical views of the term: "From an objective reflection of contemporary social life, realism has become a fictional conceit, or deceit, packaging and naturalizing an official version of the ordinary. From a style valued for its plain-speaking vernacular, realism has adopted a rhetorical sophistication that now subverts its own claims to referentiality. From a progressive force exposing the conditions of industrial society, realism has turned into a conservative force whose very act of exposure reveals its complicity with structures of power" (*Social Construction* 1). Kaplan goes on to discuss realism's relation to class struggle, the trepidation over social change, novelists' fear of powerlessness, the rise of journalism, and the emergence of a mass culture.

For the purposes of this chapter, following Howells's own ideas about realism as he describes them in "Novel-Writing and Novel-Reading" and "Criticism and Fiction" can provide the most clarity. In "Novel-Writing and Novel-Reading," Howells states that realism resides in "the novel I take to be the sincere and conscientious endeavor to picture life just as it is, to deal with character as we witness it in living people, and to record the incidents that grow out of character" (*Selected Literary Criticism* 218). Kaplan argues that to Howells "realism contests, in the name of the social whole, the elitist maintenance of an insular and exalted culture. Yet realism equally opposes the rise of a popular mass culture which unites people as consumers through the medium of the market. . . . The major work of the realist narrative is to construct a homogeneous and coherent social reality by conquering the fictional qualities of middle-class life and by controlling the specter of class conflict which threatens to puncture this vision of a unified social totality." She claims that "realism works to ensure that social difference can be ultimately effaced by a vision of a common humanity, which mirrors the readers' own commonplace, or everyday life" (*Social Construction* 21). We shall see that one of the "fictional qualities" or "specters of class conflict" that Howells will try to conquer in *An Imperative Duty* is the persistence of the tragic mulatta stereotype. But, as this chapter will reveal, Howells's conception of realism will be unable to control or resolve the tensions preserved in this staple of romanticism.[2]

In "Novel-Writing and Novel-Reading," Howells contrasts the novel with the romance, which he claims "professes like the real novel to portray actual life, but it does this with an excess of drawing and coloring which are false to nature. It attributes motives to people which do not govern real people, and its characters are of the quality of types; they are heroic, for good or for bad. It seeks effect rather than truth; and endeavors to hide in a cloud of incident the deformity and artificiality of its creations. It revels in the extravagant, the unusual, and the bizarre" (*Selected Literary Criticism* 47). According to Kaplan,

> to Howells the romance represents more than the sum of its aesthetic failings: his critique of its enslavement to past conventions, its idealization of subject matter, and its aristocratic pretensions is part of a political debate about the nature of American culture. In an essay which dubs realism "democracy in literature," Howells accuses the opponents of realism of harboring "the last refuges of the aristocratic spirit which is disappearing from politics and society, and is now seeking to shelter itself in aesthetics." Romance becomes a catchword in his lexicon for an elitist conception of culture as the inherited and well-guarded property of the upper classes. (*Social Construction* 16)

What interests me is that numerous female babes of romance wrote about interracial marriage and that, more than his realist contemporaries, Howells correlated racial questions with realism and was interested in the ways that race tests realistic representation. Concepts of heredity and racial traits were hotly debated by the scientific world in Howells's time and always were done so in terms of sexuality. Theories of race were thus often "covert theories of desire" (Robert J. C. Young 9). Since Howells was quite fluent in contemporary race theories, miscegenation fiction thereby offered him an opportunity to redress stock romantic plots by engaging objective, scientific knowledge about race that informed realism's tenets. But, as we will see, Frances Ellen Watkins Harper takes issue with Howells's supposed ironic sophistication about race in *An Imperative Duty* and rewrites many of his views in *Iola Leroy*.

My aims in this chapter are three. First, I want to construct a literary genealogy for *An Imperative Duty* that situates Howells in the middle of a call-and-response literary conversation with popular women writers about race, gender, and genre that itself crosses racial, gender, and genre lines. Second, I want to center this literary genealogy on Howells's reading of popular fiction featuring the tragic mulatta stereotype, a literary figure that conflates scientific and popular understandings of the "race question" and the "woman question."[3] Third, I want to suggest that this tragic mulatta stereotype, as a stock figure of romanticism and sentimentality, defies Howells's goal of representing her according to realism's tenets even as she usefully figures in Harper's political and aesthetic concerns. Howells wants to use his character of the doctor to diagnose and "treat" (by rewriting) unfounded romantic views of race he had read most recently in novels by Margret Holmes Bates and Alice Morris Buckner, but his theories of realism fail when he employs the tragic mulatta, a sentimental figure resistant to scientific discourse. Harper cunningly uses this figure to critique Howells's project and represent the potential of black womanhood.

Perhaps a way to unite these three aims is to ask why, at the end of Howells's *Imperative Duty*, must Olney, a nervous disorder specialist, and the mixed-race woman he loves, Rhoda Aldgate, flee to Italy? Why cannot Howells imagine the biracial couple remaining in the United States? Readers have not made explicit the connection between Howells's handling of race and genre, a connection that must be made to answer the Italy question. W. E. B. Du Bois evidently finds this ending unproblematic, for he writes that Rhoda "marries her man and goes her way as thousands have done and are doing" (218). Although thousands of blacks left the country after intermarrying, thousands did not feel it necessary to flee to Italy. In contrast, Anna Julia Cooper, another prominent black intellectual and writer, attacks the novel as a "study of a morbidly sensitive conscience hectoring over a weak, vacillating will" that ultimately does not "preach or solve problems" (202). Other early reviewers responded in a lukewarm fashion to *An Imperative Duty*, mainly because of Howells's "ignorance of the subject of race and his unlikely moral and amatory conclusions" (qtd. in Banta ix). If, as Stephen P. Knadler argues, race "served as the underground political language of realism" and Howells "simultaneously ushered into American literary history a racial identity politics whose nineteenth-century roots in whiteness have been too often neglected" (2), then what are the implications for realism of Howells's compromised novelistic exploration of racial identity?

Such influential early critics as Leslie A. Fiedler have set the tone for understanding Howells's coupling of race and genre. Fiedler, for example, notes that in over forty novels Howells does not treat the themes of adultery, violence, or seduction. Fiedler positions Howells as yet one more U.S. writer searching for "a sentimental relationship at once erotic and immaculate" that can "symbolize the union of the ego and the id, the thinking self with its rejected impulses" (260, 338–39). Olney's miscegenous union with a mulatta may very well satisfy this search, for Rhoda's blackness is cast as savagely and barbarically erotic, but this romantic stance is not without its costs to realism, as the couple's flight to Italy will attest. An attempt to answer the Italy question begins by placing *An Imperative Duty* in dialogue with popular women's novels of the time.

A Literary Genealogy

Four years before writing *An Imperative Duty*, Howells reviewed, in his April 1887 "Editor's Study" column for *Harper's Monthly*, two novels by women writers, *The Chamber over the Gate* (1886) by Margret Holmes Bates and *Towards the Gulf: A Romance of Louisiana* (1887), attributed to Alice Morris Buckner, that deal explicitly with interracial marriage. In this review, Howells focuses only on the novels' treatment of heredity, race reversion, and racial traits, thus showing a keen interest in themes he later develops and attempts to revise in *An Imperative Duty*, although his portrayal of African Americans is not much different from the "chromographic romanticism," in Alain Locke's words, of Bates's and Buckner's novels (220).[4]

Bates's and Buckner's fictions undoubtedly influenced Howells for two reasons. First, he carefully considered their literary merits and racial themes in his review, and later, in *An Imperative Duty*, offers a corrective to their claims of inherited traits and the duty and role of the tragic mulatta in U.S. society. Second, the title of *An Imperative Duty* borrows from two lines in *Towards the Gulf*. The hero John Morant ponders the "imperative" burden of his wife's racial taint and questions his "duties" to her black ancestry as well as to his white lineage (236). Scholars have suggested that Howells in turn may have influenced Harper (Warren 65–68; Bell 58). *An Imperative Duty* seems clearly to have influenced Harper's novelistic production because in *Iola Leroy*, written the year following *An Imperative Duty*'s serialization in *Harper's Monthly*, Harper so definitely reverses Howells's views. Readers of Howells have not mentioned the influence of Bates and Buckner on him, thus including them can change the conversation about women writers' influence on Howells, our understanding of the racialized woman's role in his fictions, and Howells's conception of the link between the romantic mulatta and realist representation. Furthermore, in examining the women writers' influence, we can see the gender politics of Howellsian realism: Howells uses realism paternalistically to rectify the melodramatic leanings of the babes of romance.

This literary family tree that suggests Bates and Buckner begat Howells who begat Harper has numerous curved, twisted, and broken branches, but all four authors' understanding of racialization is rooted in heredity, identity, and, most of all, the miscegenated woman's body. In all four novels a woman's body harbors a lethal secret about race; when the truth about her black ancestry becomes known, the woman decides she can no longer live.[5] In these four novels, the authorial emphasis on racial choice and marital options foregrounds anxiety about repeated miscegenation. Focusing on phenotypically white heroines whose genotype includes black ancestry, miscegenation in these novels stands, in Karen Sánchez-Eppler's words, "as a bodily challenge to the conventions of reading the body, thus simultaneously insisting that the body is a sign of identity and undermining the assurance with which that sign can be read" ("Bodily Bonds" 241). As they emphasize dilemmas of embodiment, these four novelists conflate racial, sexual, and textual problems, dramatizing Catharine MacKinnon's definition of miscegenation as a "sexual model for racial integration."

Since the biracial body in these four novels is a woman's, the novels explore the dissemination and repercussions of motherhood and maternal ideology that challenge the ruling constructions of nationhood. The woman's body is contested in race and marriage and is the site of a struggle between competing forces of social conventions for dominance, bolstering Nancy Bentley's claim that "the biracial person split apart the imagined synthesis between nature and society in bourgeois domesticity. . . . The person of mixed black and white parentage stood precisely at the place where nature and culture could come unbound" ("White Slaves" 197). Hazel Carby has discussed the mulatto figure as a "narrative device of mediation" that allowed for movement between black and white worlds and that became more popular after Reconstruction when Jim Crow laws were institutionalized (*Reconstructing Womanhood* 89–90). In a world in which bodily appearance reveals much about class, morals, and values, the mulatta's body disputes society's virtues and her own. Her body contradicts the racial and sexual absolutes that white men need to define and uphold civilization: since white society's dominance is predicated upon keeping blacks separate and inferior, an amalgamation of the two races violates this divisive logic. White societal value is also bound up in the doctrine of woman's chastity; thus, although the mulatta may be chaste, her skin indicates past sexual transgression. While she may be very light-skinned, the mulatta "signifies white but provides white men a different access to sexuality" (Berlant 556). And, since ideals of white masculinity and nationhood rely on having a home and hearth to defend, the miscegenated woman's body at once incarnates two models of white civilization: she can validate white manhood by representing the white man's all-American right to sexual conquest, yet she cannot represent white womanhood, which needs to be protected and preserved.[6] In their explorations of biracial personhood, Bates, Buckner, Howells, and Harper demonstrate a symmetry between the body politic and the body human as well as a corporeal understanding of national and literary identity.

Margret Holmes Bates's
Chamber over the Gate

Although Margret Holmes Bates was in her time a well-known and prolific writer, little of her biography is known today and her books are forgotten.[7] She merited a brief obituary in the *Indianapolis News* when she died on 25 January 1927 but not in the *New York Times*, even though she lived in that city for thirty-three years. Perhaps the most critical attention Bates received was Howells's review of her 1886 novel *The Chamber over the Gate* in his April 1887 "Editor's Study" column for *Harper's Monthly*. In this column, in which he also reviewed Alice Morris Buckner's *Towards the Gulf*, Howells values Bates's "fidelity to local circumstance" as well as her refusal to be "tempted to patronize, to satirize, or to defend her characters, and the effect of verisimilitude from her simple directness is very great" (*Editor's Study* 75). But he takes the novel to task for its "lamentable passages of stage sentiment and stage incident" and believes it resolves a miscegenation plot "too melodramatically, too helplessly" (76). What interests Howells most about Bates's novel is its concern with heredity. Howells briefly outlines the novel's study of inheritance in an Indianapolis family and mentions the "reversion to the negro type" of a child born to an army surgeon and his wife, the daughter of a slave woman (76). Howells's dissatisfaction with the novel's "too melodramatic" conclusion of its race plot is particularly compelling, because a few years later he offers a different solution in his similarly themed *An Imperative Duty*.

The theme of race and the color line announces itself early in *The Chamber over the Gate* when one principle character, the antihero Hugh Gatsimer, draws back Miriam's sleeve to comment on the whiteness of his fiancée's skin and directs this observation as an insult to his older brother, Dr. Stephen Gatsimer. Stephen and his wife had a daughter, Coral, but a few years later the wife died giving birth to a stillborn boy with negroid features. This of course means that Stephen had unwittingly married an octoroon and, convenient for all involved, mother and black baby died. His surviving daughter is a lively girl who loves black music and curiously bears a strong resemblance to June, the family's quadroon housekeeper. Obviously, June is Coral's grandmother. Because of Coral's racial stain, the Gatsimer family determines that she can never marry.

These concerns with race give way to the bulk of the novel, set in Indiana, which revolves around domestic realism. Because the novel ends tragically with the "changes wrought by intemperance" (539), Howells easily could have read the novel as a work of domestic fiction that aligns itself with the temperance movement, but instead Howells is interested exclusively in Bates's representation of the tragic mulatta. He fixates on the tangential race plot and ignores the novel's heart.

The race theme resurfaces in two notable places in the novel. One occurs when Dr. Stephen Gatsimer decides to run for elected office, but he receives an anonymous letter that threatens to reveal his wife's background. The letter urges, "Draw the color line!" and "down, lower still, with the miscegenationist!" (138). The author of the letter turns out to be Hugh, who has never forgiven his brother for staining the family line. The novel's concern with race also surfaces in Coral's suitor, Percy Langdon. Stephen feels obliged to reveal Coral's tainted heritage to Percy, who turns out to be the white half brother of Coral's dead mother. As in much miscegenation fiction, the thwarted romance gives way to restored family ties. With Coral's reconnection to her grandmother June and Uncle Percy, Bates allots Coral a degree of happiness amid the shock that she has black ancestors. For Coral to marry a black man is unthinkable; thus, her racial duty compels her to spinsterhood.

It is this dramatic reestablishment of cross-racial familial relations that Howells evidently believes resolves itself "too melodramatically, too helplessly." As we shall see, in *An Imperative Duty* Howells rewrites this ending so that his heroine does not reconnect with black relatives, and Harper in turn reverses Howells's story to make restored family ties a source of power and happiness.

Buckner's Towards the Gulf: A Romance of Louisiana

Howells is less harsh in his criticism of *Towards the Gulf*, and although he does not mention an author, he notes it is written "again by a woman" and that it deals "again with the same question" (*Editor's Study* 76). *Towards the Gulf* was published without an author's name on the title page, and although Lyle H. Wright's bibliography attributes it to Alice Morris Buckner, Werner Sollors attributes authorship to R. T. Buckner (Wright 77; Sollors, *Neither* 377).[8] Featuring descriptions of lush vegetation, French creole accents, southern plantations, and ancestral homes, *Towards the Gulf* takes place amid what Howells in his 1887 review calls "an abundance of local color" (*Editor's Study* 76). The principal characters are the brother and sister

John Morant and Isabel Morant, who live in genteel poverty in the family mansion in New Orleans. Although the novel is framed by Isabel's marriage plot, the majority of the story, and the part that interested Howells, involves John's marriage to Bamma, whom John, an avid reader of French romantic racialists, comes to suspect has black lineage. Bamma, brought up in London, was the daughter of an Englishman and his southern U.S. wife who names her daughter after the state where she grew up on a slave plantation. In this explicit link between land and a woman's body, Buckner invites comparison between the state of the nation and the state of women's sexuality, both highly contested in Reconstruction years. Although Bamma's skin is described as white, John becomes alarmed when Celine, his black housekeeper, warns John that she can detect something treacherous in Bamma's eyes and that he should not marry her. Bamma's enjoyment of creole music, especially "Danse des Negres," increases John's anxiety, as does a black taxidermist's three deep bows to Bamma as if he recognizes a "type." The taxidermist has many stuffed creatures in his shop, but the one that most strikes John is an anomaly whose surface masks its identity—a white blackbird. Suggesting a link between the white blackbird and the seemingly white Bamma, the taxidermist laments, " 'Po' lill' bird. He kin nevver fin' his own feather. He has no mate. He is ver' lonely' " (64). In a moment of symbolism and foreshadowing, John dreams that the white blackbird transforms into Bamma. John is finally convinced of his wife's ancestry when the beads Bamma has worn since she was a little girl match those found on the Morant plantation, and he increases his distance from his wife.

Bamma suspects the nature of her husband's estrangement and confides in Celine, the black maid who has been with the family for many years. Celine tells Bamma that she resembles the Morant family slaves. Shocked by this revelation, Bamma collapses and gives birth prematurely to a boy. She understands the belief that personality traits pass from one generation to the next, and since her grandfather killed himself, "it is easy for the grandchild of a suicide to commit self-murder" (274). Devastated by her lonely marriage and the ruin her racial trait has brought her husband, Bamma decides to "escape her own social isolation and restore her husband's peace of mind by the same stroke" (275). She takes her life by smelling a cloth dipped in chloroform. John recoils with disgust at the thought that his son will stain the family name and he fears "reversion of type" (290). John's worst fears are confirmed when the boy, with the "irresponsible nature" (292) of blacks, sneaks bonbons from a desk drawer and lies about it.

At the plantation, the boy accidentally falls in the gin wheel and is crushed. As his son dies, a light shines "deep into the father's heart" (308) and John overcomes his prejudice and realizes his love for his child: "In life there could have been no happy meeting face to face. Death only had made them equals—unless after death, also, the distinctions of race are preserved forever" (309). Celine also dies at the end and is called a "white-souled negress" (314), the metaphoric opposite of a white blackbird, but her dying words repeat her warning to John of the misery associated with marrying a black woman. In the triumphantly Christian ending, there is a movement toward racial sympathy, but the mammy figure warns of misery while the white man, guided by a child, leads the way toward redemption.

Romantic Racialism in *Towards the Gulf*

Towards the Gulf manifests many contemporary anxieties about race mixture, especially in its characterization of Negro types as miscegenation continues: the burly African, smirking mulatto, pathetic quadroon, and consumptive octoroon (Buckner 300).[9] Yet to become a white blackbird required much intermarriage and the intervention of the law. As one character states, " 'To become *Sanguinae clarus* had sometimes involved a legal decision' " (129–30). But this admixture is an "abomination" (228), according to the character Mr. Shriver, who is influenced by the writings of the French racial scientist Arthur de Gobineau. Mr. Shriver believes that races "differ organically and radically from each other like wine, milk, and water, and that any mingling degrades the higher type without raising the inferior type an iota" (228). This liquid metaphor for the different races echoes Gobineau's chromatic division of the races—negroid, yellow, and white— yet is certainly more generous than the theorist most admired by Gobineau, Christoph Meiners, who, in his *Grundriss der Geschichte der Menschheit* (1755), classifies humanity by the beautiful (whites) and the ugly (all others) (Gobineau 205–9, 107; Biddiss). Mr. Shriver's friend Dr. Dickson opposes this view by claiming that civilization benefits from race mixing because the inferior race melds into the superior, which "ensures the more perfect type always prevails, and assimilates all the others to itself, providing a new composite form, by which the average level of humanity is always elevated towards higher standards" (228).

The flip side to assimilation is reversion, a danger if assimilation is not complete. One of John's favorite romantic racialists, Jean Louis Armand de Quatrefages de Breau, distinguishes between atavism and reversion: "The mongrel which by atavism reassumes the characters of one of its paternal ancestors, for example, still preserves its mixed nature.... It is different in the cases of reversion displayed by hybrids, for one of the two bloods is irrevocably expelled" (77). John's father firmly believes that "hereditary descent stamps the man, and one can never be sure when race characteristics will entirely disappear. They may crop out like some hideous deformity in any generation" (Buckner 33). In considering his marriage to Bamma, John worries about passing on inferior racial qualities to his children. It is worth quoting at length his beliefs:

> His intense love for Bamma would reconcile him to their individual union; but what of their progeny? Would they not revert to the darker type? Would they not betray with successive generations the ignoble marks of African descent? ... If miscegenation should become general, would not the whole Southern race, of which he was instinctively and organically proud, be precipitated headlong into a gulf of degradation, degeneration, and despair? Was not his own unfortunate *mésalliance* a proof and a prophecy of the possibility of a general drifting towards that gulf? (246–47)

If the "gulf" signifies the chaos of racial instability, then Buckner's postulation that the hero's love is enough to overcome his prejudice is exactly Howells's testing ground. While Buckner's hero concludes that the threat of reversion is greater than the pull of love, Howells's hero determines the opposite. Howells will attempt to rewrite Buckner's unapologetic adherence to romantic racialism with his characteristic dose of corrective realism, but the romantic tragic mulatta will prove inassimilable to Howells's dictates of realism.

Another form of reversion is psychological, or the "transmission of mental qualities," particularly the "return of psychological conditions in children and grandchildren in the most unexpected manner" (230). As if to confirm his suspicions, John reads widely about race theory and finds out about "a woman seized with a sudden and irresistible desire to steal because her grandfather had been a thief; of a man affected with an unaccountable and ineradicable dread of going into water whose grandfather had been nearly drowned" (230). John suddenly recalls Bamma's dread when she first saw the abandoned slave plantation, suspects her grandmother may have been a bondswoman in that very yard, and concludes, "It was a clear case of psychological transmission. . . . 'Tis all too true! She is a white blackbird and has no mate" (231). John considers for a moment moving to Jamaica or Mexico, "where the race barriers had already been broken down to a considerable extent" (247), but instead concludes that it might be best to let his bloodline dry up: "Extinction might be, after all, the kindest destiny" (252).

All John's ideas about race are influenced by his scientific reading, not only of Gobineau's and Quatrefages's works, but also of Robert Knox's *Races of Men* (1850), Ribout's ideas on heredity, and Périer's theories of race crossing (Buckner 216). In *Towards the Gulf*, romanticism thrives despite the presentation of such racist scientific theories; in fact, Buckner uses science to strengthen the sense of romance, for racial determinism offers a thrilling and blazing destiny that highlights characters' tragic passion. "Science" and "realism" reveal themselves to be oppositional rather than complementary. While Howells extends realism to a psychological exploration of character, Frank Norris and other contemporary writers of naturalism explored the effects of heredity and the material environment on behavior. Buckner uses the same racial theories on determinism and scientific objectivity as the naturalists, but since she filters race theories through the bodily reality of the miscegenated woman, science merges into romance.

While the French men of racist science purportedly studied objective fact, they simultaneously expressed a fascination with, if not a repressed longing for, interracial sex. In his discussion of scientific racism, Robert J. C. Young remarks, "It has often been suggested that there are intrinsic links between racism and sexuality. What has not been emphasized is that the debates about theories of race in the nineteenth century, by settling on the possibility or impossibility of hybridity, focused explicitly on the issue of sexuality and the issue of sexual unions between whites and blacks" (9). Although Young's argument is valid, he does not make explicit the significance of female sexuality. In Buckner's novel, as in Bates's, Howells's, and Harper's, the "identification of racial with sexual degeneracy" is linked exclusively to a woman (Robert J. C. Young 26).

In all the discussions of race, heredity, and transmission in these four novels, it is the woman's body that is perceived as the instrument of transmission, making miscegenation and heredity literally a woman's "issue," since from her womb issue forth racial markers. Since a woman's body is the site of labor, both economic and maternal, Gayatri Chakravorty Spivak argues that "the possession of a tangible place of production in the womb situates the woman as an agent in any theory of production" (79). In *Towards the Gulf*, Mr. Byrne most effectively summarizes this point: " 'When it comes to sustaining every honorable tradition of our race, we may rely upon woman. She is the great conservator of man's wisdom. When he shall have broken down every barrier which the accumulated experience of years has erected to preserve a people from degeneracy, you will find her holding with blind instinct to the mighty restraining influences of the past' " (228). Mr. Byrne seems to be saying that if a man's lust causes him to wander across the racial divide, a white woman will revive his wisdom through race loyalty and thereby protect whites from degeneracy. Mr. Byrne's unwavering faith in white women stands in ironic contrast to Bamma, whose beauty and virtue belie her embodiment of racial treachery. The ideology Mr. Byrne espouses that pairs femininity with race and maternity with nation is the same ideology that can undo these pairings, for a white blackbird such as Bamma deceives as she conceives.

In his review of *Towards the Gulf*, Howells terms John's son's lethal accident "merciful" and concludes by calling it an "intensely touching little story" that is "immensely pathetic." He compares it with *The Chamber over the Gate* by writing that "there is no want of cleverness in any of the books on our list." But he goes on to critique Bates's and Buckner's novels by claiming that "much of the cleverness is as deplorable as the costly decoration of a house of reeds would be; for the stories are not founded in human nature" (*Editor's Study* 76). A more thorough probing convinces us that what Howells believes is "not founded in human nature" are the novels' handling of race and heredity. His approach to the race problem, however, offers a novelistic resolution informed by realism's convictions and is therefore, he believes, firmly founded in human nature. Yet, the presence of the miscegenated woman's body affects genre and demonstrates the mutability of form, for the inexorable pull of genetic destiny in naturalist texts shows the detached, scientific objectivity of the human condition. Once a biracial woman is introduced, effectively sexing scientific racism, science buckles under the pressure of romance and narrative takes on a hybrid form as naturalism "reverts" to romanticism. The presence of the biracial woman's body presents Howells with narrative quandaries and affects representation and reading by bleeding realism into romanticism.

Howells's Imperative Duty

In his early notebooks, Howells jotted down an idea for a story tentatively entitled "In Town out of Season": "Might be a story in autobiographical form of a young man, rich, cultivated, well-born who notices all those handsome negroes we saw last summer, and falls in love with an octoroon" (qtd. in Cady 156). Many years later, in 1903, he wrote in a letter that "it was in 'An Imperative Duty' that I had a man marry a woman with a faint trace of black blood. It was for a psychological, not a scientific purpose, and I merely argued that a man who really loved a woman would find his love settling any 'race question' involved" (*Selected Letters* 5:66). This letter is addressed to a Dr. Whiston, who has not been identified, but the editor of Howells's letters believes that Dr. Whiston's original letter to Howells "appears to have expressed concern that *An Imperative Duty* was a disguised scientific argument in favor of racial equality" (66). In his 1903 response Howells emphasizes the psychological, rather than the scientific, motivation for his novel, but it is significant that "race becomes a metaphor for psychology," as Henry B. Wonham identifies Howells's move (710). And, following Young's claim that race was understood in terms of sex, it is equally important that Olney is sexually interested in Rhoda because of her savage, miscegenated origins.

Since *An Imperative Duty* was Howells's first and only piece of miscegenation fiction, critics have wondered whether Howells felt obligated to address the race question posed so many times before him or, in John W. Crowley's words, "at least to show the appropriate solemnity about it" (personal letter). Howells rehearsed the theme of the tragic mulatta in 1860 with the publication of the prose poem "The Pilot's Story." The pilot tells the familiar story of a beautiful woman, "with just enough blood from her mother, / Darkening her eyes and her hair, to make her race known to a trader: / You would have thought she was white" (323–24). Her master, and father of their child, sells her to pay a gambling debt. Distraught, she commits suicide by throwing herself overboard. Other than this example, Howells had written explicitly about blacks only three times before, in "Old Brown" (1860, regarding John Brown), in his sketch "Mrs. Johnson," (1870) and in the essay "Police Report" (1882), which contains testimonies of four blacks in a Boston court. Although Howells's family's sympathies toward slaves forced them to leave their Ohio home and Howells signed a petition in favor of forming the NAACP, in his novels he portrayed African Americans as exotic, barbaric, and uncivilized.

If, as Howells stated, the plot of *An Imperative Duty* is based on a psychological literary experiment, not a scientific one, then we must pay particular attention to the characters' (and Howells's) psychological understanding of race. The first chapter of the novel reads as an ethnography of African Americans, with descriptions of black dress, lifestyle, and behavior. Olney, a specialist in nervous disorders, has returned from Italy and, in a move that exoticizes black culture, walks as a voyeur through Boston's black section as if continuing his "foreign travels in his native place" (138). Olney meditates on racial types and class and finds himself attracted to blacks who exhibit "such a smiling curiosity and such a childish simple-heartedness" (139) and who "all alike seemed shining with good-nature and goodwill" (140). The plot will later turn on such racial stereotyping when it is discovered that Rhoda, the supposedly white woman whom Olney meets and grows to love, had a black grandmother.

These stereotyped descriptions support Elsa Nettels's claim that "accepting the premises of racial determinism, [Howells] accepted the common racial stereotypes such as those by which white writers distanced themselves from the black characters they created" (87).[10] But ironically Howells's acceptance of racial stereotypes can be seen as a spurning of realism's tenet that dissuaded stock characterization. Further, his use of dialect reinforces racial clichés and violates realism's principle that human nature is universal and that character is mutable (Nettels 95). In general, the novel was not well received because, according to Martha Banta, the unappealing theme of miscegenation overshadowed its literary quality (xi).[11]

In his psychological understanding of racialization, Howells narrates race through discussions of heredity, much as Bates and Buckner did. Rhoda's aunt, Mrs. Meredith, distraught that it is her duty to reveal her niece's black ancestry, asks Olney for his opinion on heredity, the "persistence of ancestral traits; the transmission of character and tendency; the reappearance of types after several generations," and atavism. Mrs. Meredith worries about Rhoda marrying a white man and producing black babies because the miscegenation of the past and the prospect of it occurring again are fleshly realities; she turns to Olney for scientific truth. Olney dismisses such concerns and, perhaps referring to novels by Bates and Buckner, replies that " 'it's a notion that some writers rather like to toy with; but when you come to boil it down, as the newspapers say, there isn't a great deal of absolute fact there.' " To illustrate his point, Olney chooses the example of " 'reversion to the inferior race type in the child of parents of mixed blood—say a white with a mulatto or quadroon' " (160). He rejects the "scientific" idea of race reversion voiced by Bates and Buckner in favor of an equally romantic reason: " 'The natural tendency is all the other way, to the permanent effacement of the inferior type. The child of a white and an octoroon is a sixteenth blood; and the child of that child and a white is a thirty-second blood. The chances of atavism, or reversion to the black great-great-great-grandfather are so remote that they may be said hardly to exist at all' " (160). Through his scientific understanding of heredity, Olney assuages Mrs. Meredith's racism. Olney's realist narrative of heredity supplants Mrs. Meredith's romantic narrative.

With irony and humor, Howells voices and then rejects other prevailing scientific theories but ends up reinforcing social prejudices. For example, when Rhoda expresses her delight in blacks and her comedic disappointment that one can no longer buy them, her aunt, Mrs. Meredith, proclaims, " 'It is the race instinct! It must assert itself sooner or later' " (172). Olney, as the voice of enlightened thinking, counters with a sardonic, " 'I should say it was the other-race instinct that was asserting itself sooner' " (173). In another satiric incident, Howells pokes fun at Buckner's presentation of the *sanguinae clarus* idea as Rhoda wonders how many generations removed from blackness she is and pictures her great-grandmother as "a horrible old negress, a savage stolen from Africa, where she had been a cannibal" (192). Her exaggeration of her plight makes Rhoda a pitiable and laughable character. In another incident, the psychological trauma of the truth of Rhoda's ancestry makes it seem as if there were "two selves of her, one that lived before that awful knowledge, and one that had lived as long since, and again a third that knew and pitied them both" (193). In the context of the novel and Olney's supposed rational thinking, this split of selves reads as a swooning overdramatization on Rhoda's part.

Another most salient moment when Howells bangs about romantic plots is Olney's proposal to Rhoda. She rejects him violently: "'Never!' She sprang to her feet and gasped hoarsely out, 'I am a negress!'" Olney is struck by something comedic in Rhoda's great moment of vulnerability and he responds sarcastically: "'Well, not a very black one. Besides, what of it, if I love you?'" Judith R. Berzon claims that Howells's realism is most clearly shown in this instant of deflation (113). Howells himself seems to agree, for he editorializes: "As tragedy this whole affair had fallen to ruin. It could be reconstructed, if at all, only upon an octave much below the operatic pitch. It must be treated in no lurid twilight gloom, but in plain, simple, matter-of-fact noonday" (227). Distancing himself from romantic writers such as Buckner, Howells casts the climactic revelatory scene in an ironic tone and attempts to flatten romanticism's stock storyline. For Howells, the miscegenated woman's body represents a testing ground on which realism can withstand reversion to romanticism. Yet Howells is not completely successful, for her body stands as an atavistic element that defies constraint.

Olney falls in love with Rhoda but has feelings of pity for her tragic and vulnerable position and, in a moment of postbellum new paternalism, offers himself as her defender and protector. Nina Baym argues that the protection of defenseless women forms the center of white society and "that it is precisely in preserving this woman that a civilization signifies itself" (73). White men need to fight on behalf of white women, who come to symbolize the nation that also needs to be protected. Baym argues that in *The Last of the Mohicans*, the passive and weak Alice survives while her hardy sister Cora dies because "a woman's weakness *is* her strength in the white world, because it inspires men like Duncan, representative of European-American civilization, to fight for her" (77). The miscegenated woman's body complicates this idea because Olney wants to protect a woman who is not fully white and who embodies white society's rape and exploitation of blacks. The doctor romanticizes the racial taint, imagining the heroine as needing to be rescued from an ill fate. Rhoda attracts Olney because "the remote taint of her servile and savage origin gave her a kind of fascination" (223). Robert J. C. Young mentions Josiah Nott's beliefs that mulattas are delicate, unhealthy, bad breeders, and liable to miscarry (126–27). Olney tells Rhoda, "'I am going to provide for your future, and let you look after your past.' She dropped her head with a sob on his shoulder, and as he gathered her in his arm he felt as if he had literally rescued her from her own thoughts of herself" (233). While mocking romantic convention, Howells nonetheless reinscribes it because Rhoda's black parentage makes her primitive and uncivilized and therefore in need of protection. She does not need to be defended as an emblem of white society, but rather she needs to be saved from herself.

Tragic mulattas are tragic because they cannot be saved from themselves and inevitably die by novel's end. Howells attempts to correct the imperative moral duty of mulattas by reaffirming Rhoda's whiteness and providing her with a fate dissonant with the romantic tradition: marriage and a future. Yet this realist effort to redress romantic convention reverts to type: the suicide plot mandated by the tragic mulatta stereotype, but scrupulously avoided in Rhoda's case, gets deflected onto her aunt, Mrs. Meredith. Mrs. Meredith feels overwhelmingly guilty about hiding Rhoda's black ancestry from her and allowing Rhoda to pass as white. When Rhoda contemplates marriage, Mrs. Meredith decides that racial duty compels her to reveal Rhoda's black heritage. The news devastates Rhoda but Olney saves her from herself. But the miscegenated woman's body is an atavistic plot element that proves too strong: the pull of genre obliges Mrs. Meredith to overdose on sleeping medicine. Thus again, the tragic mulatta stereotype confounds Howells's effort to confront it in a realist vein.

The novel concludes with further discussion of racial duty as Olney convinces Rhoda to marry him. Rhoda considers traveling south to locate her grandmother's family, but Howells avoids restoring black family ties as Bates does in the conclusion of *The Chamber over the Gate*, and instead Olney asks Rhoda to devote to him the "fifteen-sixteenths or so of you that belong to my race by heredity," freeing her to give one-sixteenth of herself to her black relations (229). In other words, Olney's "ultimate goal is to reclassify Rhoda permanently as white so that she will no longer reconnect with black people" (Paulin 436). Olney's only regret about Rhoda is that "the sunny-natured antetypes of her mother's race had not endowed her with more of the heaven-born cheerfulness with which it meets contumely and injustice" (233). In this judgment about Rhoda, Howells again resorts to racial stereotyping that undermines realist principles. The miscegenated woman's body confounds his attempts to portray Rhoda's character in a realist light.

In *An Imperative Duty* Howells uses miscegenation fiction to reverse romantic novels' concepts of heredity by adding irony and, in theory, more sophisticated ideas about race. But the miscegenated woman's body is unable to fully accommodate the tenets of realism, as the final pages of the novel demonstrate. Olney rejects romantic, high-anxiety views of heredity, typically melodramatic in romance novels, and through his proposal to Rhoda seems to advocate racial healing and scientific objectivity. Howells's claim in his 1903 letter that love could settle the race question is validated by the novel's happy ending. Yet Olney and Rhoda understand the scorn they might face and therefore move to Italy, where Rhoda's dark beauty blends in comfortably. Howells inadvertently undermines his optimistic realism: love does *not* settle the race question, because the lovers cannot settle in the United States.

One could question whether Olney and Rhoda's move to Italy indeed constitutes a patriotic defeat because many U.S. citizens during Howells's time lived abroad for extended periods to mark their social status and acquire cultural capital. Could Olney and Rhoda's move be read as an indictment of contemporary race relations in the United States? Or perhaps one could read their move as another type of duty—in this case, Olney's duty to his wife as opposed to his duty to his country. As one critic points out, Olney's perception of his duty to his wife as being greater than his duty to his country does not necessarily imply a patriotic defeat but rather is consonant with the high regard placed on family that appears in Howells's *Silas Lapham*.[12] Kenneth W. Warren similarly attempts a positive reading of the lovers' repatriation by claiming an active role for the woman of color in *An Imperative Duty*, a role that the novel does not support:

"While Howells's novel parodied the sentimentalized self-sacrifice of the tragic mulatta figure that had already become a commonplace in U.S. fiction, his critique also drew into its orbit the belief that black women could and should play a role in combating racial oppression in a public way" (66).

Olney and Rhoda's expatriation to Italy subverts Warren's claim because Rhoda does not combat racial oppression but instead capitulates to it. Once Rhoda realizes she is biracial, she removes herself from her birth country. Although many U.S. citizens of this period did live abroad but returned home, Olney earlier in the novel expresses his belief that it is the "duty" of U.S. citizens to live in their country, and he thus hastens his return from Italy. In a peculiar circularity, the novel concludes by undermining Olney's feelings of national duty. Leaving the United States once again, this time because of his wife's racial status, therefore reaffirms that for Olney domesticity (duty to home and wife) conflicts with patriotism. Rhoda cannot be both a white wife and a U.S. resident. Iola Leroy, in contrast, chooses her black identity and can therefore be both a wife and a U.S. citizen. In this sense, miscegenation is cast as unpatriotic, for it forces Olney to shirk his stated national duty and leave the country. Howells would like to leave readers with the impression that he is a happy assimilationist, but the lovers' move to Italy compromises this vision. Diana Paulin concurs that the novel could be read as tragic since the lovers must leave their home or as romantic since the couple unite despite their racial distinctions. Ultimately, Paulin argues, "the conclusion remains indeterminate. This ambiguous ending echoes the complicated social conditions that inform Howells's representation" (437). What Paulin and other readers do not note is that, significantly, *An Imperative Duty* ends before Rhoda and Olney have children. By leaving the couple childless, Howells avoids confronting the anxiety about race for the next generation.

Nonetheless, *An Imperative Duty* has a romantic, happy ending, a marked departure from the sad endings of most tragic mulatta fiction. Specifically, Howells avoids the "too melodramatic" ending he disdained in *The Chamber over the Gate*. Although she could be labeled a "white blackbird," Rhoda is no tragic mulatta in the romantic sense. Her fate, however, is tragic in that she cannot be both biracial and a resident of the United States. In his attempt to settle the race question, Howells provides his heroine with an alternative to suicide but unwittingly reinscribes the tragic mulatta stereotype: Rhoda obliterates herself from society by killing her black ancestry and her ability to reside in the United States. Howells does not use Rhoda and Olney's expatriation as a way to critique national identity and political agency in the United States, but rather to reinvent a romantic convention.

Harper's Iola Leroy

When Howells wrote to Dr. Whiston that he wanted to explore whether love could "settle" the race question, he only considered a man's love for a woman. Howells sexualizes female racial embodiment through a lens of male desire. Frances Harper, in contrast, presents a similar story from a biracial woman's point of view in *Iola Leroy*, thus endowing miscegenation with different structural and thematic significance. By entitling her novel after her heroine, rather than after a duty larger than the individual, Harper announces the importance of a single character—and a woman no less (Peterson 99).

Although the influence of Bates and Buckner on Howells is clear, Harper's reliance on Howells is sketchier, but nonetheless present. Harper borrows freely from other writers such as Harriet Beecher Stowe, William Wells Brown, and Harriet Jacobs.[13] While Bernard Bell implies that Harper borrows from Howells, Ann du Cille argues that Harper "rewrites and subverts Howells' racist construction" (Bell 58; du Cille 161 n. 29).[14] Both Howells and Harper knew the works of Paul Laurence Dunbar and Charles Chesnutt, but while we do not have evidence that they met, there nonetheless appears to be a literary call and response between *An Imperative Duty* and *Iola Leroy*.

Harper's and Howells's textual representations of the biracial woman's body are not politically innocent—both writers charge miscegenation ideologically with different understandings of cultural practice. By complicating the politics surrounding racial heterogeneity, Howells's realist project interrogates and recasts romantic notions of heredity as dismissible concerns. Harper's politics of uplifting the black race found expression in tracing the life of a sympathetic, admirable mulatta, themes she rehearsed earlier in her novels *Minnie's Sacrifice* (1869), *Sowing and Reaping* (1876–77), and *Trial and*

Triumph (1888–89). Howells's and Harper's narratological strategies for deploying miscegenation themes parallel their desire to address such issues as character psychology, social mores, racial heredity, and genre. In Howells's campaign for realism and Harper's turn from poetry to the novel, both writers appropriate miscegenation as the vehicle for their twin concerns of social and narrative representation. Yet while Howells challenges and rewrites the romantic world of Bates and Buckner, Harper uses the very same plot and theme to rewrite Howells's realist world in turn, thereby reinstating the significance of a romantic vision but politicizing it so that the biracial woman effects social and political transformation and uplift. Thus, while the miscegenated woman's body confounds Howells's attempts to represent race realistically, Harper freely and openly draws upon the strengths of the romantic and sentimental tradition to politicize her realist social critique.

Aware of their audiences, Howells and Harper both try to appeal to the predominantly white female reading public. When read against each other, Howells's novel appeals to white notions of upward mobility and black assimilation into white culture: Rhoda's attempt to devote her life to the black cause backfires, and Dr. Olney laughs at her efforts to play the tragic but noble octoroon (Kinney 139). Since Harper's preface indicates that she wrote for a mixed-race audience, her novel addresses women's concerns such as rape and egalitarian marital relations and it valorizes black women's ability to lead and transform the race with pride. Both authors converge in their characterization of a light-skinned black woman raised white who must reconsider her racial identity when deciding whether marrying white constitutes further miscegenation.

Harper follows Howells in coupling the light-skinned heroine with a white doctor who pities her. The white Dr. Gresham falls in love with Iola because he believes that her unfortunate racial taint renders her helpless: "The deep pathos of her story, the tenderness of her ministrations, bestowed alike on black and white, and the sad loneliness of her condition, awakened within him a desire to defend and protect her all through her future life" (58). Dr. Gresham's bias compels him to see blacks as infantile and quaint, thereby bringing out the desire to protect them: "To him the negro was a picturesque being, over whose woes he had wept when a child, and whose wrongs he was ready to redress when a man. But when he saw the lovely girl who had been rescued by the commander of the post from the clutches of slavery, all the manhood and chivalry in his nature arose in her behalf, and he was ready to lay on the altar of her heart his first grand and overmastering love" (110). If Gresham's love "overmasters," then his love object is enslaved, suggesting that marriage and slavery are inextricable. Even if Gresham's love is so strong that it overmasters him, Harper still chooses loaded language suggesting hierarchy and exploitation to describe love. Yet Harper overturns Howells's vision of assimilation and etiolation: Iola refuses to marry Gresham when he balks at the possibility of not-white babies. In this point Harper seems to be specifically rewriting Howells's portrayal of a white doctor's dismissal of colored progeny. In Gresham's hesitation, Harper portrays U.S. whites' fear of reversion and corrects Howells's falsely cheerful assimilationist fantasy. Mrs. Meredith's concern with the transmission of black ancestral traits, which Olney as a man of science discounts, proves to be the issue that divides Iola and Gresham. The miscegenated woman's body, which Olney believes can be bred white with a dose of realism, serves as a point of racial pride in Harper's hands. Love cannot "settle the race question" for either Iola or Gresham.

Yet one could argue that Harper rewrites, if not avoids, Howells's race question by coupling Iola with a light-skinned black doctor. Iola's response to Dr. Latimer's proposal differs from Rhoda's response to Olney. Her immediate answer appears quite infantilizing: "'Oh, dear,' replied Iola, drawing a long breath. 'What would mamma say?'" (268). But Iola answers thus because she believes marriage would compromise her more urgent goal of serving her people. Latimer presses further with a more egalitarian question: "'Am I presumptuous in hoping that your love will become the crowning joy of my life?'" (271). Since Latimer's offer is not one of protection or defense, nor one that will restrict her race-conscious goal, Iola accepts.

Posing the question of progeny with Dr. Gresham allows Harper to take a political stand championing black pride and the choice of black husbands for light-skinned women. Instead of further etiolating her bloodline, Iola makes a self-conscious decision not to marry white. Instead, she and Dr. Latimer devote themselves to uplifting their race. Perhaps acknowledging the esteem of marrying white and any distaste her readers might feel were Iola to marry a very dark black man, Harper compromises her heroine's racial vision by marrying Iola to a very light-skinned man who passes for a white doctor. Iola, like Rhoda, therefore does get to marry the white doctor after all. Harry, Iola's brother, makes a more definitive statement by marrying the unmixed Lucille Delaney. But Dr. Latimer's deliberate choice *not* to pass for white makes him all the more admirable and a suitable mate for Iola and her political goals.[15]

It is not merely accidental or coincidental that the deceased mother of Coral Gatsimer in Bates's *Chamber over the Gate*, Rhoda, and Iola are courted by doctors. As rational scientists, physicians are supposed to have observational and diagnostic skills keen enough to read the human body. Drs. Gatsimer, Olney, and Gresham are much like detectives: they examine and investigate for clues to a (fleshly) problem. Yet for all their power to detect bodily ills, the white doctors fail to detect race mixture. They cannot claim the "racial literacy" that Michele Birnbaum attributes to them (12). Gatsimer's mistaken diagnosis is not revealed until his wife gives birth to a black baby. Rhoda's father was also a physician and his inability to read his wife's skin properly ruined his practice (166). Latimer deceives another doctor, his white colleague, Dr. Latrobe, into believing that Latimer likewise is white. Arrogantly insulted at the deception, Latrobe "thought he was clear-sighted enough to detect the presence of negro blood when all physical traces had disappeared" (239).

In these novels the doctor figure, with his presumed powers of character diagnosis, becomes a stand-in for the writer and perhaps for realism's failure to adequately treat the race question or the woman question. That the various doctors cannot properly diagnose a woman's race and that race then virtually becomes a medical problem that must be "treated" suggests that both race and femininity are pathologized. Howells's use of the doctor figure is particularly compelling because he attempts to use Dr. Olney's scientific reasoning to correct racial fallacies that lead to "too melodramatic" endings in women's fiction. Howells also had a model to follow for the ideal combination of doctor and realist: S. Weir Mitchell, an eminent physician and novelist, exchanged letters with Howells and treated his daughter, Winny.[16] Race, imagined as a property of blood, eludes white men of science specifically trained to scrutinize sanguinary conditions.

Besides the doctors, the other man of science in this quartet of novels is the black taxidermist, Emile, in Buckner's novel, who immediately recognizes Bamma's racial secret. If, in Howells's hands, the white doctor becomes a stand-in for the realist writer, the black taxidermist in *Towards the Gulf* likewise figures as an aesthetician concerned with "natural" bodily features. In Buckner's novel, the taxidermist's skills and artistry form a narrative congruent with Donna J. Haraway's claim that "taxidermy was about the single story, about nature's unity, the unblemished type specimen. Taxidermy became the art most suited to the epistemological and aesthetic stance of realism" ("Teddy Bear" 38; Seltzer 170). The taxidermist as realist triumphs over the doctor as realist in his powers of interpretation and representation. Pushing realism to an extreme, "the arts of taxidermy, dissection, and embalming allow realist representation to achieve its aim with an alarming precision, making corpses into permanent, self-evident embodiments of the essential orders of life" (Bentley, *Ethnography* 167). Perhaps because taxidermists, more than doctors, routinely investigate and probe bodies from the inside out, they more readily understand secrets beneath and within the skin. Although Bamma is still alive when she first meets the taxidermist, he nonetheless dissects her identity at once and "fixes" her into the same category as his lonely white blackbird. As representatives of their types, the bird and the woman mutually reinforce each other's hybrid, outsider condition. That Emile is black likewise suggests that blacks, not just taxidermists, may be skilled readers of racial representation and have special access to realist aesthetics, a stance that Harper's Dr. Latimer supports by his interpretation of the imperative duty of the black physician.

In Iola's rejection of the white doctor and her decision to go south in search of relatives, Harper recasts Howells's portrayal of duty. Iola's prime concern after the war is to identify herself as black and reconnect with her long-lost black family. This is, of course, the exact duty that Olney convinces Rhoda to reject. Bates, too, in *The Chamber over the Gate*, concludes her novel with the discovery of Coral and Percy's kinship, and in Buckner's *Towards the Gulf* the link between Bamma and the slaves dismantles her marriage. Because Howells deemed Bates's and Buckner's endings too melodramatic, he avoids reuniting Rhoda with her black ancestors. If the restoration of the family means tears and sentimentality, then Howells avoids sentiment by keeping his heroine white and thereby without newly discovered black relatives. Harper, however, recognizes the power and political import of having Iola reconnect with her black family and turns her readers into reformers as they weep at Iola's successful family reunions. The conclusion Howells labels "too melodramatic" becomes a source of racial pride and happiness in *Iola Leroy*.

By claiming Iola's black identity, Harper elevates the acceptance of black womanhood and the importance of the African American community. The recognition of blackness, so feared in the novels of Bates, Buckner, and Howells, is celebrated in the hands of a black woman novelist. Iola's decision to speak and act publicly as a black woman stands as a destiny Howells cannot permit his heroine.[17] Howells's most complete erasure of Rhoda's identity occurs in the novel's final pages when the couple moves to Italy, where Rhoda's dark beauty blends right in. Since the novel had opened with Olney's urgency to fulfill his patriotic duty to return to the United States from Italy, his fleeing back to Europe can be read only as unpatriotic. In Howells's vision, the United States cannot accommodate miscegenation, and the biracial woman who dares to pass as white must live in exile. Iola, by choosing blackness, is therefore more "American" than Rhoda.

Bates's and Buckner's use of the tragic mulatta stereotype that Howells attempts to challenge with realism finally undergoes revision in Harper's hands. Harper uncouples the "tragic" from "mulatta" and restores her heroine to life, bounty, and racial uplift. Although *Iola Leroy* can be viewed critically as adhering to some of realism's tenets, it unabashedly embraces the sentimentalism and romanticism that Howells resists to make urgent Harper's political and social goals.

This literary call and response that crosses racial and gender lines engages ideas about the role of the hybrid woman's body in romantic and realist aesthetics. In his paternalistic attempt to correct romantic conceptions through realist principles, Howells runs into trouble because the presence of biracial womanhood disrupts his scientific portrayals of race. When they sexualize race theory, realism and its tenets fumble: the tragic mulatta stereotype seemingly causes a reversion of genre as realism relapses into romanticism. A realist, nonromantic denouement of the tragic mulatta plot is unimaginable in the United States. Howells thus is unable to bang about the babes of romance since the mulatta figure is inassimilable to his understanding of realism. Olney and Rhoda's flight to Italy doubles as a flight from Howells's realist tenets. Their fictional heirs, however, remain in the United States in the hands of Harper, who becomes Howells's realist revisionary.

CONCLUSION

As Earl Fitz points out, "the issue of miscegenation speaks to and reflects virtually all aspects of what it has meant to be an American" ("From Blood to Culture" 244). Even though the Cuban revolutionary poet José Martí believed that race as a category of human description or experience does not exist, perceptions of race and its admixture have affected all aspects of culture and, especially for these pages, literary imagination. By focusing on hemispheric race mixture, *Race Mixture in Nineteenth-Century U.S. and Spanish American Fictions* exposes American studies to a New World perspective and suggests ways to compare questions of national, racial, and literary identity.

Part of the growing field of transamerican studies, this book establishes a previously unrealized dialogue among nineteenth-century novels of the United States, Ecuador, Peru, and Cuba about race and race mixture. This North-South conversation reveals meaningful literary affinities and transamerican relationships among writers—kinships often difficult to identify when authors are classified exclusively according to national boundaries. A broad range of disciplines in the Americas currently stands in relation to literary representations of race mixture. We need to read extensively and comparatively to engage in a robust conversation on the topic in various fields. A certain grounding or familiarity with the flexibility of the miscegenation theme in a North-South context can provide the key.

Building upon what Lois Parkinson Zamora identifies as "a shared comprehension of America and a shared mode of narrating its history" (*Writing* 34), these novels of the Americas speak in a comparative context: race mixture and its subsequent impact on national and literary identity inescapably shape both North and South America. In an effort to understand literary production in a hemispheric context, we can read against each other works that are culturally distinct but narratively analogous. Such readings demonstrate how the anxiety about race mixture is perceived politically and framed novelistically in the Americas: I have chosen each novel for its particular enunciation of a theme or concern and then engaged the novels in a dialogue to create what is perhaps a hybrid study.

For example, subjecting U.S. novels to the pressures of Andean genres reveals gaps and absences in the North's articulation of native representation. Novels from Ecuador, Peru, and Cuba challenge assumptions about North American miscegenation and intolerance to racial difference. Thus, the United States's divisive one-drop rule to determine black ancestry, as exemplified by Lydia Maria Child's *Romance of the Republic*, Margret Holmes Bates's *Chamber over the Gate*, Alice Morris Buckner's *Towards the Gulf*, and William Dean Howells's *Imperative Duty*, seems absurd next to the integrationist project of Clorinda Matto de Turner's *Aves sin nido*. The royal African descent that ennobles the hero in Gómez de Avellaneda's *Sab* stands in great contrast to the black ancestry that demonizes Margaret in Whitman's *Franklin Evans*, that primitivizes and exoticizes Rhoda in Howells's *Imperative Duty*, and that gives purpose to the eponymous heroine in Harper's *Iola Leroy*.

Juxtaposing these northern and southern novels also reveals the interdependence of miscegenation and writing. Reading hemispherically highlights for readers how race mixture is constructed as textual practice. Because nineteenth-century literature "was a site where race got manufactured, deployed, disseminated, contested, and claimed" (Stokes 3), published novels, as they circulated, influenced readers' perceptions of race and race mixture. Words, themselves black ink on a white page, solidify ideas about racial identity. Many of the writers studied in this book hoped to use the power of the printed word to challenge fixed notions of racial affinity and rewrite a new social vision. For example, Matto de Turner and Child both aimed to use interracial love as a political tool to elevate their heroines'—and therefore nonwhite women's—status.

When read together, these novels also suggest the importance of the nexus of heterosexuality and race. When anxieties about race mixture collide with a marriage plot, what happens? How do authors in the Americas resolve a marriage plot when issues of race dominate? If "heterosexuality is the means of ensuring, but also the site of endangering the reproduction" (Stokes 16) of whiteness, then heterosexuality and marriage become fraught with tension when racial difference is introduced. Marriage between whites consolidates whiteness; marriage between those perceived to be of different races threatens whiteness, with different narrative results. All the authors in this study consider how the histories of racial difference affect the way race mixture is imagined literarily in the Americas.

In *Looking Forward* (1899), Arthur Bird describes the territorial reach of the United States as "bounded on the north by the North Pole; on the south by the Antarctic Region; on the east by the first chapter of the Book of Genesis and on the west by the Day of Judgment" (qtd. in Urraca 21). Although some may smile at this as a quaint, outdated sentiment, others may claim that the United States still proffers such a vision. The appropriation of the term "America" by the United States can be traced back to the Monroe Doctrine, which, according to Orestes Brownson in 1865, states that "the United States have a proper name by which all the world knows and calls them. The proper name of the country is America. . . . The fact is significant, and foretells for the people of the United States a continental destiny, as is also foreshadowed in the so-called 'Monroe Doctrine'" (qtd. in Urraca 24).

Yet, even in the twenty-first century, problems of definition still inhere. Lois Parkinson Zamora points out that in reality "'America' encompasses thirty-five countries and fifteen territories or protectorates, four principal Indo-European languages and countless indigenous languages, 676 million inhabitants, and more than 16 million square miles of land." Further, she highlights the difficulties in using "North America" if one does not mean to include Mexico and notes the eliding of Central America in the term "South America." Even the term "inter-American" can be misleading because it can refer to relations among nations within North America or within South America or to relations between the North and the South. Finally, she argues that even the "use of the term 'U.S. fiction' is ambiguous in this comparative context because Mexico is also a 'United States'—'Los Estados Unidos de México'" (11–12). J. Michael Dash also writes about the problem of defining New World studies: the term the "*New* World, because of its Eurocentric frame of reference, not only retains the old polarization of inside versus outside, us versus them, but the less-than-useful distinction of New World versus Old World. By now the point has been made persuasively, and maybe exhaustingly, that to call this hemisphere *new* is to ignore centuries of Amerindian civilization in the Americas" (1).

To try to accommodate these exigencies, we can extend the traditional boundaries of disciplinary critical dialogues. By juxtaposing Latin American and Caribbean novels with U.S. works, this book shifts race analysis away from the nationalistic confines that historically have characterized U.S. race studies and thus discloses the profound influence of racial hybridity as a cultural force throughout the Americas. The arguments in this book build on trends within American studies and invite scholars of U.S. literature to think in more global, hemispheric terms and pursue comparative analyses that rethink categories of national culture. I focus on race mixture as a dominant cultural theme within the literature of the Americas to assert that recent race analysis within American studies has been limited by the nationalistic frameworks of identity politics and by modes of oppositional thinking. I implore readers to recall that race mixture has a long and potent history within pan-American literature.

Although our twenty-first century era of free trade, acceptance of the euro, and increasingly permeable national boundaries encourages intellectual exchanges, I do not suggest that we should engage in a wholesale free trade or cultural annexation of historic, genre, or literary contours or that we should occlude the North-South power differential by theorizing the idea of one America. Limitations certainly exist when comparing one national literature with another. Yet, as scholars increasingly look north and south rather than solely across the Atlantic for cross-cultural influences and literary communality, interracial mixing, with its implications for genre, representation, and national identity, becomes foundational for the idea of America.

Nineteenth-century anxieties about miscegenation continue into the twenty-first century. In the American hemisphere, racial fears often guide political policy and lead to barbed-wiring of borders against dark-skinned "undesirables." Although immigrants from Great Britain and the former Soviet Union look like "us," the cultural and racial influence of Mexicans, Haitians, and Cubans still carries a threat for U.S. policy makers. International political and ethnic crossings remain as perplexing as racial ones: the European Union and German reunification concern breaking down barriers; California's Proposition 187 legislates for barriers against a brown invasion; the Serbs, Croats, Kurds, Ukrainians, Québécois, Palestinians, and Irish want to establish sovereign boundaries. Worldwide border crossings become effortless in our increasingly cosmopolitan world of easy air travel, electronic communication, and global economies that often seem to anesthetize lived experience. In a time of massive global population migration, rising virulent racist nationalist movements, and unpatrollable stretches of national borders, the physical body assumes political, moral, and metaphorical dimensions.

As an agent of desire and of a particular racial history, the body and miscegenous sexual longing play an important role in many twentieth-century works, including Spike Lee's *Jungle Fever*, Lillian Smith's *Strange Fruit*, William Faulkner's *Light in August*, Eldridge Cleaver's *Soul on Ice*, Richard Wright's *Native Son*, Jorge Amado's *Tenda dos milagres*, V. S. Naipaul's *Guerillas*, Leslie Marmon Silko's *Ceremony*, Ana Castillo's *Sapogonia*, Enrique Lopez Albujar's *Matalache*, Margaret Laurence's *Diviners*, Maria Campbell's *Half-Breed*, Rudy Wiebe's *Scorched-Wood People*, Dany Laferriere's *Comment faire l'amour avec un negre sans se fatiguer*, Maryse Conde's *Moi, Tituba*, and others. David Avalos and Deborah Small's video "Ramona: Birth of a Mis-ce-ge-NATION" concatenates numerous U.S. films that feature a white protagonist's love affair with a native other. The filmmakers emphasize the familiarity of the light-dark pairing by quipping, "Don't worry, you already know the story, even though you've never heard of it. It's the *Last of the Mohicans*, *West Side Story*, and *La Bamba* all at the same time" (24).

Another major hybrid zone in the Americas is linguistic—as a multilingual hemisphere, the Americas will continue to produce literature in many languages. Across the Americas, novels are read and reread in translation. In many ways, translation and miscegenation are coextensive—both are concerned with sameness and difference, the anxiety about reproduction, and the loss of "origin." In terms of colonial powers, world "translation" meant converting native land and culture into European ideas of property and society.[1] Concerned with anthropological understandings, character psychology, and political theories of statehood, nineteenth-century themes of racial miscibility may be precursors to modernism. Anticipating later racial and political conflicts, such themes also point to modern problems of nationalism. Children of mixed heritage both resemble and differ from their parents, mimicking modernity's concern with repetition with difference. Interracial conflict may very well be an inevitable part of postcolonial modernity.

Some movement has been made to collapse the psychological distance between North and South in the Americas, as evidenced by the spate of essay collections and the increase in pan-American papers and panels at meetings of such organizations as the Modern Language Association, the International Comparative Literature Association, and the American Comparative Literature Association. Yet none of these essays or discussions specifically addresses miscegenation as an inter-American phenomenon, as I have here. If pan-American literature is to gain more prominence as a distinct field of inquiry, an understanding of race mixture's impact on the hemisphere's literary imagination is crucial.

NOTES

INTRODUCTION

1. For particularly useful discussions of race mixture in the Americas, see Berkhofer; Cohn; Esteva Fabregat; Harris; Johnston; Winthrop Jordan; Martínez-Echazábal; Morner; Solaún and Kronus; and Williamson.

2. For further reading on pan-American literary studies, see Chevigny and LaGuardia; Fitz, *Rediscovering the New World*; Fusco; García Canclini; International Comparative Literature Association; Kaup; Kaup and Rosenthal; Penn; Pérez-Firmat; Saldívar; and Spillers, *Comparative American Identities*.

3. For a further history, see Wood, especially chapter 4, "The Miscegenation Controversy of 1864," and Lemire's particularly deft reading of the 1864 pamphlet.

4. The Cuban anthropologist Fernando Oritz coined *transculturation* as a term to refer to a "one-way imposition of the dominant culture" (Spitta, *Between Two Waters* 3). See also Spitta, "Transculturation."

5. This and subsequent translations in this book, unless otherwise noted, are mine.

6. For a sophisticated discussion of "the transformation of the discourse of Romanism into a discourse of race" (229) in the nineteenth-century United States, see Fessenden.

7. It is beyond the scope of this book to survey nineteenth-century views of hybridity articulated in such works as Robert Knox's *Races of Men* (1850), Josiah Nott and George Gliddon's *Types of Mankind* (1854), Charles Darwin's *Origin of Species* (1859) and *Descent of Man* (1871), and Gobineau's *Inequality of Human Races* (1853–55). For an excellent discussion of these theorists, see Robert J. C. Young's chapter 1.

8. Carlos Gutiérrez-Jones argues that Ramona's identity does not shift because Jackson never really accepts Ramona's Indian heritage; her high-born upbringing eclipses her mestiza identity, and Ramona's daughter will grow up not knowing her Indian mother, just as Ramona never knew hers (61, 63).

9. Further discussions of mixed-race characters can be found in Berzon; Cometta Manzoni; Dearborn; Frederickson; Meléndez; Prina; Scheick; Sollors, " 'Never Was Born' "; and Yellin, *Intricate Knot*.

CHAPTER ONE

1. Examples include James Wallis Eastburn and Robert Sands's *Yamoyden, a Tale of the Wars of King Philip: In Six Cantos* (1820); Lydia Maria Child's *Hobomok* (1824); *Narrative of the Life of Mrs. Mary Jemison*, edited by James Everett Seaver (1824); Catharine Maria Sedgwick's *Hope Leslie* (1827); George Washington Custis's *Pocahontas; or, The Settlers of Virginia* (1827); and John Augustus Stone's *Metamora; or, The Last of the Wampanoags* (1829).

2. Concha Meléndez does not differentiate between the two genres. She labels as *indianista* any novel encompassing an Indian theme, whether romantic or concerned with social vindication, and considers the Argentinian poems *Santos Vega* by Hilario Ascasubi and *Martín Fierro* (1872) by José Hernández to be *literatura anti-indianista* (13).

3. Critics who struggle to describe the representation of Indians include Roy Harvey Pearce, who discusses novels by the way they represent Indians' nobility or ignobility. Richard Slotkin, in *Regeneration*, relies on such terms as the Indian war narrative, the captivity narrative, religious (missionary) literature, travel literature, and hero narratives. Reginald Horsman and Robert Berkhofer do not discuss categories at all. No critic analyzes the political vindication of Indians in a category such as *indigenismo*, and none discusses the ways miscegenation might influence the representation of Native Americans. For an overview of critical discussion about Indians, see Walker, especially 29–40.

4. Perhaps one fact that accounts for such varied representation of Native Americans is geography. For example, nineteenth-century East Coast representations of Indians in the United States differed greatly from West Coast portrayals. Indians were not a visible presence in the East, and their outsider status prompted eastern writers to assume that they would not survive long. Urban blacks lived in much closer proximity, and their presumed permanence in U.S. society motivated writers to represent them, rather than Indians, in fiction. As exceptions to this generalization, Lucy Maddox points to Emerson's and Thoreau's resistance to the Removal Act (telephone conversation). Twain would perhaps be another exception. Robert S. Levine connects these concerns to the rise of urban reform movements from 1830 to 1860 ("Fiction and Reform" 147–48).

5. For example, see Castiglia; Karcher, *First Woman* and *A Lydia Maria Child Reader*; Nelson, "Sympathy as Strategy"; and Samuels, *Romances*.

6. Cynthia Steele mistakenly argues for a parallel between writings about Indians in the United States and in Spanish America: "*Indigenista* fiction, that is, fiction treating the conflicts between native American and dominant, nation-building societies, reached its apogee in the United States during the Age of Jackson (1820–1860), as it did in Mexico after the revolution (1920–1960)" ("Fiction" 60). Steele ignores the differences between *indianismo* and

indigenismo and brands all U.S. novels with Indian themes *indigenista*, thus invoking, but not acknowledging, a substantial bibliography and critical debate on genre distinctions. By defining as *indigenista* any novel that addresses conflict between Native Americans and whites, she ignores the different political ideologies behind the various traditions. For example, Cooper's vision was very much complicit with U.S. government Indian removal policy, while much Mexican and South American *indigenista* fiction advocated integrating Indians into the dominant culture. By comparing nineteenth-century U.S. romances with the realist, activist *indigenista* novels of the twentieth century, Steele occludes the important activist dimension of *indigenista* novels and imbues romantic U.S. novels with a social critique that they do not have. She specifically labels Cooper's *Deerslayer* (1841) and R. M. Bird's *Nick of the Woods* (1837) as *indigenista*, inviting comparison to South American novels that advocate Indian vindication and consolidation into society, agendas that could not be more antithetical to Cooper's and Bird's ("Ideology").

7. For further recent discussions of the nineteenth-century Latin American novel in general, see Alegría; Corral; González Stephan; Klahn and Corral; and Regan.

8. Another valuable book is Sayer's *Les Sauvages Americains*.

9. Similarly, Luis Alberto Sánchez asserts that *indianismo* "utiliza el indio americano como un motivo decorativo. El *indigenismo*, como una bandera de protesta. Aquél se deleita en los aspectos folklóricos, dentro de un concepto esteticista o sentimental; éste se llena de indignación y convoca a la rebeldía en nombre de la justicia [uses the American Indian as a decorative object. *Indigenismo*, as a banner of protest. The former takes pleasure in the folkloric aspects, within an aesthetic or sentimental framework; the latter is full of indignation and calls for rebellion in the name of justice]" (28).

10. Mera, Child, Cooper, Sedgwick, and Jackson demonstrate an ethnographic voyeuristic interest in portraying native peoples in their own environment, as if to preserve and safeguard them from colonialism. Lee Clark Mitchell argues that this sense of urgency to record a threatened wilderness particularly defined works by U.S. writers: "In Africa, South America, and Australia, landscapes and native peoples suffered at the hands of invaders in ways strikingly similar to those in America. For reasons connected with settlement patterns, however, the invaders' perceptions of their own impact were never as conflicted. In South America, the Spanish and Portuguese clung to the coast; Africa saw only transient explorers, except in the south, where natives nevertheless outnumbered colonists; in Australia, conversely, the aborigines were few, and settlements remained coastal" (21). Coastal settlements with fewer major pushes to conquer the interior meant invaders and natives had less mutual exposure and hence less conflict over the role of miscegenation in nation building.

11. For example, the significance of interracial mixing is not emphasized by Arias, Bente, Carreras, or Pérez.

12. For a closer reading of Hawkeye's "cross," see Lemire.

13. Many critics of *Sab* examine some of the same issues raised in this chapter regarding *mestizaje*, sexuality, race, and nation building in the literature of the Americas. See especially Barreda; Benítez Rojo; Kaminsky, *Reading*; Kutzinski; Luis; Martínez-Alier; and Smith.

14. For a close examination of Sedgwick's rewriting of Puritan histories, see Gould. For a discussion of Sedgwick's questioning of women's role in the political culture, see Gossett and Bardes.

15. The novel "accents the indigenous problem in Peru, and because of this it marks the transition to novels after 1890 that have Indians as their major concern" (Meléndez 174). Many others support this claim. See Alegría; Carrillo; Castro Arenas; Cornejo Polar, *La novela indigenista* and *La novela peruana*; and Tauro.

16. For a discussion of Brace as one of Twain's many liminal figures, see Delaney.

17. See Mitchell, who connects the disappearance of the Indians with the destruction of the wilderness and frontier to speak of a more inclusive "vanishing America."

18. For further information on the frontier and the disappearing Indians, see Drinnon; Fussel; and Street.

CHAPTER TWO

1. Reynolds makes a similar point in "Black Cats."

2. For standard histories of the temperance movement, see Blocker; Blumberg; Clark; Gusfield; Rorabaugh; and Tyrrell.

3. My thanks to Jon Miller for this insight.

4. For further analysis of the black temperance movement and its bid for racial equality, see my "Deracialized Discourse."

5. I am indebted to Karen Sánchez-Eppler for this insight.

6. I am indebted to Jon Miller for drawing Sigourney to my attention.

7. When Whitman revised the novel for republication in the *Brooklyn Daily Eagle* in 1846, however, he eliminated Evans's marriage to Margaret.

8. For further reading on Whitman and race, see Aspiz and Phillips.

CHAPTER THREE

1. For example, see Cruz 43, 103, 107–9; Fox-Lockert 128; Garfield; Harter, *Gertrudis*; Kaye; and Netchinsky 213–14. Gómez de Avellaneda's treatment of Cuban slavery has not yet been compared with Martin Delany's representation of slavery and insurrection in Cuba in his novel *Blake; or, The Huts of America*, partly serialized in 1859 and then fully from 1861 to 1862.

2. See Kaminsky, "Residual" and *Reading* 98–100, 106; Kutzinski 20–27; Pratt 51; Benigno Sánchez-Eppler; Smith 2–3; and Williams.

3. Other nineteenth-century French novels about blacks in white society, which were perhaps read or known of by the Cuban writers, include Aurore Cloteaux's *Le Mulâtre* (1824), the Dutchess of Dura's *Ourika* (1824), and the Cuban writer Sophie Doin's *Blanch et noir* (1826) (see Martul Tobío xxvi). For information on Hugo's influence on Gómez de Avellaneda, see Cruz 44–47.

4. For information on these novels, I relied on Barreda; Fivel-Démoret; Gutiérrez de la Solana; and Luis. For more on Manzano, see Bremer 487–501 and Ellis.

5. See also Scott, "Shoring Up." For more biographical information, see Cotarelo y Mori; Lazo; and Marquina.

6. Benigno Sánchez-Eppler summarizes the link between slavery, sugar production, and coupling in his essay " 'Por Causa Mecánica.' "

7. For more on the *Album cubano*, see Scott, "Shoring Up."

8. For more on the reception of *Othello* in the United States, see Edelstein.

9. For a reading of Carlota and Sab as half siblings, rather than just cousins, see Bravo-Villasante 20.

10. Stacey Schlau reads the taking of the veil as an assumption of power: Teresa transcends her material and bodily self to reconcile her body/soul split and hence achieves a type of salvation (500).

CHAPTER FOUR

1. See, for example, Karcher, *First Woman*, especially chapter 19, and "Lydia"; Nelson, *The Word*, especially chapter 4; Mills; Patterson; and Yellin, *Intricate Knot* and *Women and Sisters*.

2. I am grateful to Carolyn L. Karcher for directing me to these examples.

3. For more on flowers' association with beauty, see Scarry, especially note 6.

4. The floral rhetoric of grafting and hybridity may have a different connotation when referring to human sexuality. For example, whereas the child of a racially heterogeneous couple would be a hybrid, a couple that adopts a child of a different race could be said to graft that child into the family. I am grateful to the anonymous reader for the University of North Carolina Press for these observations.

5. For more on Tulipomania and the history of the tulip, see Pavord.

CHAPTER FIVE

1. Even though the word "babe" did not appear in print referring specifically to a pretty girl until 1915, the usage nonetheless implies a subservient status, and babes were relegated to women's sphere.

2. For other explanations of Howellsian realism, see Pizer, *Documents* and *Realism and Naturalism*; and Wonham. Michael McKeon's *Origins of the En-*

glish Novel provides an unimpeachable analysis of realism vis-à-vis the novel. For further readings on realism, see Jameson.

3. For the history of the mulatto/mulatta, see Berzon; Carby, *Reconstructing Womanhood* 88–91, 140; Christian, *Black Women*; Gillman, "The Mulatto"; Winthrop Jordan; Sánchez-Eppler, *Touching*; Spillers, "The Tragic Mulatta" 147–59; Williamson; and Yellin, *Intricate Knot*.

4. Another prolific woman writer, Matt Crim, published a tragic mulatta story, "Was It an Exceptional Case?," in *Century* magazine in 1891, the same year that *An Imperative Duty* first appeared. Crim's influence on Howells is unknown. See also Crim, *In Beaver Cove*; and Jones.

5. In Bates's novel, Coral's mulatta mother, also named Coral, dies when she gives birth to an obviously black baby boy. In Buckner's novel, the heroine Bamma kills herself when she realizes the truth of her racial taint. The anxiety about miscegenation in Howells's novel is displaced from Rhoda onto Mrs. Meredith, the one who bears the burden of the secret. Mrs. Meredith kills herself after dispensing the catastrophic news to her niece. Harper's character Gracie, Iola's sister, withers away and dies when she realizes she has black ancestors and is hence a slave.

6. Nina Baym makes a similar argument regarding Indian-white relations (73).

7. Margret Holmes Ernsperger Bates (1844–1927) was born in Fremont, Ohio, to a farmer and his wife. She attended public school in Fremont and later taught school elsewhere in Ohio and Indiana. In 1865, she married Charles Austin Bates, a businessman working in Indianapolis, and had one son the following year. Bates began her literary career by writing local reports and book reviews for Indianapolis newspapers. During her career, she published many works, including *Manitou* (1881), *The Chamber over the Gate* (1886), *The Price of the Ring* (1892), *Shylock's Daughter* (1894), *Jasper Fairfax* (1897), *In the First Degree* (1907), *Hildegarde and Other Lyrics* (1911), and *Browning Critiques* (1927). She also wrote and edited ten school primers. In 1894, she moved to New York City and became a member of many writing and social organizations. See "Bates, Margret Holmes," in *The National Cyclopedia of American Biography* (New York: James T. White and Co., 1909), 10:61; "Bates, Margret Holmes," in *American Authors and Books, 1640–1940*, edited by W. J. Burke and Will D. Howe (New York: Gramercy Publishing, 1943); "Bates, Charles Austin," in *The National Cyclopedia of American Biography* (New York: James T. White and Co., 1916), 15:74; and "Bates, Margret Holmes (Ernsperger)," in *American Fiction, 1876–1900*, edited by Lyle H. Wright (San Marino, Calif.: Huntington Library, 1966), 42.

8. The 1972 reprint of the novel was made from an edition in the Fisk University Library Negro Collection. In a telephone call, a librarian at the Fisk University Library told me that the author of *Towards the Gulf* was most

likely not black but that the book made its way into the Negro Collection because of its subject matter. The novel was probably reprinted because libraries received extra funding in the 1960s and 1970s to build their holdings of materials related to African American themes.

9. For an excellent discussion of racial theories, see Robert J. C. Young, especially chapter 1. See also Gosset.

10. If Howells distanced himself from his black characters, he did not think Charles Chesnutt formulated enough distance, for Chesnutt's characters were not "black enough to contrast grotesquely with white people" ("Mr. Charles W. Chesnutt's Stories" 699). Although a supporter of Chesnutt, Howells also criticized the younger author for wanting to write didactic or "purpose fiction" to show how life should be, which breached Howells's ideas of realism (see Andrews).

11. Banta notes that *Harper's Monthly* chose not to illustrate *An Imperative Duty* even though the other novels it was serializing at the same time were illustrated: "Perhaps it was delicacy over the question of how to show Rhoda Aldgate's strange, dusky beauty" (vi n. 9).

12. I am very grateful to the anonymous reader for the University of North Carolina Press who made these astute observations.

13. Harper's poems influenced by Stowe include "To Mrs. Harriet Beecher Stowe," "Eliza Harris," and "Eva's Farewell," all found in *A Brighter Coming Day*. For a brief comparison of *Iola Leroy* with *Clotel*, see Lewis. For mention of Harper's borrowings from Jacobs, see Yellin, "Introduction" xxix.

14. For other recent readings of the novel, see Diggs; Ernest; Fabi; Foster, "Gender" and *Written by Herself*; Hubbard; Peterson; Rosenthal; Tate; and Elizabeth Young.

15. I am grateful to Frances Smith Foster for discussing this point with me (private conversation). Hazel Carby makes a similar point when she asserts that Harper represses Iola's sexuality to assure her an equitable relationship with Dr. Latimer ("Introduction" xxv).

16. For a recent account of Mitchell's treatment of Winny Howells, see Crowley, *Dean* 15.

17. In *Black and White Strangers*, Warren takes Howells to task for belittling black women's position in society in his inability to allow Rhoda to recognize her blackness: "His commonsense position apparently denied the legitimacy of the very public forum that women like Harper sought to occupy and the vocational choices they sought to endorse" (67).

CONCLUSION

1. Eric Cheyfitz argues that "translation was, and still is, the central act of European colonization and imperialism in the Americas" (104).

WORKS CITED

Alegría, Fernando. *Nueva historia de la novela hispanoamericana*. Hanover, N.H.: Ediciones del Norte, 1986.
Anderson, Benedict. *Imagined Communities: Reflections on the Origin and Spread of Nationalism*. London: Verso, 1991.
Andrews, William L. "William Dean Howells and Charles W. Chesnutt: Criticism and Race Fiction in the Age of Booker T. Washington." *American Literature* 48 (Fall 1976): 327–59.
Araujo, Nara. "Raza y género en Sab." *Casa de las Americas* 33, no. 190 (Jan.–Mar. 1993): 42–49.
Arias, Augusto. *Panorama de la literatura ecuatoriana*. Quito: Editorial Casa de la Cultura Ecuatoriana, 1971.
Aspiz, Harold. *Walt Whitman and the Body Beautiful*. Urbana: University of Illinois Press, 1980.
Avalos, David, and Deborah Small. "Ramona: Birth of a Mis-ce-ge-NATION: The Video Script." *Discourse* 18, nos. 1–2 (Winter 1995–96): 24–31.
Bakhtin, M. M. "Discourse in the Novel." In *The Dialogic Imagination: Four Essays*, edited by Michael Holquist; translated by Caryl Emerson and Michael Holquist, 259–422. Austin: University of Texas Press, 1981.
Balibar, Etienne. "The Nation Form: History and Ideology." In *Race, Nation, Class: Ambiguous Identities*, edited by Etienne Balibar and Immanuel Wallerstein, 86–106. London: Verso, 1991.
Banning, Evelyn I. *Helen Hunt Jackson*. New York: Vanguard, 1973.
Banta, Martha. "Introduction" to *"The Shadow of a Dream" and "An Imperative Duty,"* by William Dean Howells, iii–xii. Bloomington: Indiana University Press, 1970.
Baron, Dennis E. *Grammar and Good Taste: Reforming the American Language*. New Haven: Yale University Press, 1982.
Barreda, Pedro. *Black Protagonist in the Cuban Novel*. Translated by Page Bancroft. Amherst: University of Massachusetts Press, 1979.
Bates, Margret Holmes. *The Chamber over the Gate*. Indianapolis: Charles A. Bates, 1886.
Bauer, Dale M., and Susan Jaret McKinstry. *Feminism, Bakhtin, and the Dialogic*. Albany: State University of New York Press, 1991.
Baym, Nina. "How Men and Women Wrote Indian Stories." In *New Essays*

on *The Last of the Mohicans*, edited by H. Daniel Peck, 67–86. Cambridge: Cambridge University Press, 1992.

Beach, Christopher. *The Politics of Distinction: Whitman and the Discourses of Nineteenth-Century America*. Athens: University of Georgia Press, 1996.

Bell, Bernard. *The Afro-American Novel and Its Tradition*. Amherst: University of Massachusetts Press, 1987.

Benítez Rojo, Antonio. *The Repeating Island: The Caribbean and the Postmodern Perspective*. Translated by James Maraniss. Durham: Duke University Press, 1992.

Bente, Thomas O. "*Cumandá* y *Tabaré*: Dos cumbres del indianismo romántico hispano-americano." *Revista Interamericana de Bibliografía/Inter-American Review of Bibliography* 41, no. 1 (1991): 15–23.

Bentley, Nancy. *The Ethnography of Manners: Hawthorne, James, and Wharton*. Cambridge: Cambridge University Press, 1995.

———. "White Slaves: The Mulatto Hero in Antebellum Fiction." *American Literature* 65, no. 3 (Sept. 1993): 501–22.

Berkhofer, Robert. *The White Man's Indian: Images of the American Indian from Columbus to the Present*. New York: Vintage, 1978.

Berlant, Lauren. "The Queen of America Goes to Washington City." *American Literature* 65, no. 3 (Sept. 1993): 549–74.

Berzon, Judith R. *Neither White nor Black: The Mulatto Character in American Fiction*. New York: New York University Press, 1978.

Bewell, Alan. "'Jacobin Plants': Botany as Social Theory in the 1790s." *Wordsworth Circle* 20, no. 3 (Summer 1989): 132–39.

Biddiss, Michael D. *Father of Racist Ideology: The Social and Political Thought of Count Gobineau*. New York: Weybright and Talley, 1970.

Birnbaum, Michele. "Racial Hysteria: Female Pathology and Race Politics in Frances Harper's *Iola Leroy* and W. D. Howells's *An Imperative Duty*." *African American Review* 33, no. 1 (Spring 1999): 7–23.

Blair, Walter, ed. *Mark Twain's Hannibal, Huck, and Tom*. Berkeley: University of California Press, 1969.

Blocker, Jack S. *American Temperance Movements: Cycles of Reform*. Boston: Twayne, 1989.

Blumberg, Leonard. *Beware the First Drink!: The Washington Temperance Movement and Alcoholics Anonymous*. Seattle: Glen Abbey Books, 1991.

Boeckmann, Cathy. *A Question of Character: Scientific Racism and the Genres of American Fiction, 1892–1912*. Tuscaloosa: University of Alabama Press, 2000.

Bravo-Villasante, Carmen. *Una vida romántica, La Avellaneda*. Barcelona: Enrique Granados, 1967.

Bremer, Thomas. "The Slave Who Wrote Poetry: Comments on the Literary Works and the Autobiography of Juan Francisco Manzano." In *Slavery in*

the Americas, edited by Wolfgang Binder, 487–501. Würzburg, Germany: Konigshausen and Neumann, 1993.
Brooks, Peter. *Reading for the Plot: Design and Intention in Narrative*. New York: Vintage, 1984.
Brown, Herbert Ross. *The Sentimental Novel in America, 1789–1860*. Durham: Duke University Press, 1940.
Brushwood, John S. *Genteel Barbarism: Experiments in Analysis of Nineteenth-Century Spanish-American Novels*. Lincoln: University of Nebraska Press, 1981.
[Buckner, Alice Morris]. *Towards the Gulf: A Romance of Louisiana*. Freeport, N.Y.: Books for Libraries Press, 1972.
Cable, George Washington. *The Grandissimes*. New York: Scribner, 1880.
Cady, Edwin H. *The Realist at War: The Mature Years (1885–1920) of William Dean Howells*. Syracuse: Syracuse University Press, 1958.
Carby, Hazel. "Introduction" to *Iola Leroy*, by Frances Harper, ix–xxvi. Boston: Beacon, 1987.
———. *Reconstructing Womanhood: The Emergence of the Afro-American Woman Novelist*. New York: Oxford University Press, 1987.
Carmichael, Tami Skinner. "Catharine Maria Sedgwick's Literary Miscegenation: Transcending Boundaries in Nineteenth-Century American Literature." Ph.D. diss., University of Georgia, 1988.
Carreras, Marcela, Maria Candelaria de Olmos, and Paula Gigena. "Romanticismo e indianismo en *Cumandá* de J. L. Mera." *Estudios filológicos* 32 (1997): 57–71.
Carrillo, Francisco. *Clorinda Matto de Turner y su indigenismo literario*. Lima: Ediciones de la Biblioteca Universitaria, 1967.
Castiglia, Christopher. *Bound and Determined: Captivity, Culture Crossing, and White Womanhood from Mary Rowlandson to Patty Hearst*. Chicago: University of Chicago Press, 1996.
Castro Arenas, Mario. *La novela peruana y la evolución social*. 2d ed. Lima: José Godard, 1967.
Channing, William. "Essay on American Language and Literature." *North American Review* 1 (Sept. 1815): 1.
Chateaubriand, François-René de. *"Atala" and "René."* Translated by Walter J. Cobb. New York: Signet, 1971.
Chevigny, Bell Gale, and Gary LaGuardia, eds. *Reinventing the Americas: Comparative Studies of Literature of the United States and Latin America*. Cambridge: Cambridge University Press, 1986.
Cheyfitz, Eric. *The Poetics of Imperialism: Translation and Colonization from "The Tempest" to "Tarzan."* New York: Oxford University Press, 1991.
Child, Lydia Maria. *An Appeal in Favor of That Class of Americans Called Africans*. Boston: Allen and Ticknor, 1833.

———. *Flowers for Children*. 1st and 2d ser. New York: C. S. Francis, 1844.
———. *Flowers for Children*. 3d ser. New York: C. S. Francis, 1846.
———. *History of the Condition of Women, in Various Ages and Nations*. Boston: John Allen, 1835.
———. *"Hobomok" and Other Writings on Indians*. Edited by Carolyn L. Karcher. New Brunswick: Rutgers University Press, 1986.
———. "A Legend of the Falls of St. Anthony." In *"Hobomok" and Other Writings on Indians*, edited by Carolyn L. Karcher, 203-12. New Brunswick: Rutgers University Press, 1986.
———. *Lydia Maria Child: Selected Letters, 1817–1880*. Edited by Milton Meltzer and Patricia G. Holland. Amherst: University of Massachusetts Press, 1982.
———. *A New Flower for Children*. New York: C. S. Francis, 1856.
———. "The Quadroons." In *Rediscoveries: American Short Stories by Women, 1832–1916*, edited by Barbara H. Solomon, 88–98. New York: Penguin, 1994.
———. *A Romance of the Republic*. Edited by Dana D. Nelson. Lexington: University Press of Kentucky, 1997.
———. "The Tulip and Tri-Colored Violet." *Juvenile Miscellany* 1 (1826): 37–39. In *American Periodical Series, 1800–1850*, 389–90, microfilm.
Christian, Barbara. *Black Women Novelists: The Development of a Tradition*. Westport, Conn.: Greenwood Press, 1980.
———. "Introduction" to *The Hazeley Family*, by Mrs. A. E. Johnson, xxvii–xxxvii. New York: Oxford University Press, 1988.
Clark, Norman. *Deliver Us from Evil*. New York: Norton, 1976.
Cmeil, Kenneth. "Whitman the Democrat." In *A Historical Guide to Walt Whitman*, edited by David S. Reynolds, xxvii–xxxvii. New York: Oxford University Press, 2000.
Cohn, Deborah N. *History and Memory in the Two Souths: Recent Southern and Spanish American Fiction*. Nashville: Vanderbilt University Press, 1999.
Cometta Manzoni, Aída. *El indio en la poesía de América española*. Buenos Aires, 1939.
Cooper, Anna Julia. *A Voice from the South*. New York: Oxford University Press, 1988.
Cooper, James Fenimore. *The Last of the Mohicans*. New York: Penguin, 1986.
Cornejo Polar, Antonio. *La novela indigenista*. Lima: Editorial Lasontay, 1980.
———. *La novela peruana: Siete estudios*. Lima: Editorial Horizonte, 1977.
Corral, Wilfrido. "Hacia una poética hispanoamericana de la novela decimonónica." *Modern Language Notes* 110, no. 2 (1995): 385–415.
Cotarelo y Mori, Emilio. *La Avellaneda y sus obras*. Madrid: Tipografía de Archivos, 1930.

Crim, Matt. *In Beaver Cove and Elsewhere*. New York: Charles L. Webster, 1892.
Croly, David. *Miscegenation: The Theory of the Blending of the Races, Applied to the American White Man and Negro*. New York: H. Dexter, Hamilton, 1864.
Crowley, John W. *The Dean of American Letters: The Late Career of William Dean Howells*. Amherst: University of Massachusetts Press, 1999.
———. Letter to the author. 1995.
Cruz, Mary. "Prólogo" to *Sab*, by Gertrudis Gómez de Avellaneda. Havana: Editorial Arte y Literatura, 1976.
Dash, J. Michael. *The Other America: Caribbean Literature in a New World Context*. Charlottesville: University Press of Virginia, 1998.
Davidson, Cathy. *Revolution and the Word: The Rise of the Novel in America*. New York: Oxford University Press, 1986.
Dearborn, Mary. *Pocahontas's Daughters: Gender and Ethnicity in American Culture*. New York: Oxford University Press, 1986.
Delaney, Paul. "The Genteel Savage: A Western Link in the Development of Mark Twain's Transcendent Figure." *Mark Twain Journal* 21, no. 3 (Spring 1983): 29–31.
DelCampo, Kelly Phipps. "Sacrifice and National Identity: Foundational Discourse in Nineteenth-Century Cuban Antislavery Texts." Ph.D. diss., Emory University, 1995.
Diggs, Marylynne. "Surveying the Intersection: Pathology, Secrecy, and the Discourses of Racial and Sexual Identity." In *Critical Essays: Gay and Lesbian Writers of Color*, edited by Emmanuel S. Nelson, 1–20. New York: Haworth Press, 1993.
Dippie, Brian. *Vanishing American: White Attitudes and U.S. Indian Policy*. Middletown, Conn.: Wesleyan University Press, 1982.
Dix, Dorothea. *Garland of Flora*. Boston: S. G. Goodrich and Carter and Hendee, 1829.
Dixon, Thomas, Jr. *The Clansman: An Historical Romance of the Ku Klux Klan*. Lexington: University Press of Kentucky, 1970.
Drinnon, Richard. *Facing West: The Metaphysics of Indian-Hating and Empire Building*. Minneapolis: University of Minnesota Press, 1980.
Du Bois, W. E. B. "As a Friend of the Colored Man." In *Critical Essays on W. D. Howells, 1866–1920*, edited by Edwin H. Cady and Norma W. Cady, 217–18. Boston: G. K. Hall, 1983.
du Cille, Ann. *The Coupling Convention: Sex, Text, and Tradition in Black Women's Fiction*. New York: Oxford University Press, 1993.
Echevarría, Evelio. "La novela indigenista hispanoamericana: Definición y bibliografía." In *Revista Interamericana de Bibliografía/Inter-American Review of Bibliography* 35, no. 3 (1985): 289–96.

Edelstein, Tilden G. "*Othello* in America: The Drama of Racial Intermarriage." In *Interracialism: Black-White Intermarriage in American History, Literature, and Law*, edited by Werner Sollors, 356–68. New York: Oxford University Press, 2000.

Eley, Geoff. "Nations, Publics, and Political Cultures: Placing Habermas in the Nineteenth Century." In *Habermas and the Public Sphere*, edited by Craig Calhoun, 289–339. Cambridge: MIT Press, 1992.

Ellis, Robert R. "Reading through the Veil of Juan Francisco Manzano: From Homoerotic Violence to the Dream of a Homoracial Bond" *PMLA* 113, no. 3 (May 1998): 422–35.

Erkkila, Betsy. *Whitman the Political Poet*. New York: Oxford University Press, 1989.

Ernest, John. *Resistance and Reformation in Nineteenth-Century African-American Literature: Brown, Wilson, Jacobs, Delany, Douglass, and Harper*. Jackson: University Press of Mississippi, 1995.

Esteva Fabregat, Claudio. *El mestizaje en Iberoamérica*. Madrid: Editorial Alhambra, 1988.

Fabi, M. Giulia. "Taming the Amazon?: The Price of Survival in Turn-of-the-Century African American Women's Fiction." In *The Insular Dream: Obsession and Resistance*, edited by Kristiaan Versluys, 228–41. Amsterdam: VU University Press, 1995.

Fanon, Franz. *Black Skin, White Masks*. Translated by Charles Lam Markmann. New York: Grove, 1967.

Fern, Fanny. *Fern Leaves from Fanny's Portfolio*. Auburn, N.Y.: Derby and Miller, 1853.

Fessenden, Tracy. "From Romanism to Race: Anglo-American Liberties in *Uncle Tom's Cabin*." *Prospects* 25 (2000): 229–68.

Fiedler, Leslie A. *Love and Death in the American Novel*. New York: Stein and Day, 1982.

Figarola Caneda, Domingo. *Gertrudis Gómez de Avellaneda*. Madrid: Sociedad General Española de Librería, 1929.

Fitz, Earl. "From Blood to Culture: Miscegenation as a Metaphor of the Americas." In *Mixing Race, Mixing Culture: Inter-American Literary Dialogues*, edited by Monika Kaup and Debra J. Rosenthal, 243–72. Austin: University of Texas Press, 2002.

———. *Rediscovering the New World: Inter-American Literature in a Comparative Context*. Iowa City: University of Iowa Press, 1991.

Fivel-Démoret, Sharon Romeo. "The Production and Consumption of Propaganda Literature: The Cuban Anti-Slavery Novel." *Bulletin of Hispanic Studies* 66, no. 1 (Jan. 1989): 1–12.

Folsom, Ed. "Lucifer and Ethiopia: Whitman, Race, and Poetics before the

Civil War and After." In *A Historical Guide to Walt Whitman*, edited by David S. Reynolds, 45–96. New York: Oxford University Press, 2000.

Foster, Frances Smith. "Gender, Genre, and Vulgar Secularism: The Case of Frances Ellen Watkins Harper and the AME Press." In *Recovered Writers, Recovered Texts: Race, Class, and Gender in Black Women's Literature*, edited by Dolan Hubbard, 46–59. Knoxville: University of Tennessee Press, 1997.

———. Private conversation. Toronto, 29 Dec. 1993.

———. *Written by Herself: Literary Production by African American Women, 1746–1892*. Bloomington: Indiana University Press, 1993.

Fox-Lockert, Lucía. *Women Novelists in Spain and Spanish America*. Metuchen, N.J.: Scarecrow Press, 1979.

Frederickson, George. *The Black Image in the White Mind*. New York: Harper and Row, 1971.

Freimarck, Vincent, and Bernard Rosenthal, eds. *Race and the American Romantics*. New York: Schocken Books, 1971.

Fusco, Coco. *English Is Broken Here: Notes on Cultural Fusion in the Americas*. New York: New Press, 1995.

Fussel, Edwin. *Frontier: American Literature and the American West*. Princeton: Princeton University Press, 1965.

García Canclini, Néstor. *Hybrid Cultures: Strategies for Entering and Leaving Modernity*. Translated by Christopher L. Chiappari and Silvia L. López. Minneapolis: University of Minnesota Press, 1995.

Garfield, Evelyn Picon. *Poder y Sexualidad: El discurso de Gertrudis Gómez de Avellaneda*. Amsterdam: Rodopi, 1993.

Gelder, Ann. "Reforming the Body: 'Experience' and the Architecture of Imagination in Harriet Jacobs's *Incidents in the Life of a Slave Girl*." In *Inventing Maternity: Politics, Science, and Literature, 1650–1865*, edited by Susan C. Greenfield and Carol Barash, 252–66. Lexington: University Press of Kentucky, 1999.

Gillman, Susan. "The Mulatto, Tragic or Triumphant?: The Nineteenth-Century American Race Melodrama." In *The Culture of Sentiment: Race, Gender, and Sentimentality in Nineteenth-Century America*, edited by Shirley Samuels, 221–43. New York: Oxford University Press, 1992.

———. "*Ramona* in 'Our America.'" In *José Martí's "Our America": From National to Hemispheric Cultural Studies*, edited by Jeffrey Belnap and Raul Fernández, 91–111. Durham: Duke University Press, 1998.

———. "The Squatter, the Don, and the Grandissimes in Our America." In *Mixing Race, Mixing Culture: Inter-American Literary Dialogues*, edited by Monika Kaup and Debra J. Rosenthal, 140–60. Austin: University of Texas Press, 2002.

Gips, Kathleen. *Flora's Dictionary: The Victorian Language of Herbs and Flowers*. Chagrin Falls, Ohio: TM Publications, 1995.

Gobineau, Arthur de. *The Inequality of the Human Races*. Translated by Adrian Collins. New York: Howard Fertig, 1967.

Gold, Janet. "The Feminine Bond: Victimization and Beyond in the Novels of Gertrudis Gómez de Avellaneda." *Letras femeninas* 15, nos. 1–2 (1989): 83–89.

Gold, Peter J. "Indianismo and Indigenismo." *Romance Notes* 14, no. 3 (Spring 1973): 460–64.

Gómez de Avellaneda, Gertrudis. *Sab*. Havana: Editorial Arte y Literatura, 1976.

———. *"Sab" and "Autobiography."* Edited and translated by Nina M. Scott. Austin: University of Texas Press, 1993.

González, Eduardo. "American Theriomorphia: The Presence of *Mulatez* in Cirilo Villaverde and Beyond." In *Do the Americas Have a Common Literature?*, edited by Gustavo Pérez-Firmat, 177–97. Durham: Duke University Press, 1990.

González Stephan, Beatriz, Javier Lasarte, Graciela Montaldo, and María Julia Daroqui, eds. *Esplendores y miseria del siglo XIX: Cultura y sociedad en américa latina*. Caracas: Monte Avila Editores, 1994.

Goody, Jack. "The Secret Language of Flowers." *Yale Journal of Criticism* 3, no. 2 (1990): 133–52.

Gosset, Thomas. *Race: The History of an Idea in America*. New York: Oxford University Press, 1997.

Gossett, Suzanne, and Barbara Ann Bardes. "Women and Political Power in the Republic: Two Early American Novels." *Legacy* 2, no. 2 (Fall 1983): 13–30.

Gould, Philip. "Catharine Sedgwick's 'Recital' of the Pequot War." *American Literature* 66, no. 4 (Dec. 1994): 641–62.

Greenfield, Susan C. "'Abroad and at Home': Sexual Ambiguity, Miscegenation, and Colonial Boundaries in Edgeworth's *Belinda*." *PMLA* 112, no. 2 (Mar. 1997): 214–28.

Greenwood, Grace. *Greenwood Leaves*. Boston: Ticknor and Fields, 1850.

Gruesz, Kirsten Silva. *Ambassadors of Culture: The Transamerican Origins of Latino Writing*. Princeton: Princeton University Press, 2002.

Guerra, Lucia. "Estratégias femeninas en la elaboración del sujeto romántico en la obra de Gertrudis Gómez de Avellaneda." *Revista iberoamericana* 51 (July–Dec. 1985): 707–22.

Gusfield, Joseph. *Symbolic Crusade*. Urbana: University of Illinois Press, 1963.

Gutiérrez de la Solana, Alberto. "*Sab y Francisco*: Paralelo y contraste." In *Homeaje a Gertrudis Gómez de Avellaneda: Memorias del simposio en el centenario de su muerte*, edited by Gladys Zaldívar and Rosa Martínez de Cabrera, 301–17. Miami: Ediciones Universal, 1981.

Gutiérrez-Jones, Carlos. *Rethinking the Borderlands: Between Chicano Culture and Legal Discourse.* Berkeley: University of California Press, 1995.

Hale, Sarah Josepha. *Flora's Interpreter; or, The American Book of Flowers and Sentiments.* 11th ed. Boston: Marsh, Capen, Lyon, and Webb, 1842.

———. *Flora's Interpreter and Fortuna Flora.* Boston: Benjamin B. Mussey, 1850.

Handley, George. *Postslavery Literatures in the Americas: Family Portraits in Black and White.* Charlottesville: University Press of Virginia, 2000.

Haraway, Donna J. *Primate Visions: Gender, Race, and Nature in the World of Modern Science.* New York: Routledge, 1989.

———. *Simians, Cyborgs, and Women.* New York: Routledge, 1991.

Harper, Frances Ellen Watkins. *A Brighter Coming Day: A Frances Ellen Watkins Harper Reader.* Edited by Frances Smith Foster. New York: Feminist Press, 1990.

———. *Iola Leroy; or, Shadows Uplifted.* Boston: Beacon, 1987.

———. *"Minnie's Sacrifice," "Sewing and Reaping," "Trial and Triumph": Three Rediscovered Novels by Frances E. W. Harper.* Edited by Frances Smith Foster. Boston: Beacon, 1994.

Harris, Marvin. *Patterns of Race in the Americas.* New York: Norton, 1974.

Harris, Susan. *Nineteenth-Century American Women's Novels: Interpretive Strategies.* New York: Cambridge University Press, 1990.

Harter, Hugh A. "Gertrudis Gómez de Avellaneda." In *Spanish American Women Writers*, edited by Diane E. Marting, 210–25. Westport, Conn.: Greenwood Press, 1990.

———. *Gertrudis Gómez de Avellaneda.* Boston: Twayne, 1981.

Holland, Norman S. "Fashioning Cuba." In *Nationalisms and Sexualities*, edited by Andrew Parker, Mary Russo, Doris Summer, and Patricia Yaeger, 147–56. New York: Routledge, 1992.

Hooper, Lucy, ed. *The Lady's Book of Flowers and Poetry, to which Are Added a Botanical Introduction, a Complete Floral Dictionary, and a Chapter on Plants in Rooms.* New York: Derby and Jackson, 1858.

Horsman, Reginald. *Race and Manifest Destiny: The Origins of American Racial Anglo-Saxonism.* Cambridge, Mass.: Harvard University Press, 1981.

Howells, William Dean. "April, 1887." In *Editor's Study*, edited by James W. Simpson, 73–77. Troy, N.Y.: Whitston, 1983.

———. "Criticism and Fiction." In *Criticism and Fiction and Other Essays*, edited by Clara Marburk Kirk and Rudolf Kirk, 9–87. New York: New York University Press, 1959.

———. "False and Truthful Fiction." In *Documents of American Realism and Naturalism*, edited by Donald Pizer, 70–98. Carbondale: Southern Illinois University Press, 1998.

———. *An Imperative Duty*. In *"The Shadow of a Dream" and "An Imperative Duty,"* edited by Edwin H. Cady. Albany: New College and University Press, 1962.

———. "Mr. Charles W. Chesnutt's Stories." *Atlantic Monthly* 85 (May 1900): 699.

———. "The Pilot's Story." *Atlantic Monthly* 6 (Sept. 1860): 323–24.

———. *Selected Letters*. Vol. 3, *1882–1891*. Edited by Robert Leitz. Boston: Twayne, 1980.

———. *Selected Letters*. Vol. 5, *1902–1911*. Edited by William C. Fischer. Boston: Twayne, 1983.

———. *Selected Literary Criticism*. Vol. 3, *1898–1920*. Edited by Ulrich Halfmann, Donald Pizer, and Ronald Gottesman. Bloomington: Indiana University Press, 1993.

Hubbard, Dolan. *The Sermon and the African American Literary Imagination*. Columbia: University of Missouri Press, 1994.

Hulme, Peter. *Colonial Encounters: Europe and the Native Caribbean, 1492–1797*. London: Methuen, 1986.

Hurston, Zora Neale. *Their Eyes Were Watching God*. New York: HarperCollins, 1998.

International Comparative Literature Association. *Inter-American Literary Relations*. Edited by Mario J. Valdés. New York: Garland, 1985.

Jackson, Helen Hunt. *Ramona*. Introduction by Michael Dorris. New York: New American Library, 1988.

Jackson, Richard L. *The Black Image in Latin American Literature*. Albuquerque: University of New Mexico Press, 1976.

Jackson, Shirley M. "Fact from Fiction: Another Look at Slavery in Three Spanish-American Novels." In *Blacks in Hispanic Literature*, edited by Miriam DeCosta, 83–89. Port Washington, N.Y.: Kennikat Press, 1977.

Jacobs, Harriet A. *Incidents in the Life of a Slave Girl*. Edited by Jean Fagin Yellin. Cambridge, Mass.: Harvard University Press, 1987.

Jameson, Fredric. *Marxism and Form: Twentieth-Century Dialectical Theories of Literature*. Princeton: Princeton University Press, 1971.

JanMohamed, Abdul R. "Sexuality on/of the Racial Border: Foucault, Wright, and the Articulation of 'Racialized Sexuality.'" In *Discourses of Sexuality: From Aristotle to AIDS*, edited by Domna C. Stanton, 94–116. Ann Arbor: University of Michigan Press, 1992.

Johnson, Mrs. A. E. *The Hazeley Family*. New York: Oxford University Press, 1988.

Johnston, James Hugo. *Race Relations in Virginia and Miscegenation in the South, 1776–1860*. Amherst: University of Massachussetts Press, 1970.

Jones, W. Powell. "Matt Crim: Forgotten Georgia Writer." *Emory University Quarterly* 20 (Fall 1962): 149–59.

Jordan, Cynthia S. *Second Stories: The Politics of Language, Form, and Gender in Early American Fictions*. Chapel Hill: University of North Carolina Press, 1989.

Jordan, Winthrop. *White over Black: American Attitudes toward the Negro, 1550–1812*. Baltimore: Penguin, 1969.

Kaminsky, Amy. *Reading the Body Politic: Feminist Criticism and Latin American Women Writers*. Minneapolis: University of Minnesota Press, 1993.

———. "Residual Authority and Gendered Resistance." In *Critical Theory, Cultural Politics, and Latin American Narrative*, edited by Steven M. Bell, Albert H. LeMay, and Leonard Orr, 103–21. Notre Dame: University of Notre Dame Press, 1993.

Kaplan, Amy. "Nation, Region, and Empire." In *The Columbia History of the American Novel*, edited by Emory Elliott, 240–66. New York: Columbia University Press, 1991.

———. *The Social Construction of American Realism*. Chicago: University of Chicago Press, 1988.

Kaplan, Sidney. *American Studies in Black and White*. Amherst: University of Massachusetts Press, 1991.

Karcher, Carolyn L. *First Woman in the Republic: A Cultural Biography of Lydia Maria Child*. Durham: Duke University Press, 1994.

———. *A Lydia Maria Child Reader*. Durham: Duke University Press, 1997.

———. "Lydia Maria Child's *A Romance of the Republic*: An Abolitionist Vision of America's Racial Destiny." In *Slavery and the Literary Imagination*, edited by Deborah McDowell and Arnold Rampersad, 81–103. Baltimore: Johns Hopkins University Press, 1989.

Kaup, Monika. *Rewriting North American Borders in Chicano and Chicana Narrative*. New York: Peter Lang, 2001.

Kaup, Monika, and Debra J. Rosenthal, eds. *Mixing Race, Mixing Culture: Inter-American Literary Dialogues*. Austin: University of Texas Press, 2002.

Kaye, Jackeline. "La esclavitud en América: *Cecilia Valdés* y *La Cabana del tío Tom*." Translated by Ana Pual. *Casa de las Américas* 22, no. 129 (Nov.–Dec. 1981): 74–83.

Kilgour, Maggie. *From Communion to Cannibalism: An Anatomy of Metaphors of Incorporation*. Princeton: Princeton University Press, 1990.

Kime, Wayne R. "Huck among the Indians: Mark Twain and Richard Irving Dodge's *The Plains of the Great West and Their Inhabitants*." *Western American Literature* 24, no. 4 (Feb. 1990): 321–33.

Kinney, James. *Amalgamation!: Race, Sex, and Rhetoric in the Nineteenth Century Novel*. Westport, Conn.: Greenwood Press, 1985.

[Kirkland], C[aroline]. M., ed. *Poetry of the Flowers*. New York: Thomas Y. Crowell, n.d.

Kirkpatrick, Susan. *Las Románticas: Women Writers and Subjectivity in Spain, 1835–1850*. Berkeley: University of California Press, 1989.

———. "Toward a Feminist Textual Criticism: Thoughts on Editing the Work of Coronado and Avellaneda." In *The Politics of Editing*, edited by Nicholas Spadaccini and Jenaro Talens, 125–38. Minneapolis: University of Minnesota Press, 1992.

Klahn, Norma, and Wilfrido Corral, eds. *Los novelistas como críticos*. Mexico: Fondo de Cultura Económico, 1991.

Klammer, Martin. *Whitman, Slavery, and the Emergence of Leaves of Grass*. University Park: Pennsylvania State University Press, 1995.

Knadler, Stephen P. "Strangely Re-abolitionized: William Dean Howells and Racial Representation." *Arizona Quarterly* 53, no. 1 (Spring 1997): 1–24.

Kolodny, Annette. *The Land before Her: Fantasy and Experience of the American Frontiers, 1630–1860*. Chapel Hill: University of North Carolina Press, 1984.

———. *The Lay of the Land: Metaphor as Experience and History in American Life and Letters*. Chapel Hill: University of North Carolina Press, 1975.

Koppelman, Susan. *The Other Woman: Stories of Two Women and a Man*. Old Westbury, N.Y.: Feminist Press, 1984.

Kutzinski, Vera M. *Sugar's Secrets: Race and the Erotics of Cuban Nationalism*. Charlottesville: University Press of Virginia, 1993.

Lazo, Raimundo. *Gertrudis Gómez de Avellaneda: La mujer y la poesía lírica*. Mexico City: Porrua, 1972.

Lemire, Elise. *"Miscegenation": Making Race in America*. Philadelphia: University of Pennsylvania Press, 2002.

Levine, Robert S. "Fiction and Reform." In *The Columbia History of the American Novel*, edited by Emory Elliott, 130–54. New York: Columbia University Press, 1991.

———. "'Whiskey, Blacking, and All': Temperance and Race in William Wells Brown's *Clotel*." In *The Serpent in the Cup: Temperance in American Literature*, edited by David S. Reynolds and Debra J. Rosenthal, 93–114. Amherst: University of Massachusetts Press, 1997.

Lewis, Vashti. "The Near-White Female in Frances Ellen Harper's *Iola Leroy*." *Phylon: A Review of Race and Culture* 45, no. 4 (Winter 1984): 314–22.

Lincoln, Almira H. *Familiar Lectures on Botany, Including Practical and Elementary Botany, with Generic and Specific Descriptions of the Most Common Native and Foreign Plants and a Vocabulary of Botanical Terms for the Use of Higher Schools and Academies*. Hartford, Conn.: F. J. Huntington, 1832.

Locke, Alain. "American Literary Tradition and the Negro." *Modern Quarterly* 3, no. 3 (May–July 1926): 215–22.

Lomnitz, Claudio. "Nationalism as a Practical System: Benedict Anderson's Theory of Nationalism from the Vantage Point of Spanish America." In

The Other Mirror: Grand Theory through the Lens of Latin America, edited by Miguel Angel Centeno and Fernando López-Alves, 329–60. Princeton: Princeton University Press, 2001.

Luis, William. *Literary Bondage: Slavery in Cuban Narrative.* Austin: University of Texas Press, 1990.

MacKinnon, Catharine. Public lecture. Princeton University, 7 Apr. 1992.

Maddox, Lucy. *Removals: Nineteenth-Century American Literature and the Politics of Indian Affairs.* New York: Oxford University Press, 1991.

———. Telephone conversation. 13 Apr. 1994.

Marcet, Jane Haldimand. *Conversations on Vegetable Physiology; Comprehending the Elements of Botany, with Their Application to Agriculture.* Boston: Crocker and Brewster, 1830.

Mariátegui, José Carlos. *Seven Interpretive Essays on Peruvian Reality.* Translated by Marjory Urquidi. Austin: University of Texas Press, 1971.

Marquina, Rafael. *Gertrudis Gómez de Avellaneda.* Havana: Editorial Trópico, 1939.

Martínez-Alier, Verena. *Marriage, Class, and Colour in Nineteenth-Century Cuba: A Study of Racial Attitudes and Sexual Values in a Slave Society.* London: Cambridge University Press, 1974.

Martínez-Echazábal, Lourdes. *Para una semiótica de la mulatez.* Madrid: Ediciones José Porrúa Turanzas, 1990.

Martul Tobío, Luis. "Introducción" to *Sab*, by Gertrudis Gómez de Avellaneda. Lewiston, N.Y.: Edwin Mellen Press, 1993.

Mathes, Valerie Sherer. *Helen Hunt Jackson and Her Indian Reform Legacy.* Austin: University of Texas Press, 1990.

Matto de Turner, Clorinda. *Aves sin nido.* Buenos Aires: Ediciones Solar, 1968.

———. *Birds without a Nest: A Novel.* Translated by J. G. Hall in 1904; emended by Naomi Lindstrom. Austin: University of Texas Press, 1996.

———. *Torn from the Nest.* Translated by John H. R. Polt. New York: Oxford University Press, 1998.

McKeon, Michael. *The Origins of the English Novel, 1600–1740.* Baltimore: Johns Hopkins University Press, 1988.

Meléndez, Concha. *La novela indianista en Hispanoamérica.* Río Piedras: Universidad de Puerto Rico, 1961.

Mera, Juan León. *Cumandá; o, Un drama entre salvajes.* Madrid: Espasa-Calpe, 1976.

Miller, Beth. "Gertrude the Great: Avellaneda, Nineteenth-Century Feminist." In *Women in Hispanic Literature: Icons and Fallen Idols*, edited by Beth Miller, 201–14. Berkeley: University of California Press, 1983.

Millones-Figueroa, Luis. "Alma blanca, cuerpo negro: La construcción ideológica del mulato en la novela antiesclavista." *Lucero* 5 (1994): 77–87.

Mills, Bruce. *Cultural Reformations: Lydia Maria Child and the Literature of Reform.* Athens: University of Georgia Press, 1994.
Mitchell, Lee Clark. *Witness to a Vanishing America: The Nineteenth-Century Response.* Princeton: Princeton University Press, 1981.
Montes-Huidobro, Matías. "Cuba." In *Handbook of Latin American Literature,* 2d ed., edited by David William Foster, 227–70. New York: Garland Press, 1992.
Moon, Michael. *Disseminating Whitman: Revision and Corporality in Leaves of Grass.* Cambridge, Mass.: Harvard University Press, 1991.
Morner, Magner. *Race Mixture in the History of Latin America.* Boston: Little, Brown, 1967.
Morse, Richard M. *New World Sounding: Culture and Ideology in the Americas.* Baltimore: Johns Hopkins University Press, 1989.
Muñoz, Braulio. *Sons of the Wind: The Search for Identity in Spanish American Indian Literature.* New Brunswick: Rutgers University Press, 1982.
Murphy, Gretchen. "Enslaved Bodies: Figurative Slavery in the Temperance Fiction of Harriet Beecher Stowe and Walt Whitman." *Genre* 28 (Spring–Summer 1995): 95–118.
Nelson, Dana. "Sympathy as Strategy in Sedgwick's *Hope Leslie.*" In *The Culture of Sentiment: Race, Gender, and Sentimentality in Nineteenth-Century America,* edited by Shirley Samuels, 191–202. New York: Oxford University Press, 1992.
———. *The Word in Black and White: Reading "Race" in American Literature, 1638–1867.* New York: Oxford University Press, 1992.
Netchinsky, Jill Ann. "Engendering a Cuban Literature: Nineteenth-Century Antislavery Narrative." Ph.D. diss., Yale University, 1986.
Nettels, Elsa. *Language, Race, and Social Class in Howells's America.* Lexington: University Press of Kentucky, 1988.
Norwood, Vera. *Made from This Earth: American Women and Nature.* Chapel Hill: University of North Carolina Press, 1993.
Olalquiaga, Celeste. *Megalopolis: Contemporary Cultural Sensibilities.* Minneapolis: University of Minnesota Press, 1992.
Osgood, Frances Sargent. *The Floral Offering, a Token of Friendship.* Philadelphia: Carey and Hart, 1846.
———. *The Poetry of Flowers and Flowers of Poetry, to which Are Added a Simple Treatise on Botany, with Familiar Examples, and a Copious Floral Dictionary.* New York: J. C. Riker, 1848.
———. *A Wreath of Wild Flowers from New England.* London: E. Churton, 1838.
Palfrey, John Gorham. Review of *Yamoyden, a Tale of the Wars of King Philip: In Six Cantos,* by James W. Eastburn. *North American Review* 12 (1821).
Parsons, S[amuel] B[owne]. *The Rose: Its History, Poetry, Culture, and Classification.* New York: John Wiley, 1860.

Patterson, Mark R. "Surrogacy and Slavery: The Problematics of Consent in Baby M, *Romance of the Republic*, and *Pudd'nhead Wilson*." *American Literary History* 8, no. 3 (Fall 1996): 449–70.

Paulin, Diana. "Representing Forbidden Desire: Interracial Unions, Surrogacy, and Performance." *Theatre Journal* 49, no. 4 (1997): 417–39.

Pavord, Anna. *The Tulip*. New York: Bloomsbury Press, 1999.

Pearce, Roy Harvey. *The Savages of America: A Study of the Indian and the Idea of Civilization*. Baltimore: Johns Hopkins University Press, 1965.

Peluffo, Ana. "El poder de las lágrimas: Sentimentalismo, género, y nación en *Aves sin nido* de Clorinda Matto de Turner." In *Indigenismo hacia el fin del milenio: Homenaje a Antonio Cornejo-Polar*, edited by Mabel Mora, 119–38. Pittsburgh: Biblioteca de América, 1998.

Penn, William S. *As We Are Now: Mixblood Essays on Race and Identity*. Berkeley: University of California Press, 1997.

Pérez, Galo René. *Pensamiento y literatura del Ecuador*. Quito: Editorial Casa de la Cultura Ecuatoriana, 1972.

Pérez-Firmat, Gustavo. "Introduction: Cheek to Cheek." In *Do the Americas Have a Common Literature?*, edited by Gustavo Pérez-Firmat, 1–6. Durham: Duke University Press, 1990.

———, ed. *Do the Americas Have a Common Literature?* Durham: Duke University Press, 1990.

Peterson, Carla. " 'Further Liftings of the Veil': Gender, Class, and Labor in Frances E. W. Harper's *Iola Leroy*." In *Listening to Silences: New Essays in Feminist Criticism*, edited by Elaine Hedges and Shelley Fisher Fishkin, 97–112. New York: Oxford University Press, 1994.

Petrino, Elizabeth. *Emily Dickinson and Her Contemporaries: Women's Verse in America, 1820–1885*. Hanover, N.H.: University Press of New England, 1998.

Phillips, Dana. "Nineteenth-Century Racial Thought and Whitman's 'Democratic Ethnology of the Future.' " *Nineteenth-Century Literature* 49, no. 3 (Dec. 1994): 289–320.

Pizer, Donald. *Realism and Naturalism in Nineteenth-Century American Literature*. Carbondale: Southern Illinois University Press, 1966.

———, ed. *Documents of American Realism and Naturalism*. Carbondale: Southern Illinois University Press, 1998.

Pollak, Vivian. *The Erotic Whitman*. Berkeley: University of California Press, 2000.

Pratt, Mary Louise. *Imperial Eyes: Travel Writing and Transculturation*. London: Routledge, 1992.

———. "Women, Literature, and National Brotherhood." In *Women, Culture, and Politics in Latin America*, by Seminar on Feminism and Culture in Latin America. Berkeley: University of California Press, 1990.

Prina, Zulma Esther. *El mestizaje en América: Mito y realidad en José María Arguedas*. Buenos Aires: Editorial Encuentro, 1989.
Quatrefages de Breau, Jean Louis Armand de. *The Human Species*. New York: D. Appleton, 1881.
Rama, Angel. *Transculturación narrative en América Latina*. Mexico City: Siglo Veintiuno, 1987.
Regan, Stephen, ed. *The Nineteenth-Century Novel: A Critical Reader*. London: Routledge, 2001.
Reynolds, David S. "Black Cats and Delirium Tremens." In *The Serpent in the Cup: Temperance in American Literature*, edited by David S. Reynolds and Debra J. Rosenthal, 22–59. Amherst: University of Massachusetts Press, 1997.
———. *Walt Whitman's America: A Cultural Biography*. New York: Vintage, 1995.
Reynolds, David S., and Debra J. Rosenthal, eds. *The Serpent in the Cup: Temperance in American Literature*. Amherst: University of Massachusetts Press, 1997.
Ritvo, Harriet. "Barring the Cross: Miscegenation and Purity in Eighteenth- and Nineteenth-Century Britain." In *Human, All Too Human*, edited by Diana Fuss, 37–58. New York: Routledge, 1996.
Robinson, Forrest G. "Uncertain Borders: Race, Sex, Civilization in *The Last of the Mohicans*." *Arizona Quarterly* 47, no. 1 (Spring 1991): 1–28.
Rodríguez-Luis, Julio. *Hermenéutica y praxis del indigenismo: La novela indigenista de Clorinda Matto a José María Arguedas*. Mexico City: Fondo de Cultura Económica, 1980.
Rorabaugh, W. J. *The Alcoholic Republic: An American Tradition*. New York: Oxford University Press, 1979.
Rosemberg, Fernando. "Dos actitudes literarias: Indianismo e indigenismo." *Revista Interamericana de Bibliografía/Inter-American Review of Bibliography* 36, no. 1 (1986): 52–57.
Rosenthal, Debra J. "Deracialized Discourse: Temperance and Racial Ambiguity in Harper's 'The Two Offers' and *Sowing and Reaping*." In *The Serpent in the Cup: Temperance in American Literature*, edited by David S. Reynolds and Debra J. Rosenthal, 153–64. Amherst: University of Massachusetts Press, 1997.
Rowson, Susanna. *Charlotte Temple*. New York: Oxford University Press, 1986.
Saco, José Antonio. *Historia de la esclavitud*. Santiago, Chile: Editorial Orbe, n.d.
Sacoto, Antonio. *The Indian in the Ecuadorian Novel*. New York: Las Americas, 1967.
Said, Edward. *Culture and Imperialism*. New York: Alfred A. Knopf, 1993.
Saks, Eva. "Representing Miscegenation Law." *Raritan* 8, no. 2 (Fall 1988): 39–69.

Saldívar, José David. *The Dialectics of Our America: Genealogy, Cultural Critique, and Literary History*. Durham: Duke University Press, 1991.

Samuels, Shirley. "Generation through Violence: Cooper and the Making of Americans." In *New Essays on "The Last of the Mohicans,"* edited by H. Daniel Peck, 87–114. Cambridge: Cambridge University Press, 1992.

———. *Romances of the Republic: Women, the Family, and Violence in the Literature of the Early American Nation*. New York: Oxford University Press, 1996.

Sánchez, Luis Alberto. *Del naturalismo al posmodernismo*. Vol. 3 of *Historia comparada de las literaturas americanas*. Buenos Aires: Editorial Losada, 1974.

Sánchez-Eppler, Benigno. "*Por Causa Mecánica*: The Coupling of Bodies and Machines and the Production and Reproduction of Whiteness in *Cecilia Valdés* and Nineteenth-Century Cuba." In *Thinking Bodies*, edited by Juliet Flower MacCannell and Laura Zakarin, 78–86. Stanford: Stanford University Press, 1994.

Sánchez-Eppler, Karen. "Bodily Bonds: The Intersecting Rhetorics of Feminism and Abolition." In *The New American Studies: Essays from Representations*, edited by Philip Fisher, 60–92. Berkeley: University of California Press, 1991.

———. "Temperance in the Bed of a Child: Incest and Social Order in Nineteenth-Century America." In *The Serpent in the Cup: Temperance in American Literature*, edited by David S. Reynolds and Debra J. Rosenthal. Amherst: University of Massachusetts Press, 1997.

———. *Touching Liberty: Abolition, Feminism, and the Politics of the Body*. Berkeley: University of California Press, 1993.

Sartiliot, Claudette. *Herbarium Verbarium: The Discourse of Flowers*. Lincoln: University of Nebraska Press, 1993.

Sarver, Stephanie L. *Uneven Land: Nature and Agriculture in American Writing*. Lincoln: University of Nebraska Press, 1999.

Sayer, Gordon M. *Les Sauvages Americains: Representations of Native Americans in French and English Colonial Literature*. Chapel Hill: University of North Carolina Press, 1997.

Scarry, Elaine. "Imagining Flowers: Perceptual Mimesis (Particularly Delphinium)." *Representations* 37 (Winter 1997): 90–115.

Scheick, William J. *The Half-Blood: A Cultural Symbol in Nineteenth-Century American Fiction*. Lexington: University Press of Kentucky, 1979.

Schlau, Stacey. "Stranger in a Strange Land: The Discourse of Alienation in Gómez de Avellaneda's Abolitionist Novel *Sab*." *Hispania* 69, no. 3 (Sept. 1986): 495–503.

Schulman, Ivan A. "The Portrait of the Slave: Ideology and Aesthetics in the Cuban Antislavery Novel." In *Comparative Perspectives on Slavery in New*

World Plantation Societies, edited by Vera Rubin and Arthur Tuden, 356–67. New York: New York Academy of Sciences, 1977.

Scott, Nina M. "Introduction" to *Sab and Autobiography*, by Gertrudis Gómez de Avellaneda; edited and translated by Nina M. Scott, xi–xxi. Austin: University of Texas Press, 1993.

———. "Shoring Up the 'Weaker Sex': Avellaneda and Nineteenth-Century Gender Ideology." In *Reinterpreting the Spanish American Essay: Women Writers of the Nineteenth and Twentieth Centuries*, edited by Doris Meyer, 57–67. Austin: University of Texas Press, 1995.

Sedgwick, Catharine Maria. *Hope Leslie*. Edited by Mary Kelley. New Brunswick: Rutgers University Press, 1987.

Seltzer, Marc. *Bodies and Machines*. New York: Routledge, 1992.

Sigourney, L[ydia] H. *Water-Drops*. New York: Robert Carter, 1848.

Sizer, Lyde Cullen. "Still Waiting: Intermarriage in White Women's Civil War Novels." In *Sex, Love, Race: Crossing Boundaries in North American History*, edited by Martha Hodes, 254–66. New York: New York University Press, 1999.

Slotkin, Richard. *The Fatal Environment: The Myth of the Frontier in the Age of Industrialization, 1800–1890*. New York: Atheneum, 1985.

———. *Regeneration through Violence: The Mythology of the American Frontier, 1600–1860*. Middletown, Conn.: Wesleyan University Press, 1973.

Smith, Paul Julian. *The Body Hispanic: Gender and Sexuality in Spanish and Spanish American Literature*. New York: Oxford University Press, 1989.

Solaún, Mauricio, and Sidney Kronus. *Discrimination without Violence: Miscegenation and Racial Conflict in Latin America*. New York: Wiley, 1973.

Sollors, Werner. *Neither Black nor White Yet Both: Thematic Explorations of Interracial Literature*. New York: Oxford University Press, 1997.

———. "'Never Was Born': The Mulatto, an American Tragedy?" *Massachusetts Review* 27, no. 2 (Summer 1986): 293–316.

Sommer, Doris. *Foundational Fictions: The National Romances of Latin America*. Berkeley: University of California Press, 1991.

———. Letter to the author. 27 Oct. 1994.

Spillers, Hortense J. *Comparative American Identities*. New York: Routledge, 1991.

———. "The Tragic Mulatta: Neither/Nor—Toward an Alternative Model." In *The Difference Within: Feminism and Critical Theory*, edited by Elizabeth A. Meese and Alice Parker, 147–59. Philadelphia: J. Benjamins, 1989.

Spitta, Silvia. *Between Two Waters: Narratives of Transculturation in Latin America*. Houston: Rice University Press, 1995.

———. "Transculturation, the Caribbean, and the Cuban-American Imaginary." In *Tropicalizations: Transcultural Representations of Latinidad*, edited by Frances R. Aparicio and Susan Chávez-Silverman, 160–82. Hanover, N.H.: University Press of New England, 1997.

Spivak, Gayatri Chakravorty. *In Other Worlds: Essays in Cultural Politics*. New York: Methuen, 1987.

Steele, Cythnia. "The Fiction of National Formation: The *Indigenista* Novels of James Fenimore Cooper and Rosario Castellanos." In *Reinventing the Americas: Comparative Studies of Literature of the United States and Spanish America*, edited by Bell Gale Chevigny and Gary LaGuardia, 60–67. Cambridge: Cambridge University Press, 1986.

———. "Ideology and the *Indigenista* Novel in the Nineteenth-Century United States and in Twentieth-Century Mexico." *Proceedings of the Tenth Congress of the International Comparative Literature Association 1982*, 3:76–81. New York: Garland Press, 1985.

Stein, Rachel. *Shifting the Ground: American Women Writers' Revisions of Nature, Gender, and Race*. Charlottesville: University Press of Virginia, 1997.

Stokes, Mason. *The Color of Sex: Whiteness, Heterosexuality, and the Fictions of White Supremacy*. Durham: Duke University Press, 2001.

Street, Brian V. *The Savage in Literature: Representations of "Primitive" Society in English Fiction, 1858–1920*. London: Routledge, 1975.

Sundquist, Eric. *Faulkner: The House Divided*. Baltimore: Johns Hopkins University Press, 1983.

Tate, Claudia. *Domestic Allegories of Political Desire: The Black Heroine's Text at the Turn of the Century*. New York: Oxford University Press, 1993.

Tauro, Alberto. *Clorinda Matto de Turner y la novela indigenista*. Lima: Universidad Nacional Mayor de San Marcos, 1976.

Thomas, Brook. *American Literary Realism and the Failed Promise of Contract*. Berkeley: University of California Press, 1997.

Trachtenberg, Alan. "Jerome Loving: *Walt Whitman: The Song of Himself*." *Walt Whitman Quarterly Review* 17, no. 3 (Winter 2000): 124–28.

Traubel, Horace. *With Walt Whitman in Camden*. Vol. 5, *March 28–July 14, 1888*. New York: Mitchell Kennedy, 1915.

Twain, Mark. "Huck Finn and Tom Sawyer among the Indians." In *Mark Twain's Hannibal, Huck, and Tom*, edited by Walter Blair, 92–140. Berkeley: University of California Press, 1969.

———. *"Huck Finn and Tom Sawyer among the Indians" and Other Unfinished Stories*. Berkeley: University of California Press, 1989.

———. *Mark Twain's Notebooks and Journals*. Edited by Frederick Anderson, Michael B. Frank, and Kenneth M. Sanderson. Berkeley: University of California Press, 1975.

———. "The Noble Red Man." In *Collected Tales, Sketches, Speeches, and Essays, 1852–1890*, 442–46. New York: Library of America, 1992.

———. *Roughing It*. New York: Airmont, 1967.
Tyrrell, Ian. *Sobering Up: From Temperance to Prohibition in Antebellum America, 1800–1860*. Westport, Conn.: Greenwood Press, 1979.
Unzueta, Fernando. "The Nineteenth-Century Novel: Toward a Public Sphere or a Mass Media?" In *Latin American Literature and Mass Media*, edited by Edmundo Paz-Soldán and Debra A. Castillo, 21–40. New York: Garland, 2001.
Urraca, Beatriz. "A Textbook of Americanism: Richard Harding Davis's *Soldiers of Fortune*." In *Tropicalizations: Transcultural Representations of Latinidad*, edited by Frances R. Aparicio and Susana Chávez-Silverman, 21–50. Hanover, N.H.: University Press of New England, 1997.
van Ravenswaay, Charles. *A Nineteenth-Century Garden*. New York: Main Street Press, 1977.
Walker, Cheryl. *Indian Nation: Native American Literature and Nineteenth-Century Nationalisms*. Durham: Duke University Press, 1997.
Ward, Thomas. "Nature and Civilization in *Sab* and the Nineteenth-Century Novel in Latin America." *Hispanofila* 126 (May 1999): 25–40.
Warner, Michael. "Whitman Drunk." In *Breaking Bounds: Whitman and American Cultural Studies*, edited by Betsy Erkkila and Jay Grossman, 30–43. New York: Oxford University Press, 1996.
Warren, Kenneth W. *Black and White Strangers*. Chicago: University of Chicago Press, 1993.
Wasserman, Renata. *Exotic Nations: Literature and Cultural Identity in the United States and Brazil, 1830–1930*. Ithaca: Cornell University Press, 1994.
Whitman, Walt. *Complete Poetry and Collected Prose*. Edited by Justin Kaplan. New York: Library of America, 1982.
———. *The Early Poems and the Fiction*. Edited by Thomas L. Brasher. New York: New York University Press, 1963.
———. *Notebooks and Unpublished Prose Manuscripts*. Vol. 6. Edited by Edward F. Grier. Collected Writings of Walt Whitman. New York: New York University Press, 1984.
Williams, Lorna Valerie. *The Representation of Slavery in Cuban Fiction*. Columbia: University of Missouri Press, 1994.
Williamson, Joel. *New People: Miscegenation and Mulattoes in the U.S.* New York: Free Press, 1980.
Winch, Julie. *Philadelphia's Black Elite: Activism, Accommodation, and the Struggle for Autonomy, 1787–1848*. Philadelphia: Temple University Press, 1988.
Wirt, Mrs. E. W. *Flora's Dictionary*. Baltimore: Fielding Lucas, 1832.
Wonham, Henry B. "Writing Realism, Policing Consciousness: Howells and the Black Body." *American Literature* 67, no. 4 (Dec. 1995): 701–24.
Wood, Forrest G. *Black Scare: The Racist Response to Emancipation and Reconstruction*. Berkeley: University of California Press, 1968.

Wright, Lyle H. *American Fiction, 1876–1900: A Contribution toward a Bibliography.* San Marino, Calif.: Huntington Library, 1966.
Yellin, Jean Fagin. *The Intricate Knot: Black Figures in American Literature, 1776–1863.* New York: New York University Press, 1972.
———. "Introduction" to *Incidents in the Life of a Slave Girl*, by Harriet Jacobs; edited by Jean Fagin Yellin, xiii–xxxiv. Cambridge, Mass.: Harvard University Press, 1987.
———. *Women and Sisters.* New Haven: Yale University Press, 1989.
Young, Beth. "But Are They Any Good?: Women Readers, Formula Fiction, and the Sacralization of the Literary Canon." Ph.D. diss., University of Southern California, 1995.
Young, Elizabeth. "Warring Fictions: *Iola Leroy* and the Color of Gender." *American Literature* 64, no. 2 (June 1992): 273–97.
Young, Robert J. C. *Colonial Desire: Hybridity in Theory, Culture, and Race.* New York: Routledge, 1995.
Zamora, Lois Parkinson. "The Usable Past: The Idea of History in Modern U.S. and Latin American Fiction." In *Do the Americas Have a Common Literature?*, edited by Gustavo Pérez-Firmat, 7–41. Durham: Duke University Press, 1990.
———. *Writing the Apocalypse: Historical Vision in Contemporary U.S. Latin American Fiction.* Cambridge: Cambridge University Press, 1989.
Ziff, Larzer. "Literature and Politics: 1884." In *American Literature, Culture, and Ideology: Essays in Memory of Henry Nash Smith*, edited by Beverly Voloshin, 219–33. New York: Peter Lang, 1990.

INDEX

Adventures of Huckleberry Finn (Twain), 42, 45, 46
"American Primer" (Whitman), 61
Anderson, Benedict, 12–13
Antislavery narratives, 15, 69–75, 81, 84–85, 87
Autobiography (Gómez de Avellaneda), 76
Aves sin nido (Matto de Turner), 8, 9, 13, 19, 21, 26, 29, 37–41

Bakhtin, M. M., 11, 82–83
Bates, Margret Holmes, 18, 121–22, 136, 154 (n. 7); *Chamber over the Gate*, 16, 119–23, 128, 133, 135, 139–44; influence on Howells, 119–21
Brown, William Wells, 63
Buckner, Alice Morris, 16, 118, 135; influence on Howells, 119–20; *Towards the Gulf*, 16, 119–29, 140–41, 144, 154 (n. 8)

Cable, George Washington, 100
Cannibalism, 48–49
Century of Dishonor (Jackson), 42, 45
Chamber over the Gate (Bates), 16, 119–23, 128, 133, 135, 139–44
Chateaubriand, François-René de, 9–10, 13, 22, 25, 69
Chesnutt, Charles, 155 (n. 10)
Child, Lydia Maria, 4, 5, 15, 24, 26, 31, 34, 44, 51, 64, 95–115 passim, 151 (n. 10); *History of the Condition of Women*, 96; *Hobomok*, 13, 20, 31–37, 41, 43–44, 96, 150 (n. 1); *Juvenile Miscellany*, 101; "Legend of the Falls of St. Anthony," 32; "Quadroons," 100, 112; *Romance of the Republic*, 8, 9, 15, 17, 95–114, 144; "Tulip and the Tri-Color Violet," 101
Comparative literature of the Americas, 1, 2, 13, 14, 16, 17, 21
Cooper, Anna Julia, 118
Cooper, James Fenimore, 4, 5, 20, 22, 24–34, 42, 44, 46, 50, 51, 151 (n. 10); *Last of the Mohicans*, 13, 20, 21, 25–31, 37, 41, 132
Criticism and Fiction (Howells), 116
Cumandá (Mera), 3, 8, 9, 19, 21–31, 37–40, 51

Dixon, Thomas, 100
Du Bois, W. E. B., 118

Franklin Evans (Whitman), 14, 17, 52–69, 144

Gómez de Avellaneda, Gertrudis: *Autobiography*, 76; biography, 75–80; and censorship, 74, 79–80; compared to Stowe, 69–72, 87; *Guatimozín*, 69; and race mixture, 70–71, 75, 80–96; *Sab*, 8–10, 15, 17, 29, 69–96, 152 (n. 13)

Guatimozín (Gómez de Avellaneda), 69

Harper, Frances E. W., 15, 64, 117, 155 (n. 13); influenced by Howells, 120, 136; *Iola Leroy*, 16, 117–21, 135–42, 144
Heteroglossia, 11, 82–83
History of the Condition of Women (Child), 96
Hobomok (Child), 13, 20, 31–37, 41, 43–44, 96, 150 (n. 1)
Hope Leslie (Sedgwick), 13, 20–21, 34–37, 41, 43, 150
Howells, William Dean, 15, 45, 64, 115–42 passim; and Bates, 119–20, 122, 128, 133, 135, 140; and Buckner, 119–20, 122, 128, 140; *Criticism and Fiction*, 116; and Harper, 120, 136–38; *Imperative Duty*, 16, 17, 115–23, 129–42 passim, 144, 155 (nn. 11, 17); "Mrs. Johnson," 130; "Novel-Writing and Novel-Reading," 116, 117; "Old Brown," 130; "Pilot's Story," 130; "Police Report," 130; and race mixture, 117–19, 130–36; and realism, 116–20, 126–39 passim; *Rise of Silas Lapham*, 115
"Huck and Tom among the Indians" (Twain), 13, 21, 41, 45–51
Hugo, Victor, 69, 73
Hurston, Zora Neale, 105
Hybrids/hybridity, 6–8, 15, 82–83, 149 (n. 7); in animals, 99–100; definitions, 99; in plants, 15, 104, 106–8, 113–14, 127

Imperative Duty (Howells), 16, 17, 115–23, 129–42 passim, 144, 155 (nn. 11, 17)
Incest: in *Aves sin nido*, 39–41, 86; in *Cumandá*, 29–30, 39–41; in *Sab*, 86–88; as literary theme, 8–10, 14
Indianismo and *indianista* literature and writers, 14, 19–26, 30–34, 37, 41, 150 (nn. 2, 6), 151 (n. 9)
"Indian question," 21–22, 42
Indian Removal Act, 4, 26, 42
Indigenismo and *indigenista* literature and writers, 14, 19–24, 37–38, 41, 44, 50, 150 (nn. 3, 6), 151 (n. 9)
Iola Leroy (Harper), 16, 117–21, 135–42, 144
"I Sing the Body Electric" (Whitman), 65

Jackson, Andrew, 36
Jackson, Helen Hunt, 24, 26, 41–46, 151 (n. 10); *Century of Dishonor*, 42, 45; *Ramona*, 11, 20, 21, 39, 41–46, 49, 51, 149 (n. 8)
Johnson, Mrs. A. E., 105
Juvenile Miscellany (Child), 101

Last of the Mohicans (Cooper), 13, 20, 21, 25–31, 37, 41, 132
Leaves of Grass (Whitman), 54, 61
"Legend of the Falls of St. Anthony" (Child), 32

Manzano, Juan Francisco, 73
Martí, José, 21, 143
Matto de Turner, Clorinda, 3, 19, 37–41, 51, 144; *Aves sin nido*, 8, 9, 13, 19, 21, 26, 29, 37–41
Mera, Juan León, 24–26, 41, 44, 151 (n. 10); *Cumandá*, 3, 8, 9, 19, 21–31, 37–40, 51
Mestizaje, 5–6, 11, 23, 83, 152 (n. 13)
Miscegenation. *See* Race mixture
Mixed race. *See* Race mixture
"Mrs. Johnson" (Howells), 130

Natives: representation of, 13–14, 18–24, 39, 42, 44, 46, 150 (n. 4)
"Negro question," 22
"Noble Red Man" (Twain), 42
"Noble savage," 20, 22, 33, 42, 46
"Novel-Writing and Novel-Reading" (Howells), 116, 117

"Old Brown" (Howells), 130

"Pilot's Story" (Howells), 130
"Police Report" (Howells), 130

"Quadroons" (Child), 100, 112

Race mixture: and antislavery writing, 14–15; and blood purity, 6–7, 90–91; as cannibalism, 48–49; and death, 27–28, 30, 36, 47; definitions of, 4–6; as failure of literary imagination, 28, 36; and genre, 19–24, 49–51, 52, 118; and hybrid plants, 15, 96, 104, 106–8, 110, 113; literary anxiety over, 3, 11, 21, 29, 47, 72, 85, 120, 125, 144; as literary theme, 1, 2, 7–8, 11–18 passim, 21, 26–27, 71, 85, 117, 122, 123, 136–37, 143; as melodrama, 115, 122; and national identity, 1, 2, 3, 12, 13, 14, 18, 30, 34–37, 113–14, 121; as rape, 46–50, 70, 81, 84–85; as scientific knowledge, 117, 118; and sexuality, 12, 32, 128; as social critique or reform, 2, 7, 15, 30, 40, 95–96, 111, 113–14, 136; as unpatriotic, 135; and Vanishing American, 51; and women's bodies, 43, 46, 98, 120–21, 124, 132–38 passim, 141; and women writers, 12–13. *See also* Comparative literature of the Americas; Hybrids/Hybridity; Incest; *Indianismo* and *indianista* literature and writers; *Indigenismo* and *indigenista* literature and writers; *Mestizaje*; Realism; Romanticism; Temperance; Tragic mulatto

Racial detection, 28–29
Ramona (Jackson), 11, 20, 21, 39, 41–46, 49, 51, 149 (n. 8)
Realism, 15–16, 22, 26, 38; and Bates, 122; definitions, 116–17, 153–54 (n. 2); and Howells, 116–20, 126–42 passim; and Twain, 45–46, 50–51
Reconstruction, 4, 15
Rise of Silas Lapham (Howells), 115
Romance of the Republic (Child), 8, 9, 15, 17, 95–114, 144
Romanticism, 13, 16, 19–20, 22, 26, 38, 86, 117–20; and Howells, 117–20, 129–42 passim; and Jackson, 46; and tragic mulatto, 117–20, 133–36
Romantic racialism, 124–28
Roughing It (Twain), 45
Rousseau, Jean-Jacques, 10, 13, 22
Rowson, Susanna, 62

Sab (Gómez de Avellaneda), 8–10, 15, 17, 29, 69–96, 152 (n. 13)
Sedgwick, Catharine Maria, 4, 5, 24, 26, 34–35, 44, 51, 151 (n. 10), 152 (n. 14); *Hope Leslie*, 13, 20–21, 34–37, 41, 43, 150
Sigourney, Lydia, 60
Slave narratives or novels. *See* Antislavery narratives
"Song of Myself" (Whitman), 65, 66
Stowe, Harriet Beecher, 22, 45, 136; *Uncle Tom's Cabin*, 15, 43, 69–72, 87

Temperance, 14, 16–17; and African Americans, 56, 60; as formula, 52; and *Franklin Evans*, 52–68; history of temperance movement, 55–56; and race mixture, 52–53, 61–65, 68; temperance literature, 57–61; and women, 59–60
Tom Sawyer (Twain), 45
Towards the Gulf (Buckner), 16, 119–29, 140–41, 144, 154 (n. 8)
Tragic mulatto, 16, 17, 64, 117–23, 126, 133–36, 141–42, 154 (n. 3)
"Tulip and the Tri-Color Violet" (Child), 101
Twain, Mark, 20, 26, 44–51; *Adventures of Huckleberry Finn*, 42, 45, 46; "Huck and Tom among the Indians," 13, 21, 41, 45–51; "Noble Red Man," 42; *Roughing It*, 45; *Tom Sawyer*, 45

Uncle Tom's Cabin (Stowe), 15, 43, 69–72, 87

Vanishing American, 51
Villaverde, Cirilo, 74–75, 84

Whitman, Walt: "American Primer," 61; as editor of *Brooklyn Daily Eagle*, 65; *Franklin Evans*, 14, 17, 52–69, 144; "I Sing the Body Electric," 65; *Leaves of Grass*, 54, 61; and race mixture, 52–53, 61–65; "Song of Myself," 65, 66; and temperance, 52–68 passim

www.ingramcontent.com/pod-product-compliance
Lightning Source LLC
Chambersburg PA
CBHW020651300426
44112CB00007B/327